The Way Of THE DRAGON
BRUCE INTRODUCTION BRUCE
By Rick Baker

"Return of the Dragon" or The Way of the Dragon (Chinese:猛龍過江, originally released in the United States as Return of the Dragon) is a 1972 Hong Kong martial arts action-comedy film written, co-produced and directed by Bruce Lee, who also stars in the lead role. This is Lee's only complete directorial film and the last one released during his lifetime. The film co-stars Nora Miao, Robert Wall, and Wei Ping-ou, with Chuck Norris playing his debut screen role. The Way of the Dragon was released in Hong Kong on 30 December 1972 and in the United States in August 1974 UK, 4 June 1974, (London) ; UK, 14 June.
The film went on to gross an estimated US$130 million worldwide (equivalent to over $700 million adjusted for inflation), against a tight budget of $130,000, earning a thousand times its budget. It was the highest-grossing Hong Kong film up until Lee's next film, Enter the Dragon (1973). Welcome once again to another bumper packed Bruce Lee special edition. After the success of the G.O.D special edition we decided to go this time for Bruce Lee's directorial Debut "Way of the Dragon". What I found most interesting was the amount of related memorabilia that was submitted for this edition from various collectors.
I saw Way of the Dragon back in 1975 (UK Theatrical release) and was disappointed that the B.B.F.C had once again, took their scissors and made cuts not just to the "Nuchaku" fight scenes but also some other slight cuts that would only become complete when a restored version from "Hong Kong legends" DVD hit the high street stores. Even the British quad poster had the "nunchakus" airbrushed out! I was lucky enough in the late 80s to obtain a Hong Kong bootleg release on VHS to finally see the movie in its entirety. Way of the Dragon, represents Bruce Lee's very best cinematic work, well-reflecting his meticulous nature and ambition as a humble creative. Way of the Dragon is very much an international feature film; this brought Bruce outside his own Hong Kong comfort zone, travelling to Rome to tell the story of a man who visits his relatives in Italy, only to find him defending them against a gang of brutal gangsters. Much of the film follows the familiar route of a martial arts movie, spiked with moments of exemplary action (of which Lee himself choreographed), concluding in one of the finest endings in film history where Bruce Lee and Chuck Norris go face-to-face taking 45 hours to film.

I talk to Alan Canvan, and take a deep dive into W.O.D putting questions to Alan on his personal thoughts, after the success in the last issue where we talked about his Redux game of Death 2.0. Plus we have so much more in this edition that should whet the appetite of fan of this movie.

SOME FUN FACTS

This was the last movie, to be filmed in the actual Roman Coliseum.

Part of the music in this film is actually originally from the Ennio Morricone score for the Sergio Leone western C'era una volta il West (1968).

The whole thing was shot without sound, with the actors looping their lines in post-production.

Was billed "Return of the Dragon" during its western release in order to cash in on the success of "Enter the Dragon" as its "sequel".

Bruce Lee dubbed almost all of the English speaking characters in this film including one line for the boss. That line is: "Take him out, but be careful with that gun in public".

Bruce Lee wrote the death threat note which the Mafia gave to Uncle Wang.

Bruce Lee and Chuck Norris allegedly made real contact during their fight scenes

According to the Bruce Lee documentary, this is Linda Lee Cadwell's favourite of all her husband's films.

Bruce Lee had Chuck Norris put on weight to appear larger and more formidable.

This was the highest grossing film in Hong Kong in 1972, beating the records set by Bruce Lee's previous films.

Bruce Lee turned down the lead role in Slaughter in San Francisco (1974), directed by Wei Lo, in order to concentrate on making this movie.

Bruce Lee hoped to cast boxer Joe Lewis as an opponent in the film, but he declined.

Bruce Lee's character name of Tang Lung is Chinese for "China Dragon."

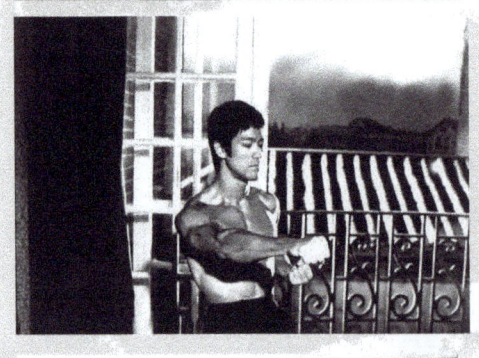

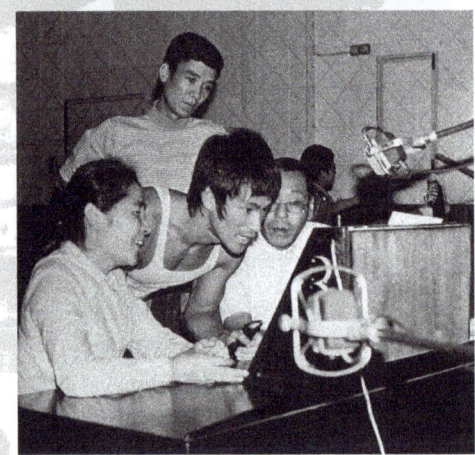

Rick Baker & Alan Canvan
take a deep dive into Bruce's

THE WAY OF THE DRAGON

RB: Let's jump right in. How do you rate Bruce's directorial debut?

AC: Way of the Dragon is an anomaly in Bruce's adult filmography because it allowed him to infuse comedy into his performance. This type of role wasn't new to Bruce and, if you pay close attention, the Tang Lung character he created shares DNA with one of his early childhood roles, Kid Cheung, in The Kid. Lee loved comedy and his performance in both movies is a tribute to the era of silent pictures – particularly the work of Charlie Chaplin. Additionally, the first fifty-five minutes of the film served as a template for the Kung Fu comedy sub-genre that Jackie Chan would effectively adopt and use to brand his cinematic persona, even going as far as updating the film's story years later with Rumble in the Bronx. Ultimately though, Way of the Dragon was born out of Lee's lack of faith in Hong Kong filmmakers, regarding their skill level as substandard compared to the cinema

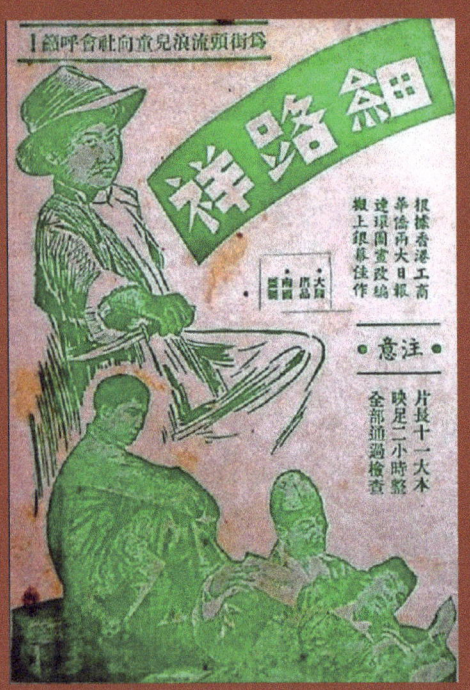

auteurs he was exposed to in Hollywood. Matthew Polly refers to Way as Bruce's Spaghetti Eastern – and for good reason. Bruce wanted to duplicate Clint Eastwood's success in America by producing the equivalent of a low budget Leone picture and have it cross over to the West.

RB: Critics reviews when this was first screened, referred to this as

a comedy! Although some of the more comedic scenes where cut for the Western market as they felt they would not understand his "fish out of water" moments during the opening scenes at the restaurant and the toilet sequence. Despite this being an intended international movie, it remains very much a Hong Kong movie throughout.

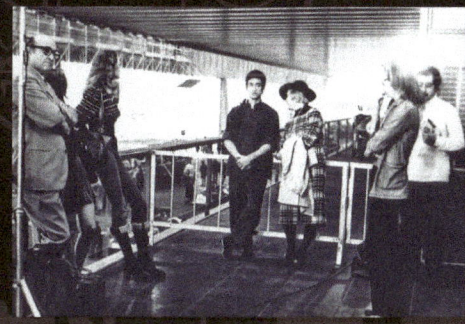

AC: The "fish out of water" angle is a relatable trope that's been seen in many popular films like Crocodile Dundee. I think what sealed Way of the Dragon's fate was that, as a film, it can't quite decide what it wants to be. The early part of the film does play to Chinese audiences in a way that affirms Lee's real-life experience with culture shock upon first arriving in the US in 1959. Some of the airport scenes feel like they could be autobiographical. In that respect, Way is equally as nationalistic as Fist of Fury in that it sees Lee embrace his "Chinese-ness" in a manner that he'd have been far less comfortable with in a Western picture.

RB: Originally Bruce was to shoot the entire movie in Italy, but despite his due diligence on prepping the movie he overlooked the visas for the crew and getting permission to film at the Coliseum. Do you feel that having to go back to Hong Kong to shoot the film derailed his thoughts and produced a weaker film?

AC: Initially, Way of the Dragon was going to be a nineteenth century period piece based in San Francisco that borrowed numerous elements from Lee's Warrior TV series treatment. Production costs prevented it from going that way (pun intended). Instead, Bruce looked at various parts of Europe, eventually settling on Rome because he was keen to have a battle scene take place in the Coliseum – the symbolic pinnacle of warriorhood. The crew only shot in Italy for twelve days but that had little to do with his dissatisfaction with the overall film. You have to remember that the project was in many ways Lee's equivalent of going to film school, and he made mistakes that rookie filmmakers often make with their first feature. Because of this, he felt that the end result didn't quite capture his vision as a writer or director.

RB: For his directorial debut Bruce produced and wrote the script. I would be interested to hear your thoughts on his scriptwriting. Do you think Bruce was wearing too many hats for his first outing and should he just have concentrated on directing? Although he was obviously a competent writer would he have benefitted in bringing in another writer to shape his script up or do you think it was a case of it being his baby and him wanting complete control?

AC: Well, unlike The Silent Flute, where Lee contributed ideas to a story that was eventually written by Stirling Silliphant, Way didn't have the safety net of an award-winning screenwriter to save it. This was Bruce's first solo screenplay, and it's evident in both the story structure as well as the dialogue (which frequently comes across as stiff and cartoony.) Except for the "kick me/don't think, feel/finger pointing to the moon" portion in Enter the Dragon (which he partially lifted from the teachings of the Buddha), Bruce's strength was in concepts, not dialogue. On the other hand, as an actor, director and fight choreographer, his brilliance shone through in his ability to tell stories – fables that relayed triumphs of the flesh and spirit – through combat, and equally, in his ability to physically perform and give them sex appeal. It's an arena in which he's unmatched to this day.

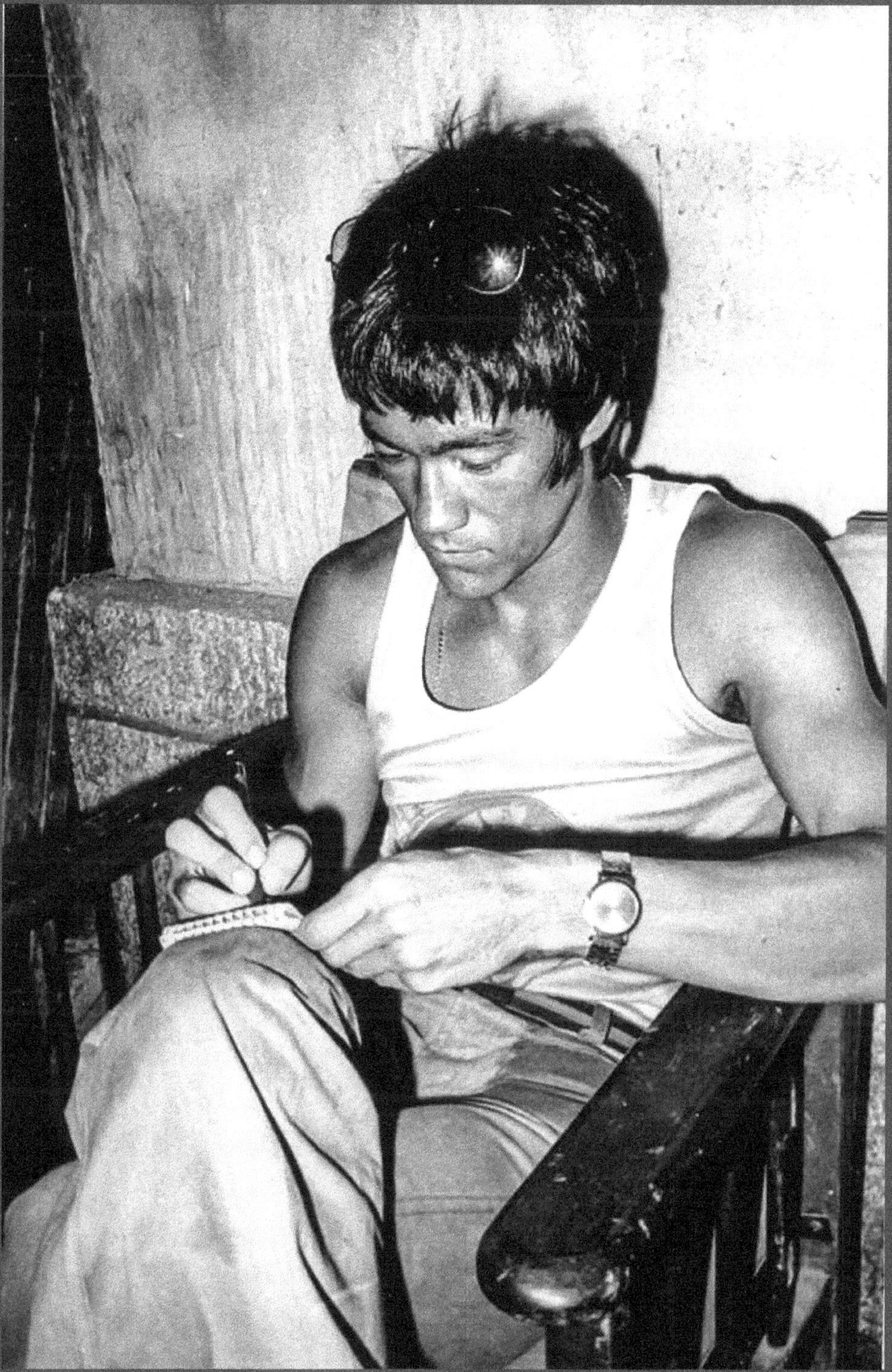

RB: What do you think the meaning of Bruce's company Concord Productions with Raymond Chow means and why he picked that name.

AC: I can tell you with full confidence that it had nothing to do with the Concord Jet. Bruce named it after Concordia, the Roman goddess of Harmony, and highlighted this by incorporating an animated version of the red and gold yin-yang symbol that he'd used as his JKD logo since the early 60's.

RB: I believe you feel that Way of the Dragon has one of Bruce's best fight scenes with Chuck Norris.

AC: To me, the clash in the Colosseum is really the center piece of the movie, with the fight itself touching on several philosophical themes – namely trial through adversary as a conduit for self-reflection and rite of passage. This plays out equally for both Bruce and Norris's characters. From both a technical and artistic perspective, the sequence is damn near perfect, though I feel, at times, the inserts of the kitten during the battle could have been used more effectively. That's a minor quibble though.

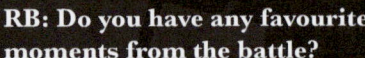

RB: Do you have any favourite moments from the battle?

AC: Several, but there is one sequence that I feel doesn't get enough recognition: the medium shot where Bruce advances on Chuck and flows into a series of strikes that culminate with him chain punching and side kicking Norris out of the camera frame. The choreography incorporates elements of classical Wing Chun techniques and is lifted almost verbatim from the Bob Baker fight in Fist of Fury. Lo Wei shot the movements with the men positioned in profile to capture the full movements of the action. Lee, on the other hand, specifically frames the action to be partially hidden behind Chuck's torso – effectively putting the viewer in Chuck's character and on the receiving end of the blows.

RB: That's a great observation.

AC: Another piece of the finale that stands out to me is the aftermath of the fight: Tang pays respect to a fellow warrior for giving him a platform to truly test himself – to dig deep and discover the stuff he's made of, not only as a fighter, but as a man. It's a wonderful moment, packed with emotion that relays the larger story within the battle.

RB: Great stuff Alan. You've also said that the film also contains his poorest fight scene. Could you go into detail about this.

AC: Yeah. The skirmish in Jon Benn's office, in my mind, is the weakest in Lee's choreography. The performance is the antithesis of what we normally experience with a Bruce Lee fight scene. My view is that it was mainly hampered by the people he hired in the henchmen roles who were not stuntmen and had virtually no experience with fight choreography. Despite it being the same players in the alleyway fight that takes place earlier in the film, it's far inferior because it doesn't have the flashy weapons to distract the audience. Lee put himself in a bit of a pickle because the scene needed Caucasian stuntmen, of which there were not an abundance of in Hong Kong at the time. Had the script called for Chinese thugs, the result would have been completely different. Few people then, or now, could compete with the HK stuntmen of that era.

RB: So, you like the fight in the alley?

AC: I view both fights to be close in tone

to what you might see in a Bud Spencer/ Terence Hill flick. One done well, the other not.

RB: Aside from the fight choreography, what elements do you particularly enjoy in Way of the Dragon?

AC: For me, it's the subtle nods to Lee's inspiration from what some would consider the least likely of sources. For example, Bruce sets up the Coliseum battle by having Tang navigate the maze-like structure of the amphitheatre as Ho taunts him with death threats and maniacal laughter that echo throughout the ruins. It plays like something straight out of a Giallo film (a genre in Italian cinema that's known for horror and suspense.) Another scene is when Lee executes backfists and kicks while studying himself in the mirror of Malissa Longo's apartment. To me, that moment is a precursor to DeNiro's "Are you talking to me?" bit in Taxi Driver.

RB: Funny you should mention the mirror scene, It jogged my memory to the first time I saw the movie. I had a wardrobe that had a mirror on the inside of the door, when I got back and put my P-jays on, I remember standing there trying to rein-act that moment. I was studying Shoukokia Karate at the time and I would often come home and check myself kicking etc.
Watching the film later in my more adult life, I felt Bruce's actions were more macho, knowing there was a woman about to seduce him, his mirror display was reinforcing his alpha male position, building confidence to deal with this alien situation that he had been led into by the beautiful Malissa Longo. I also smile now at the end he pulls down his bottom eyelid, maybe checking after his long haul flight, that his eyes did not look tired or bloodshot. The whole scene for me now depicts the typical actions of fish out of water trying to adapt to his new environment whether facing confrontation in the deadly act of violence, or the deadly persuasion of a femme fatal
What elements do you not enjoy?

AC: The premise of the story is absurd – even by the standards of movie logic.

as Director? Do you think this was a good opening project?

AC: Way of the Dragon borrowed its plot from Lo Wei's Yellow Faced Tiger (eventually released as A Man Called Tiger with Jimmy Wang Yu), which, as you know, was initially going to be Lee and Wei's third collaboration. I've always viewed the parallels, along with Hai Tien's fighting moniker "Yellow Faced Tiger" in Game of Death, as Lee's less than subtle jab at Lo. Beyond that, Bruce includes a trope from his first two films that seem motivated by "if it ain't broke, don't fix it" rationale: 1). the outsider joining a surrogate family in a foreign land and having to prove his worth and 2). the villain hiding in plain sight amongst the tribe and using an interpreter as a go between. Of course, the devil is in the details – a European location, the slapstick comedy, Lee's short haircut – give it a certain freshness, but the film still feels like a retread of what came before. That is, until we arrive at the Coliseum, where it becomes something else, wider in scope and larger than life. To circle back to your question - was it a good opening project? I'd say yes, because he was able to familiarize himself with his strength and weaknesses as filmmaker, which in turn gave him more confidence with Game of Death.

RB: Why do you suppose Lee chose to give Wei Ping-ao's character an effeminate look and mannerisms?

AC: My feeling is that Lee threw in a wild card to have some fun with an openly homosexual character. Bruce enjoyed doing impressions of gay stereotypes and was known to play pranks that involved baiting guys to pick a fight with him, only to lay them out by feigning spastic moves and giving the impression that he did it by accident. It was highly amusing to him. I think giving Ho those traits added a bit of coarse humor to the proceedings and complimented some of the gaudy imagery in the film.

**RB: This is a broader question but also relevant to "Way of the Dragon". What are your thoughts on the sex scenes in Bruce's movies? We have the prostitutes in "The Big Boss", the Japanese geisha frolicking in "Fist of Fury", Malisa Longo bearing all in "Way of the

Why is Jon Benn's character hell bent on acquiring this Chinese restaurant and, as ruthless as he purports to be, why not "just pull out a .45 and bang…?" The answer is obvious: because if he'd done so then there'd be no movie (laughter.) But, even so, the set up feels contrived and exists purely as a plot device to get Tang Lung to the Coliseum. In that respect, it's similar to the Game of Death outline where the more compelling portion of the story took place inside the pagoda. Additionally, the Shakespearean twist with the villainous Uncle isn't earned, despite the moment of foreshadowing where he reflects on being a far away from home. From a technical perspective, the sloppy continuity and out of focus camera shots reveal that Way is the work of a beginner. That said, I must admit that all this is a huge part of the movie's charm.

**RB: What do you think Bruce was trying to achieve with his first movie

Dragon" and Ahna Capri parading a bevy of girls to entertain the guests in "Enter the Dragon". Do you think this was just for light titillation?

AC: The earlier films didn't shy away from sexuality. By contrast, Way of the Dragon seems to have kicked off Bruce's PG rated image, whereby nearly all of his sexual activity on screen was neutered. This would be repeated in Enter the Dragon, though Clouse did shoot an extended scene that was cut of Lee putting on his catsuit in the darkness as Mei Ling watches, which was extremely suggestive. While I'm aware that the characters in those films were not sexually active for specific reasons, I can't help but think, in the long run, that this contributed to the absurd notion that a warrior needs to be chaste in order to be pure or good. Prior to the 20th Century, this wasn't necessarily a virtue of warriorhood. The Big Boss, of course, is the only film that allows him to be sexually uninhibited on screen. In the end, this hardly mattered because Lee's chemistry with the camera allowed his physique to sexualize him in way that would essentially substitute for the carnal activity.

RB: Our good friend Michael Worth is doing a piece on Japanese cinematographer Tadashi Nishimoto, who was brought onto the project by Bruce. His unprecedented style of photography to Hong Kong films would influence many Hong Kong filmmakers for years to come. I would be interested to hear your thoughts as a filmmaker on his work on Way of the Dragon and the benefits he brought to this project.

AC: Tadashi Nishimoto was an inspired choice for cinematographer. I think what Bruce loved about Nishimoto was his daring approach to composition. For example, one of my favourite shots is the profile of Lee's face looking up at the adjacent buildings in search of the sniper. Frame right of the composition uses black as negative space while frame left bathes Lee's features in blue, gold and amber lighting. It's highly Western and stylistic in its execution, which contributed to the illusion of the film being fully shot in Rome. I would have been very interested to see his approach to the non-pagoda scenes in Game of Death. I always come back to the shot at the end of Lee's battle with Jabbar: Nishimoto frames both men in a medium close-up that begins with Bruce's face, slowly tracks across Kareem struggling against Lee's headlock and continues through the back of the sofa panel before landing on the veins of Kareem's hand gripping the cushion. Not only do I consider it to be one of the most beautifully composed shots in cinema history, it's also a perfect illustration of an entire story encapsulated in a single image.

RB: How do you compare Joseph Koo's soundtrack to John Barry's score of Game of Death? Although Barrys theme is without doubt the better score ever, shall we pay respect to Joseph Koo who is well respected in Hong Kong?

AC: Joseph Koo's main theme is a wonderful hybrid of Ennio Morricone, Middle Eastern jazz and tribal warrior

chants that create a haunting and hypnotic score. The coda cleverly incorporates a pulsating percussion (which Lee played) alongside the indigenous shouts to build a sense of urgency in a relatively mellow arrangement. Elsewhere in the film, the score is inspired by Henry Mancini's Pink Panther theme. Koo did a great job with it, though as you noted, it doesn't hold the dramatic weight of Barry's score for Game of Death or Schifrin's score for Enter the Dragon.

RB: Out of his five movies including the uncompleted Game of Death, where does Way of the Dragon fall for you?

AC: It's tough to pin down because I love Bruce's movies for different reasons. To me, The Big Boss and The Orphan contain his best acting performances. Game of Death and Enter the Dragon, his best fight choreography. Way of the Dragon is appealing because it's consistently entertaining – sometimes for the wrong reasons. That said, I would rank the Chuck Norris, Bob Wall and double nunchaku alley fight scenes amongst the best of Lee's on-screen battles.

RB: How do you compare Bruce's direction in Way of the Dragon to your cut of Redux and highlighting his aesthetic eye behind the camera?

AC: It's not a fair comparison. My sensibilities as a filmmaker are different than what Lee's were in 1972. Growing up in the late 70's/early 80's exposed me to the work of directors that Bruce never knew (and would certainly have influenced him.) But unquestionably, his directorial skills grew considerably in the relatively short time between the two projects. Much of that was a result of him identifying the mistakes he made with Way along with his almost preternatural ability to absorb things quickly as has did with dance and martial arts.
I have no doubt that had Lee finished Game it would have been superior film to Way in almost every respect, but I'm not convinced that the non-combat scenes would have hit the bid for an international film release.

RB: You don't think so ?

AC: I think Bruce needed more experience with seasoned filmmakers to understand

what made them great. I'm of the opinion that if he'd completed Game of Death post Enter the Dragon in 1973, it would've been a better movie than if he'd completed it in 1972. Why? Because he'd have experienced four solid months of working with Robert Clouse. If he'd made films with Kurosawa or Scorsese, he'd have had a much better understanding of how to execute narratives all the way through.

RB: How does Way of the Dragon compare now to the first time you watched it, seeing it through the eyes of a young unknowledgeable fan verses 2022 Alan with a deeper understanding as a film maker?

AC: Great question. My initial experience with Way of the Dragon was surreal because it was tied to specific elements in the Game of Death 1978 film. I instantly recognized shots that were lifted and used for Clouse's production, so, to me, the Coliseum fight felt like "lost" footage. But what really made it strange was all the audio cues that I was fluent with from repeated viewings of Game of Death were completely missing. So, it took a minute to get used to. Over the years, I've come to embrace Way for what it is: a quirky, flawed and occasionally brilliant piece of film making. More importantly, I recognize what a milestone it was for Bruce in terms of his evolution as an artist, even as I'm able to readily identify what works in it and what doesn't.

RB: Alan, Once again, thank you for

taking time out to take a deep dive into "Way of the Dragon" highlighting many good answers to my questions, and raising some very valid points.
I am looking forward to taking a deep dive into the reaming tiles in future issues, also looking at his childhood movies and his TV career examining his philosophy in "Long Street"

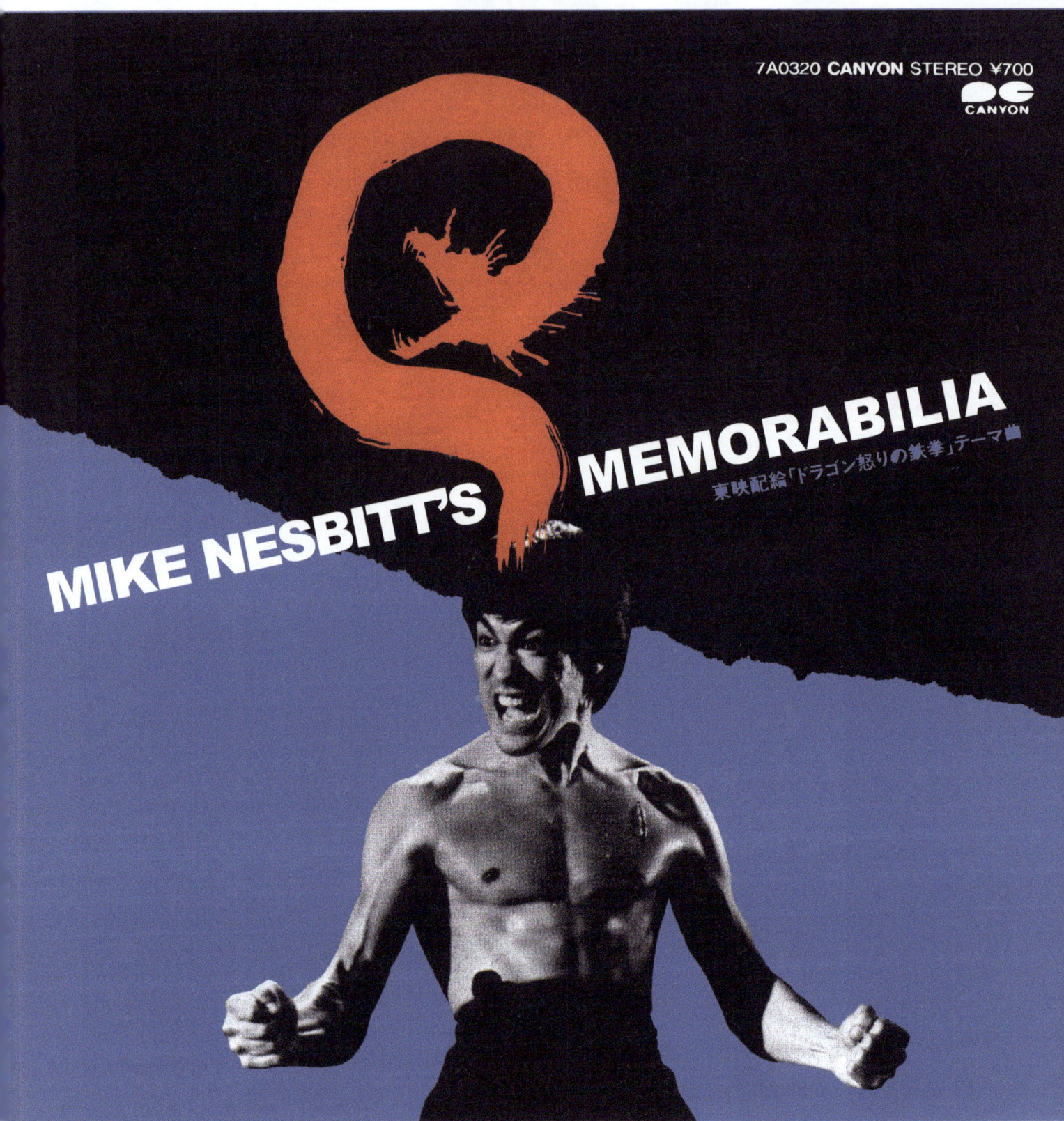

MIKE NESBITT'S MEMORABILIA

The Way of the Dragon has the distinction of being the only movie that Bruce Lee not only starred in but also wrote, produced and directed. At the time, it was considered Bruce's biggest project, and he, along with Raymond Chow, Concord Production and Golden Harvest was highly invested in its success. Having been released on the 1st of June 1972 in Hong Kong and on the 14th of August 1972 in America, it took nearly 2 years for it to be released in the UK, finally getting released on the 4th of June 1974 in London, nearly a year after Bruce Lee's untimely death. The film cost $130,000 to make and went on to gross over $130 million worldwide. Still, The Way of the Dragon is not considered to be Bruce Lee's best movie, and is only saving factor for many people was because of two reasons, and they were: the first ever filmed, double nunchaku scene, and for having the classic finale fight scene against real-life American Karate Champion, Chuck Norris.

I have always considered one of the greatest successes of The Way of the Dragon, was to be the introduction of Chuck Norris as Colt, the main bad guy in the movie. There is no doubt that the iconic white karate Gi, huge sideburns, and hairy chest, along with the flawless finale fight scene against Tang Lung (Bruce), kick-started Chuck Norris's acting career, and made him one of the most beloved action movie stars of the 1970s and 80s. And of course, Chuck Norris's image along with Bruce on numerous magazines, books, posters, videos, records and a host of other memorabilia, also helped in the success of

The Way of the Dragon. In fact, anything depicting Bruce's image on memorabilia is always considered collectable, especially if it shows an iconic image of Bruce from one of his movies, for example, Bruce Lee wearing his Game of Death tracksuit, or Bruce with the iconic scratch marks on his face and chest from Enter the Dragon, and of course Bruce facing off against Chuck Norris or holding the double nunchaku in The Way of the Dragon. These types of images on memorabilia would keep Bruce Lee's memory alive, even now, nearly 50 years after his passing.

The following pages show a collection of memorabilia relating to The Way of the Dragon, from countries as far and wide as the UK, America, Italy, France, Japan, and Hong Kong, and range in date from 1973 to the present day. Some of the collection will be recognisable to long-time Bruce Lee fans, but there are also some rarer items some may not have seen before, including signed photos and original artwork.

UK Lobby cards

"THE WAY OF THE DRAGON" x
STARRING BRUCE LEE
Colour Scope   A Golden Harvest Production   Released through Cathay Films

"THE WAY OF THE DRAGON" x
STARRING BRUCE LEE
Colour Scope   A Golden Harvest Production   Released through Cathay Films

"THE WAY OF THE DRAGON" x
STARRING BRUCE LEE
Colour Scope   A Golden Harvest Production   Released through Cathay Films

"THE WAY OF THE DRAGON" x
STARRING BRUCE LEE
Colour Scope   A Golden Harvest Production   Released through Cathay Films

"THE WAY OF THE DRAGON" x
STARRING BRUCE LEE
Colour Scope   A Golden Harvest Production   Released through Cathay Films

"THE WAY OF THE DRAGON" x
STARRING BRUCE LEE
Colour Scope   A Golden Harvest Production   Released through Cathay Films

Cinema Tickets

Japanese Flyers

猛龍生誕80周年

世界は今も、彼を中心に回っている。

BRUCE LEE 4K

最高画質と最強音声で更新された無敵の絶対聖典！

ブルース・リー
4Kリマスター復活祭 2020

「ドラゴン危機一発」 THE BIG BOSS 　「ドラゴン怒りの鉄拳」 FIST OF FURY 　「ドラゴンへの道」 THE WAY OF THE DRAGON 　「死亡遊戯」 GAME OF DEATH

©2010 Fortune Star Media Limited. All Rights Reserved.
配給：ツイン TWIN

brucelee4k.com

ドラゴンへの道
最後のブルース・リー
世紀の闘神ブルース・リー！
鮮烈必殺技のすべてを叩き込んで
宿敵ヨーロッパの群雄を打ち砕く
唸り飛ぶ迫真のダブル・ヌンチャク
壮麗ローマ・コロシアム大遺跡の一騎打ち
烈昂の叫びと共に噴きあげる《クン・フー》クライマックス！
Bruce Lee in
THE WAY OF THE DRAGON
Co-Starring CHUCK NORRIS. NORA MIAO
Directed by BRUCE LEE Produced by RAYMOND CHOW
for A Concord Production
カラー作品
監督・脚本・音楽・武術指導そして主演
ブルース・リー
ノラ・ミアオ チャック・ノリス
撮影・西本 正 コンコルド・プロダクション作品／東映洋画
東映
日本版
ブルース・リー
大型ポスター

Chinese Press Books

Japanese Yamakatsu Cards

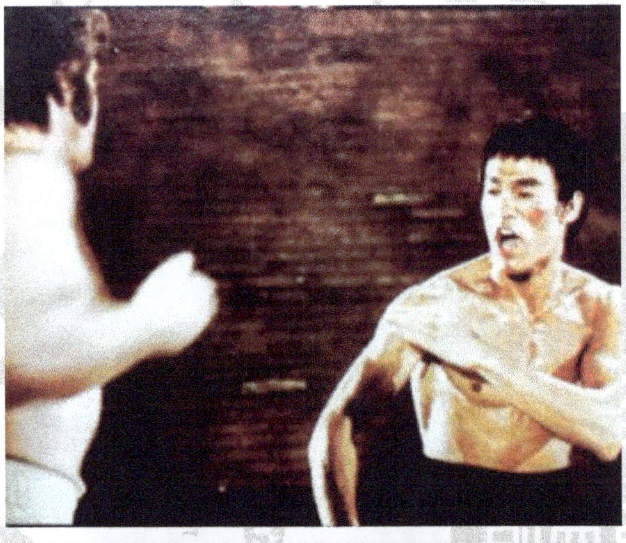

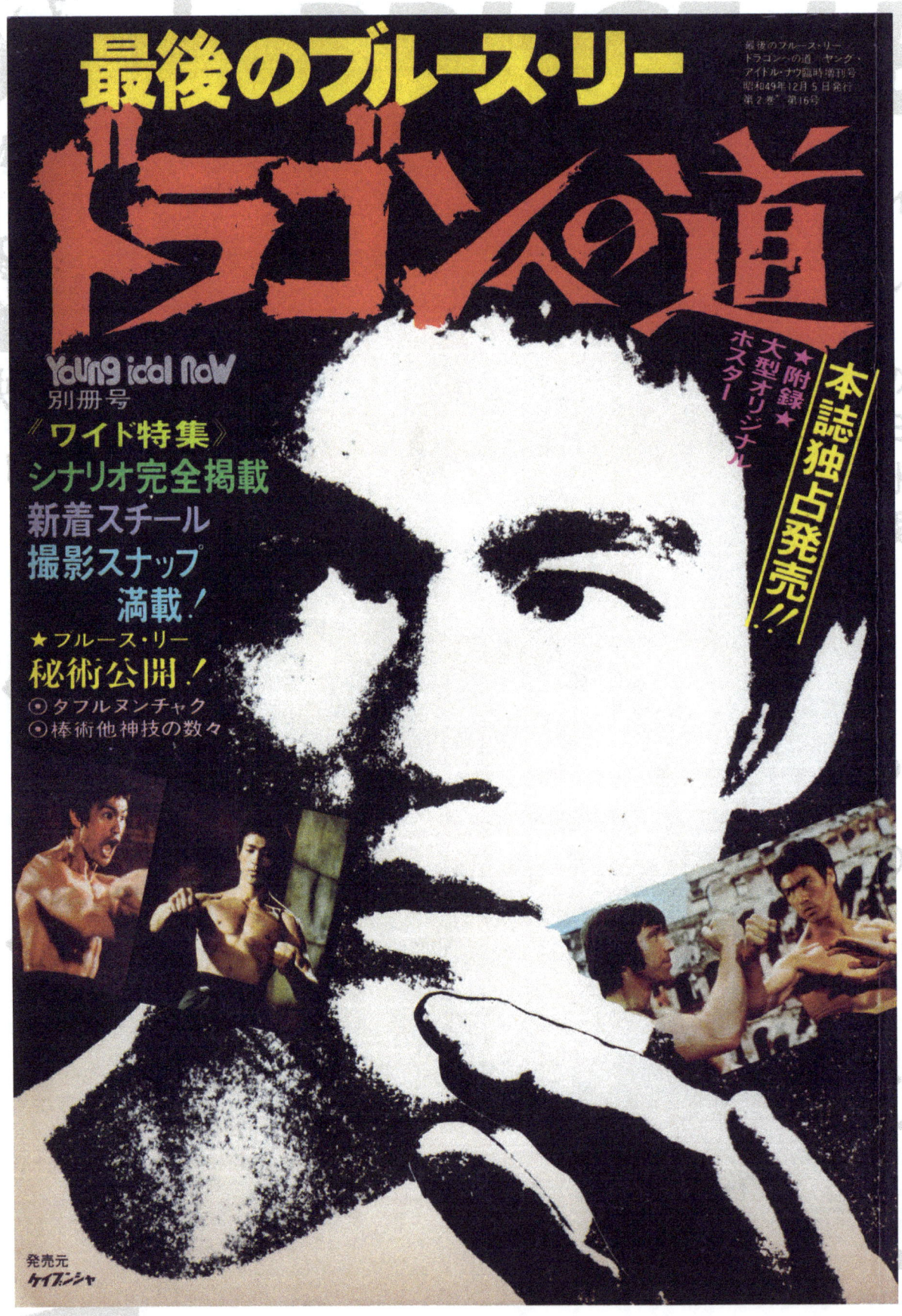

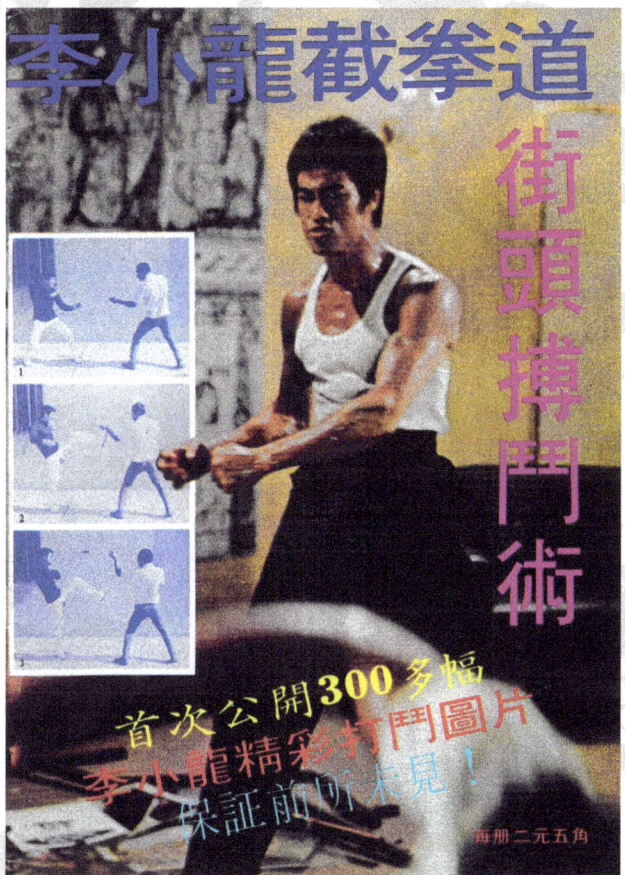

卓上用
特選場面スチール集

★

ブルース・リー映画と
「小さな恋のメロディ」
傑作場面

★

スクリーン 8月号第1付録

スクリーン8月号第1付録　昭和53年8月1日発行　第33巻第9号通巻444号　昭和53年2月24日国鉄首都特別扱承認雑誌第3809号

「ドラゴンへの道」

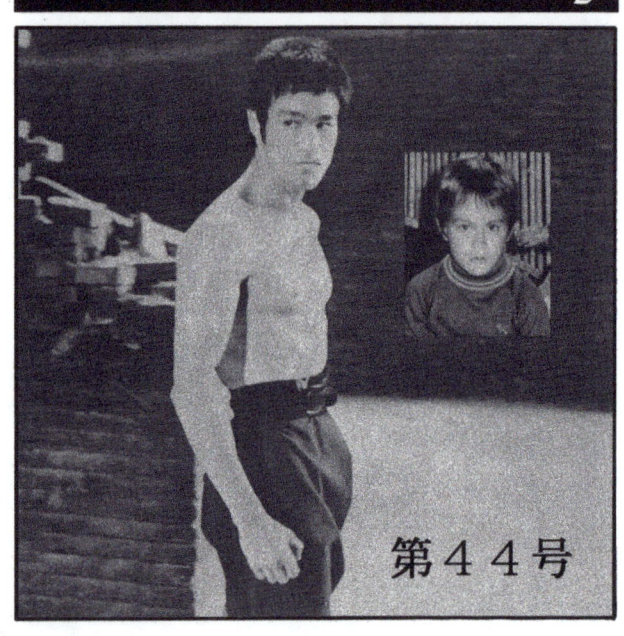

BRUCE LEE
POSTER MAGAZINE

発行・編集／ブルース・リーファンクラブ
発 行 日／昭和55年1月20日(陽月20日)
©ユウワ・東映洋画／ファイル ポップ

創刊号

NO. 1 '80 1/20

「小龍問路」
The Dragon Set
'Little Dragon Seekin

特集・ドラゴンへの道
THE WAY OF THE DARGON

Fanclub Fanzines

BRUCE LEE ★ KING OF KUNG FU ★

LITTLE DRAGON

ISSUE 1

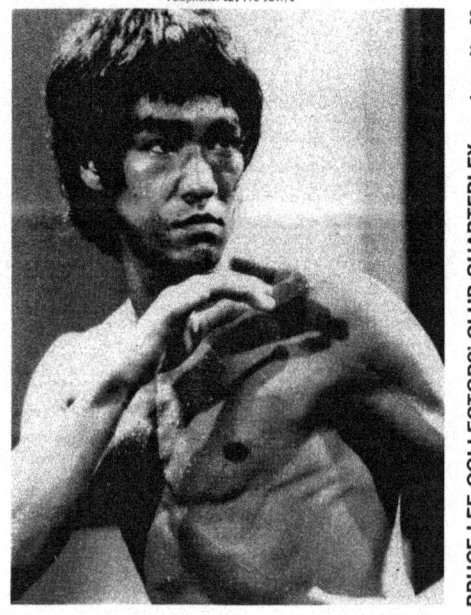

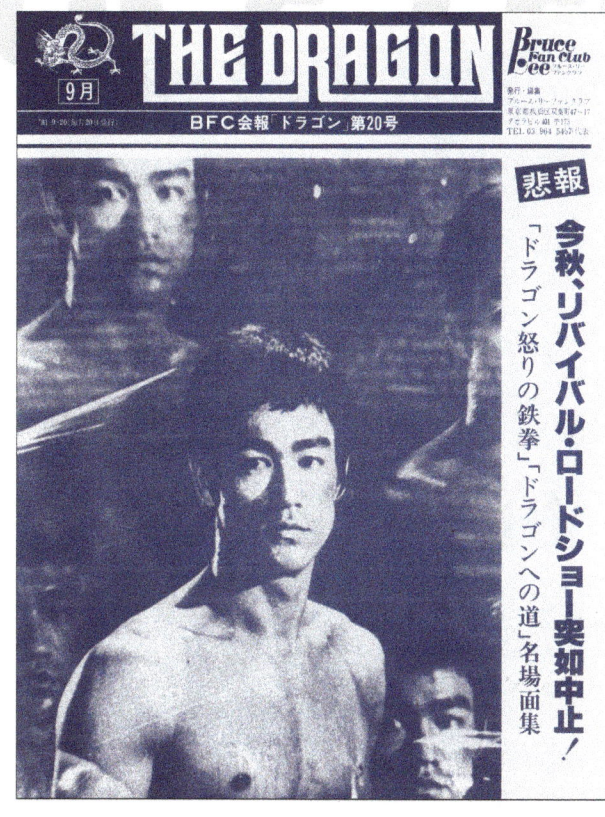

 **CHUCK NORRIS Enterprises**

#7 Empty Saddle Road / Rolling Hills Estates, California 90274

May 5, 1980

Dear Shelagh,

Emil Farkas sent your letter to me. I hope I spelled your name right. I am not sure what you want to know. I'll tell you about my movies. "Return of the dragon" with Bruce Lee. "Breaker Breaker". "Good Guys wear black." "Force of one." and my new one "the Octogon".

I am sorry I don't have any posters at this time. I will send you a picture. Thanks for writing. Best Wishes.

Your Friend

Chuck Norris

Chuck Norris Letter 1980's

CHUCK NORRIS FAN CLUB

904 SILVER SPUR RD.
SUITE #380
ROLLING HILLS ESTATES, CA 90274

Dear Dot Branham,

Thank you for your interest and support. Fans are very important to an actor, for without all of you, there would be no CHUCK NORRIS.

The road to recognition has not been an easy one. It has taken me years of hard work and training. As they say, nothing worth achieving is ever easy or without sacrifice. The best advice I can give you is never lose sight of your goals and always strive to your ultimate potential. If you really believe in what you are doing, you will fulfill your dreams.

The greatest benefit I have received from my years in karate is the philosophy I've learned that any goal can be achieved if first you get a visual picture in your mind of the goal you want. Then be determined to stick with it until the goal is realized, you must study or train accordingly. If you do this, I do not think there is a goal in the world you cannot accomplish. That is the great thing about America; every dream is a possibility.

The growth of the CHUCK NORRIS FAN CLUB depends on the people like you. As a member you will receive an official membership card, an 8 x 10 autographed photo, and a biography of CHUCK NORRIS. You will also receive a quaterly newsletter. The fee for joining the CHUCK NORRIS FAN CLUB IS $15.00 to cover postage and will be renewable annually.

If you would like to become a member of the fan club please complete the enclosed application form and return it with a check or money order for $15.00 payable to CHUCK NORRIS FAN CLUB, c/o Century Martial Arts Supply, 1705 National Blvd., Oklahoma City, Ok 73110.

Warmest regards,

Chuck Norris

CHUCK NORRIS

Chuck Norris Letter 1980's

Signed Folder & Photo's

Page: 54 Eastern Heroes - Way of the Dragon Special

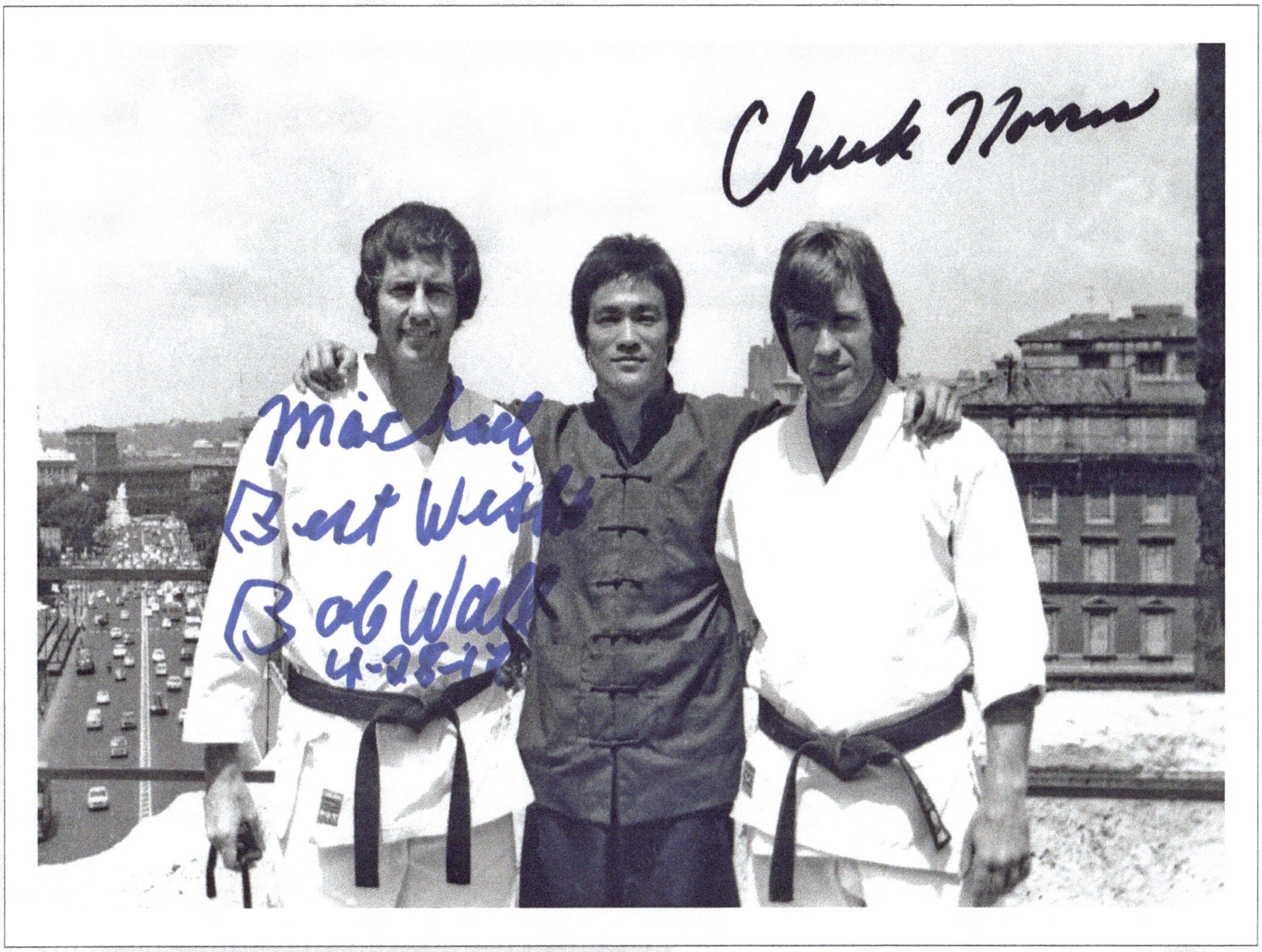
Chuck Norris
Michael
Best Wishes
Bob Wall
4-28-17

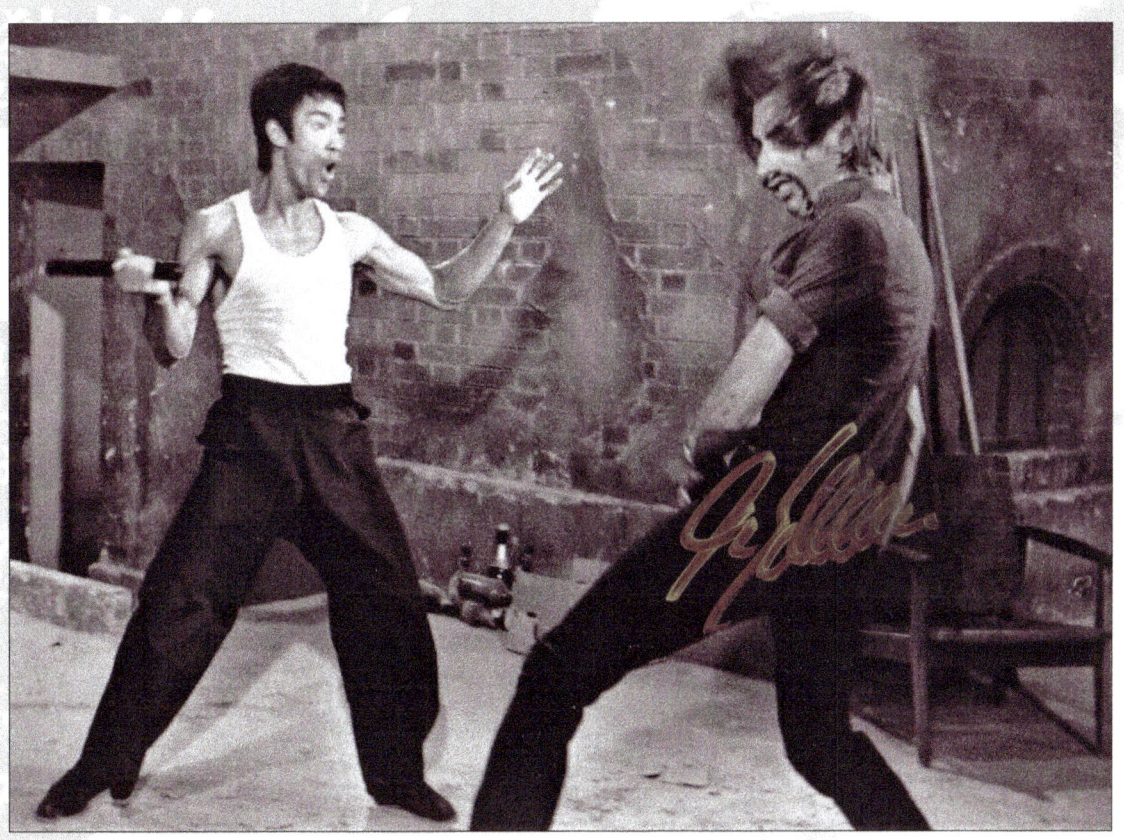

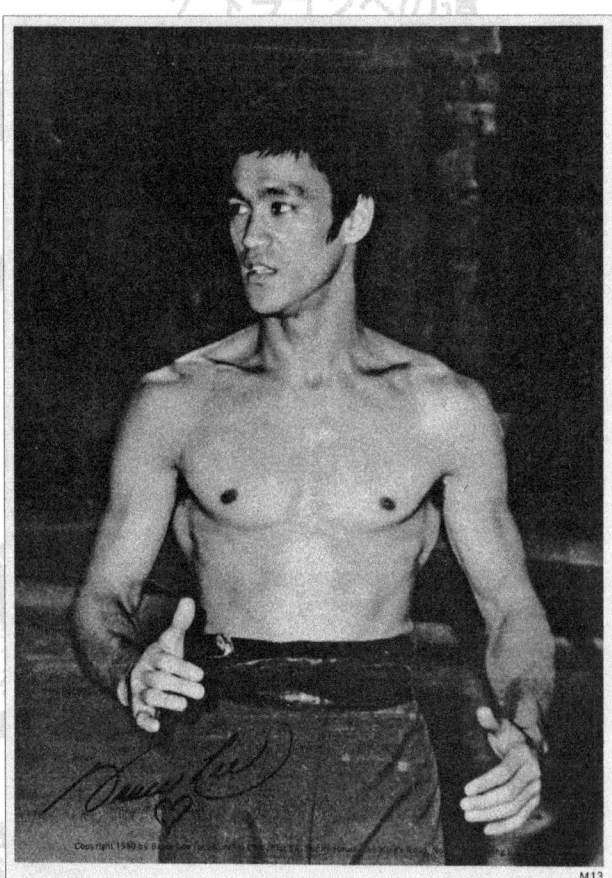

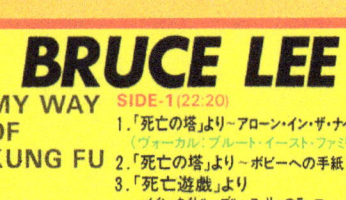

Cassette EPs & LPs

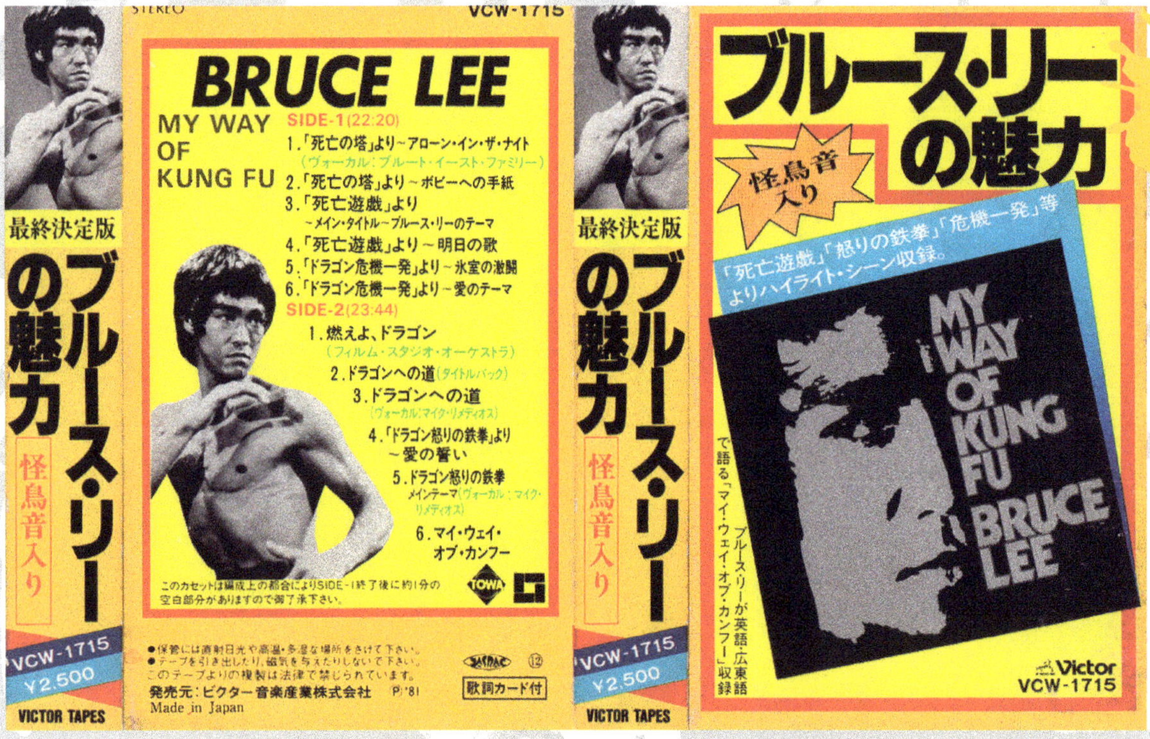

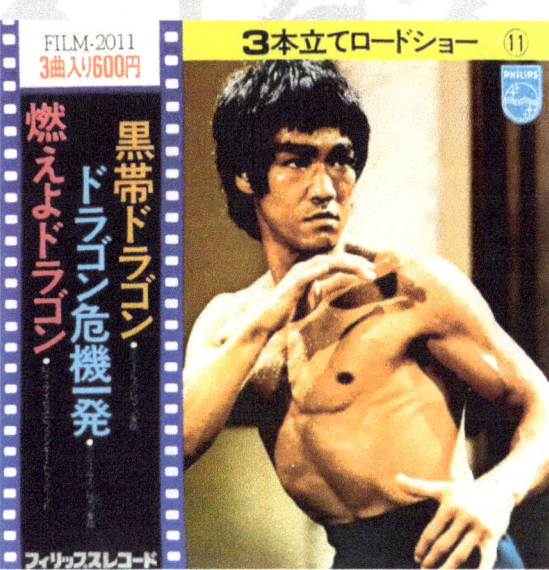

Transfers

Stereo
CBS
SONY
ACTION & SPECTACLE MOVIE THEMES

BRUCE LEE
BIG SPECIAL
THE WAY OF THE DRAGON
Enter The Dragon
THE BIG BOSS
FIST OF FURY
ブルース・リー専科

ORIGINAL SOUNDTRACK RECORDING
THE WAY OF THE DRAGON
ドラゴンへの道

燃えよドラゴン/ドラゴンへの道
不滅の鉄拳・ドラゴン大全集

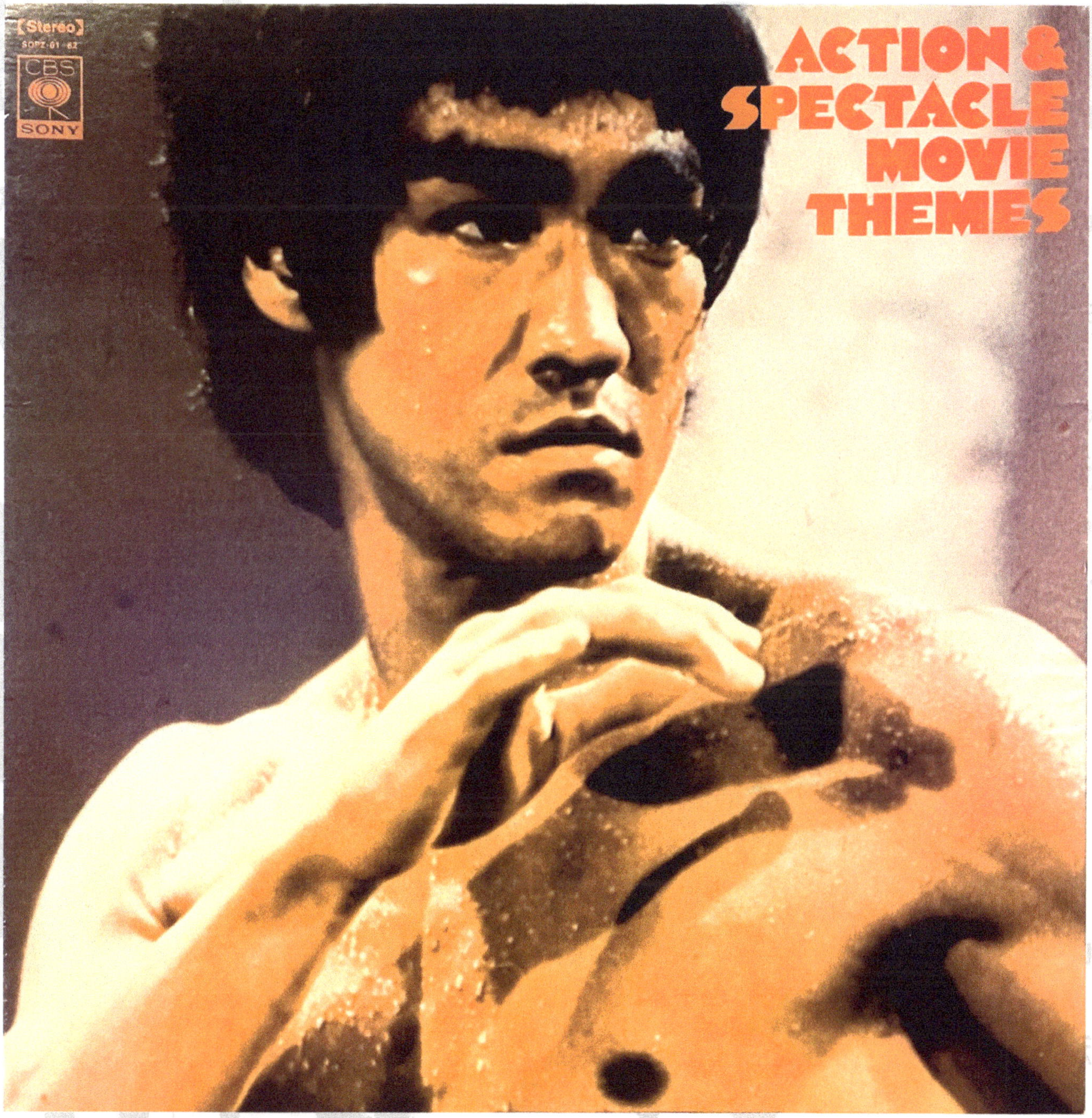

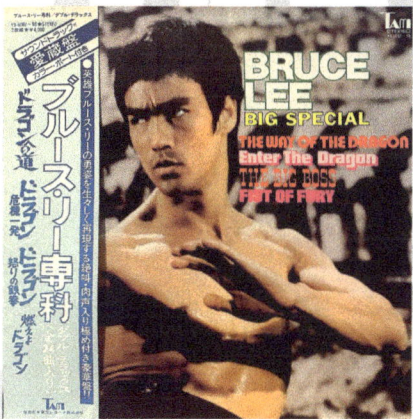

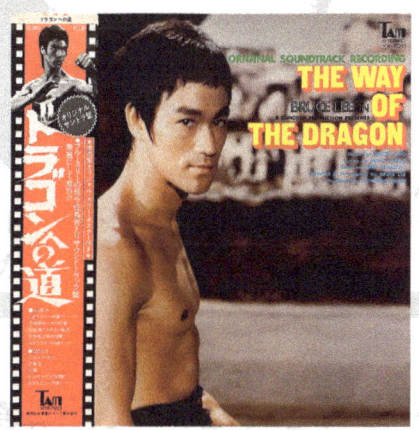

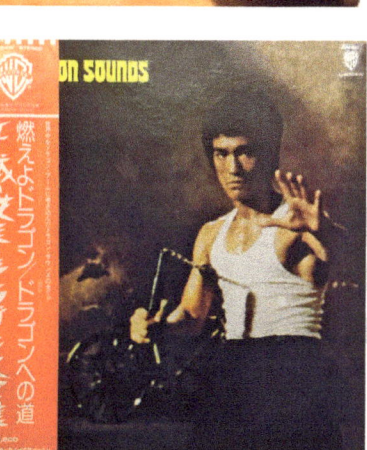

RCA
¥1,300
ドラゴンへの道 燃えよドラゴン
ブルース・リー・スペシャル
Bruce Lee

RCA
SCREEN Action THEME SPECIAL
RICHARD HUNTER AND HIS ORCHESTRA

SCREEN MUSIC BEST 100 SERIES
ACTION

ブルース・リー／ドラゴン・サウンド大全集
YX-7025〈STEREO〉¥2,500
ブルース・リー
ポスター（死亡遊戯）付き
怪鳥音入り
サウンドトラック他
●これが最新にして最高のドラゴン・サウンド魅力のすべて!!
ブルース・リー／ドラゴン・サウンド大全集
●ドラゴンへの道●カトーのテーマ●ドラゴン怒りの鉄拳●燃えよドラゴン
●ドラゴンへの道●吼えろ!ドラゴン●鏡の中の決闘●大激闘●フォーエバー!
ブルース・リー●ブラック・ビューティ号のテーマ●ドラゴン危機一発●踊れ!ドラゴン
●ブルース・リーのグリーン・ホーネット●ドラゴンへの道／全14曲
Tam
発売元■東宝レコード株式会社
BRUCE LEE
GON SOUNDS SPECIAL
Tam
STEREO
YX-7025

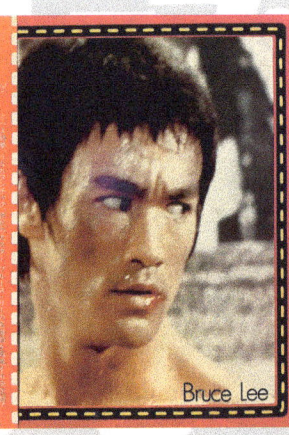

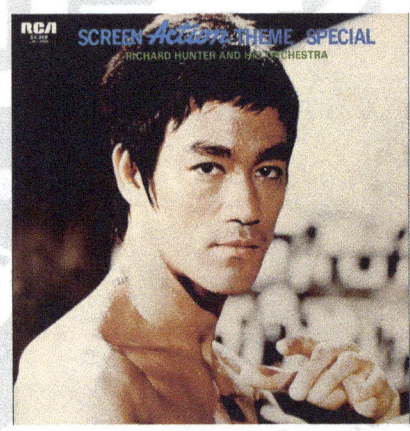

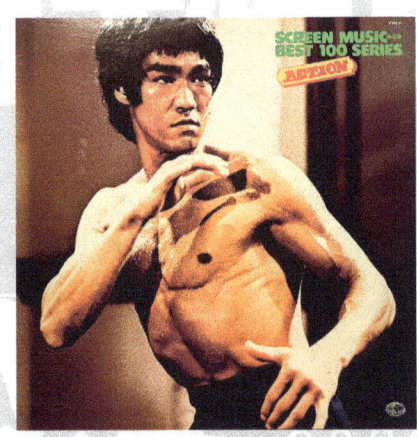

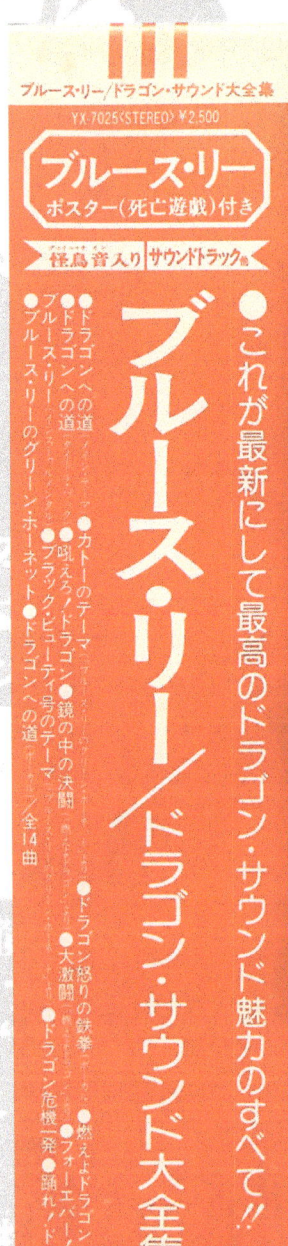

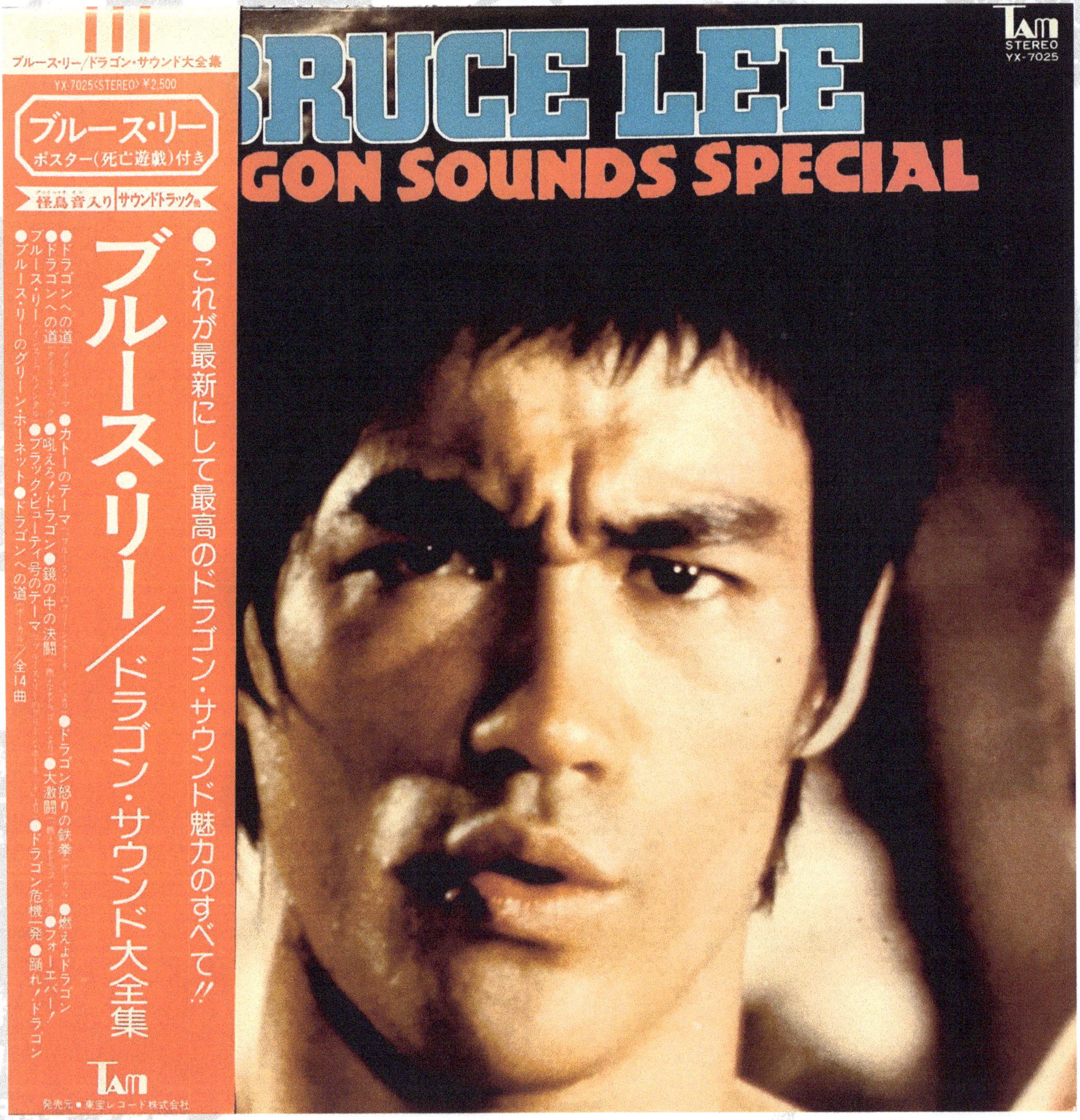

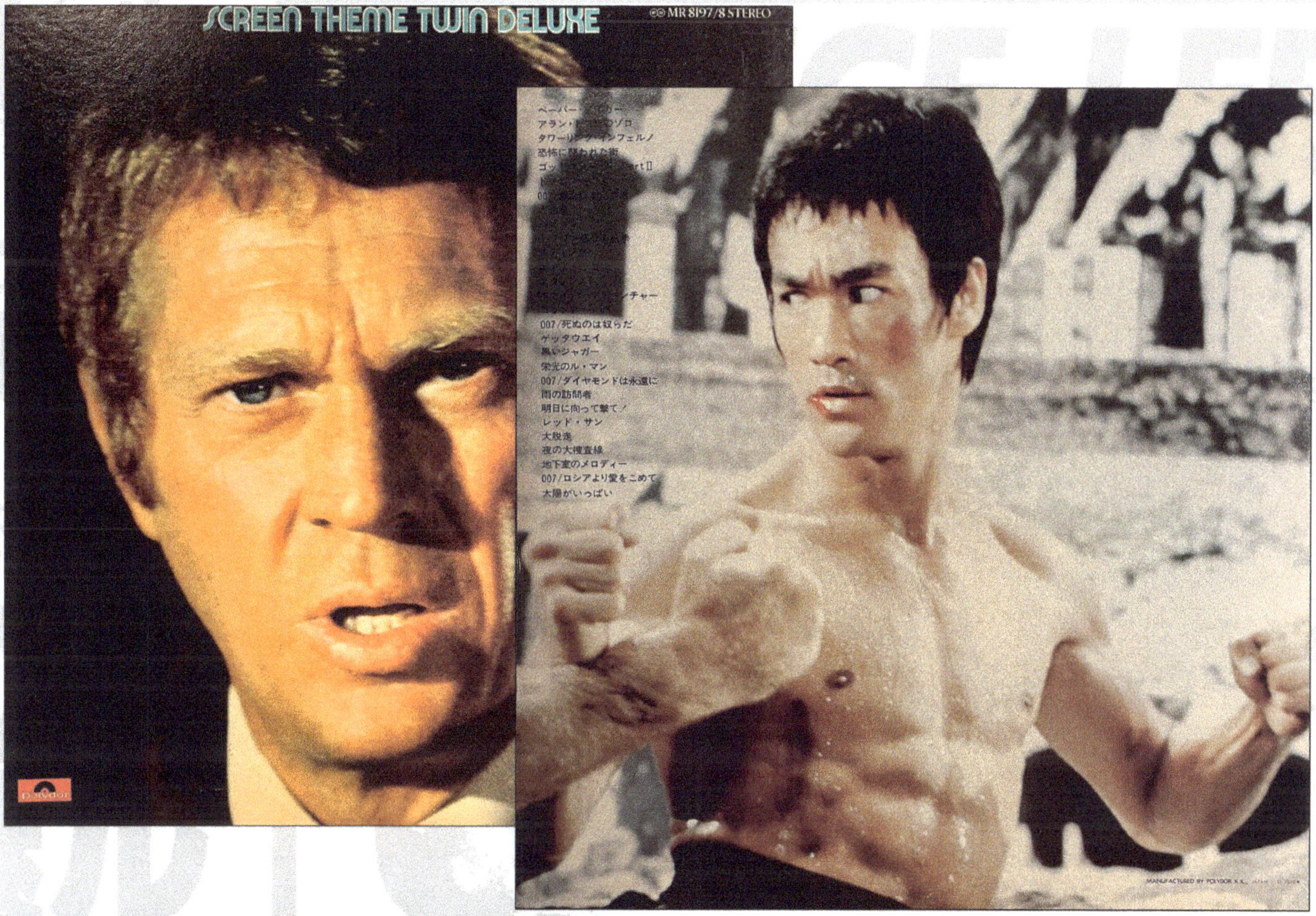

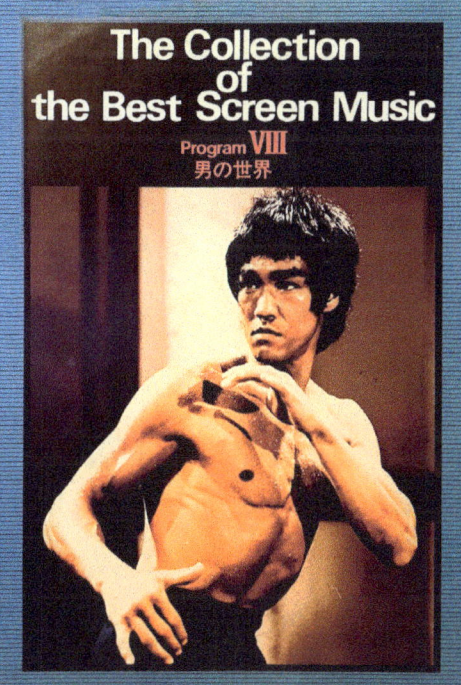

THE WAY OF THE DRAGON
STARRING: BRUCE LEE
Produced by Raymond Chow
Directed by Bruce Lee
A Raymond Chow's Golden Harvest Group Release
Distributed through Golden Communications
RANK VIDEO
BRUCE LEE
BRUCE LEE THE WAY OF THE DRAGON
Once more the Colosseum echoes the sound of a fight to the death!
THE WAY OF THE DRAGON
VHS

FIST OF FURY
BRUCE LEE · NORA MIAO
1973/Colour/approx. 100 mins.
The kung fu adventure considered by many to be the best of all the Bruce Lee films.
The story is set in Shanghai in 1908. Bruce Lee plays the martial arts expert who unleashes a "fist of fury" in a one-man vendetta against the gang that kills his kung fu master and terrorises his former school. Non-stop action and stunning fight sequences are the hallmarks of Bruce Lee films, and this one weaves them all into a classic tale of a man putting his life on the line to save his friends.
Produced by Raymond Chow
Directed by Lo Wei
No. 1 The Big Boss
No. 3 The Way of the Dragon
No. 4 Game of Death
Other titles in the Bruce Lee Collection.
Golden Harvest Group
Distributed through Golden Communications
Rank Home Video
BRUCE LEE
BRUCE LEE COLLECTION No 2
FIST OF FURY
18
VHS
5 014847 007127

ブルース・リーが自ら
メガフォンをとった貴重な作品。
GOLDEN HARVEST PRESENTS A RAYMOND CHOW PRODUCTION
BRUCE LEE in THE WAY OF THE DRAGON
頼りなさそうな中国人青年タン(ブルース・リー)が実はクンフーの達人でダブルヌンチャクを使い大活躍。圧巻は後半の白人武闘家ワン(チャック・ノリス)とのローマコロシアムでの対決シーン。華麗なアクション・シーンでブルース・リーの美学をあますところなく見せてくれる文字通りのワンマン映画。
●スタッフ
製作:レイモンド・チョウ(鄒文懐)
企画・監督・脚本・音楽・武術指導:ブルース・リー(李小龍)
●キャスト
ブルース・リー(李小龍)
ノラ・ミャオ(苗可秀)
チャック・ノリス、他
原題:猛龍過江
(The Way of the Dragon)
1972年/香港映画/広東語版日本語字幕入り/シネマスコープ/カラー/日本公開1975年
This motion picture is protected by copyright and this recording may be used only in private homes in Japan.
©1972 GOLDEN HARVEST (INT'L) LTD. All Rights Reserved.
製造・発売元 (株)ポニー キャニオン C-6-21
SELL ONLY
税込¥3,800 税抜¥3,689
MADE IN JAPAN
PONY CANYON
最後のブルース・リー
ドラゴンへの道
Golden Harvest
字幕スーパー
PCVP-10241
98分 Hi-Fi MONO
税抜¥3,689
最後のブルース・リー
ドラゴンへの道
GOLDEN HARVEST PRESENTS A RAYMOND CHOW PRODUCTION
BRUCE LEE in THE WAY OF THE DRAGON

Game of Death
Bruce Lee
Bruce Lee
Game of Death
Game of Death
THE 1978 ACTION CLASSIC
18
054 166 3
Manufactured, sold and distributed in the U.K. by PolyGram Video Ltd.

VHS

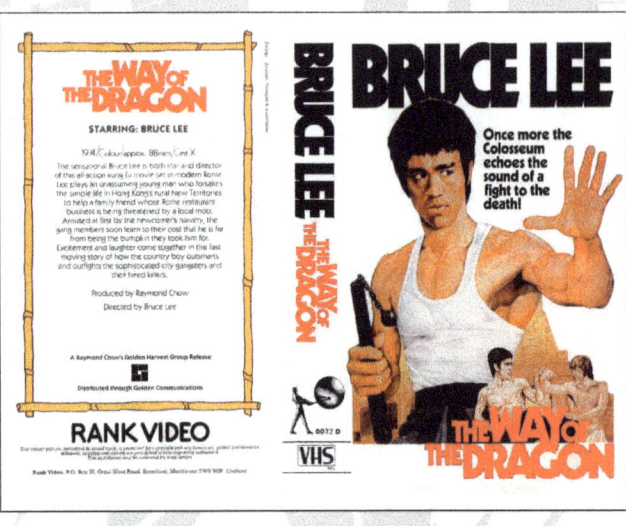

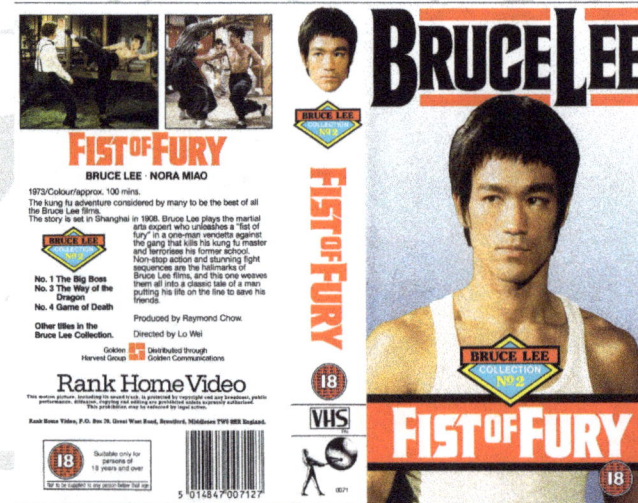

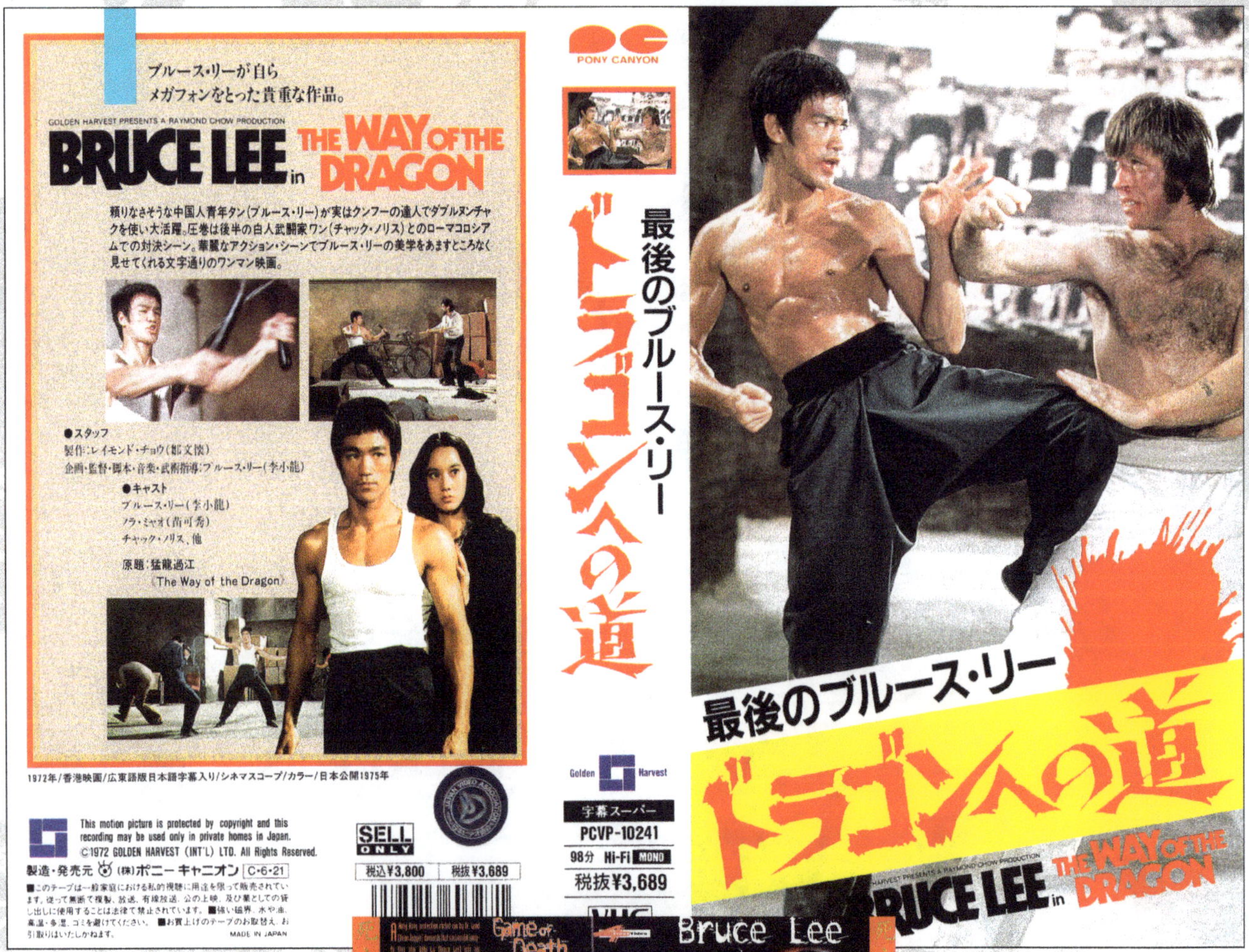

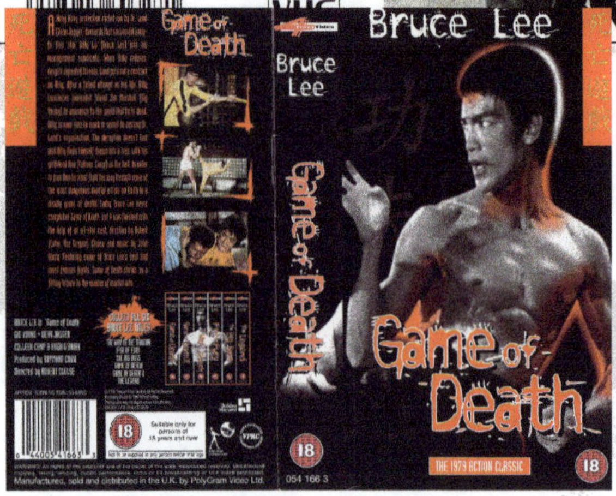

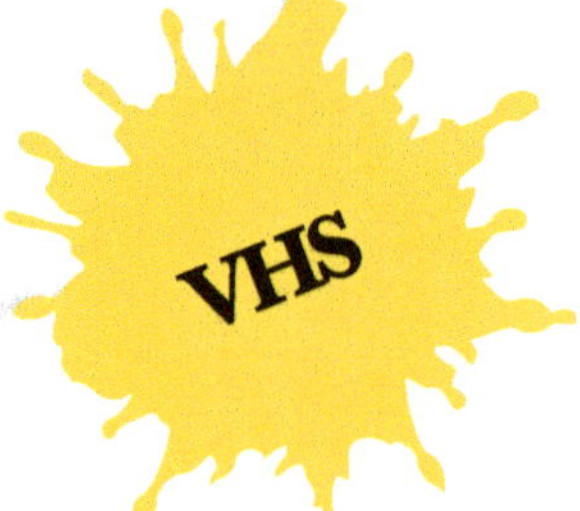

Tsing On Tsui Original Artwork

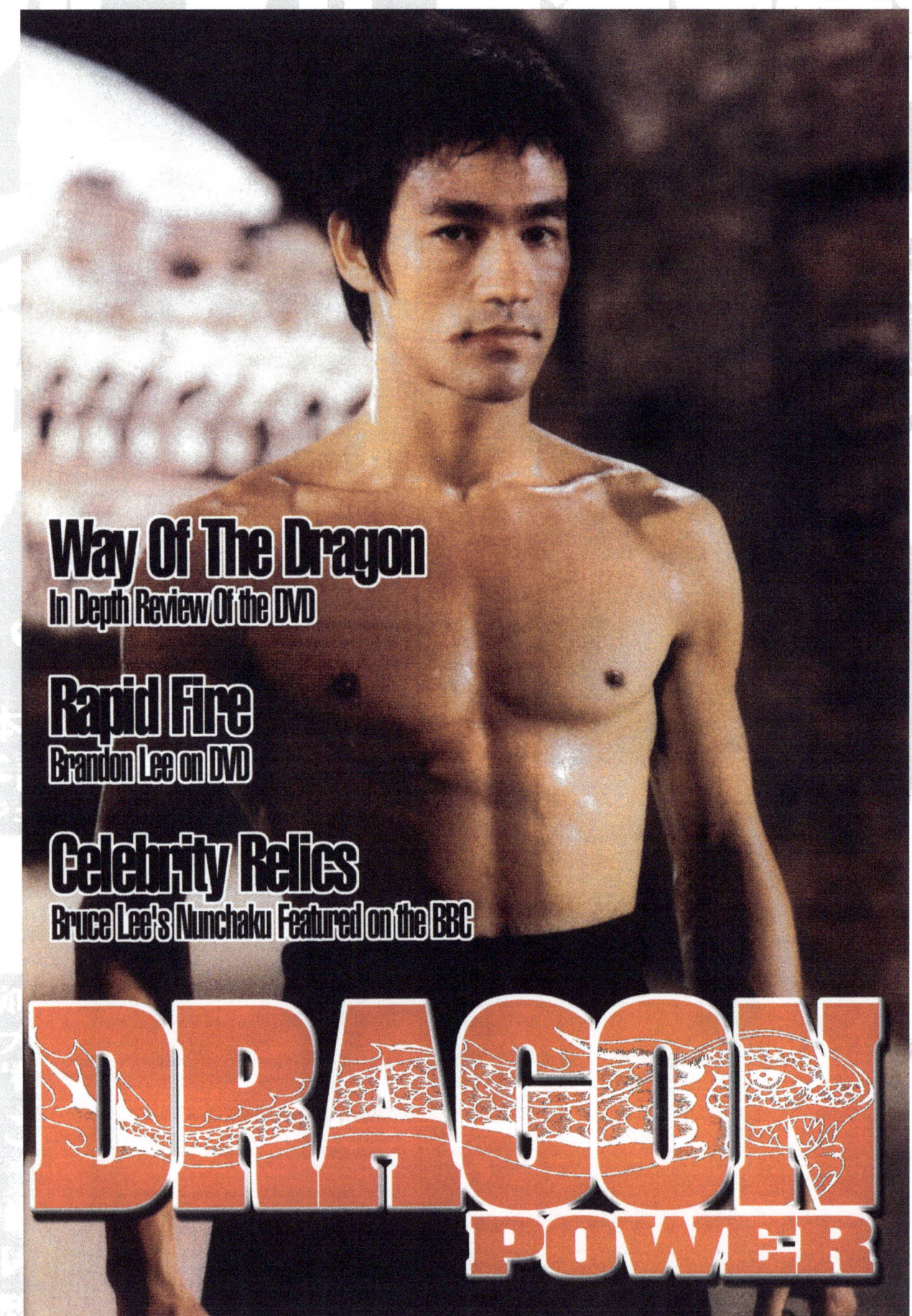

DRAGON

THE BEST IN KUNG FU — VOL 2 No.7 30p EVERY MONTH

THE GREAT MARTIAL ARTS MAGAZINE FOR THE GREAT MARTIAL ARTISTS

Street Fight- Don't be a mug!

BRUCE LEE SUFFERS HIS ONE AND ONLY BLOW!

Kung Fu Cinema- Bruce Lee and the Supermen

Kung-Fu Fighters

Vol 1 No 1
50p

PACKED WITH KUNG-FU SUPERSTARS

Ed Parker – the man who discovered BRUCE LEE

TECHNIQUES OF KUNG-FU:

T'ai Chi Chuan

The Dragon was Silent: BRUCE LEE'S LIFE & DEATH

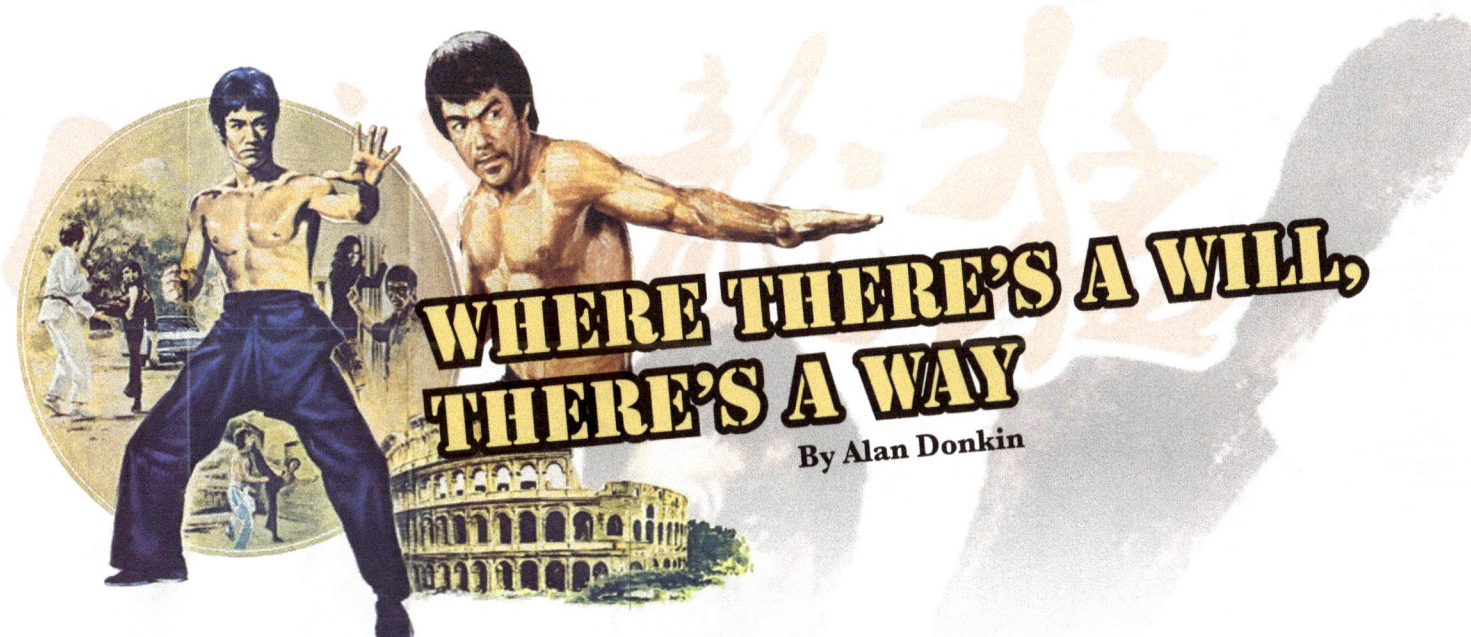

WHERE THERE'S A WILL, THERE'S A WAY

By Alan Donkin

I've never seen Way of the Dragon. Yes, that's right. A person writing about Way of the Dragon in a magazine dedicated to Way of the Dragon has never seen Way of the Dragon.

If you are judging, I don't blame you. Bruce Lee's work is Kung Fu Cinema 101. The nuts and bolts of a fan's education. The platinum standard of the genre. So, what happened? I entered the genre via Drunken Master and Snake in the Eagle's Shadow. After that, it was low budget indies on the old satellite channel, movies4men2. I watched Duel of the Seven Tigers and, wowed by the quality of Phillip Ko, Cliff Lok and Casanova Wong, ordered my own copy. That opened the door to Vengeance Video, and a world of titles that were more obscure than those accessible to the average punter. I threw myself into watching those. Bruce's work seemed like it would always be there. The dvds taking their place on the shelf, always accessible. Something I'd get round to when I wanted a guaranteed dose of quality. If I watched too many crappy films, I could cleanse my palate with the finest of the genre.

There's also the fact that they held a mythical status for me, and I really didn't want to be disappointed in any way. As such, Bruce's films almost became unwatchable. Too precious to indulge in, and too commonplace to be curious about. It's a level of logic that's absurdly flawed, but we all have our classics that we haven't watched, haven't we? I'm not just on about films in this genre. Think of the wider medium. Consider the lists of 100 best films you see, put out every year or decade by magazines and institutions. How many have you actually seen? Hands up who's genuinely seen Citizen Kane. Can you hear the sound of straws being clutched? Way of the Dragon is, in fact, the only one that I haven't seen now. I've watched the rest. Fist of Fury is the best. Sorry, Enter the Dragon fans.

When Rick asked me if I'd like to do a piece for this magazine, a little klaxon sounded in my mind: 'Hypocrite Alert! You haven't even SEEN the film!' Instead of shirking from the offer, though, I decided to use my ignorance as a starting point. Now was the time to watch it.

I don't just want to do a review, though. There's thousands of those, from people a lot more knowledgeable than me. I needed an angle that's (hopefully) a little bit fresh. So, I've decided to use, as a starting point, my great passion: poster collecting. I thought, 'What is the purpose of a theatrical poster'? Fundamentally, it's to advertise the movie. To encourage people to spend money to go and watch it. To provide the viewer with an idea of what the film is about. With this in mind, I've decided to look at a selection of Way of the Dragon posters. What do they tell me, and what expectations do they create? When I first thought of the idea, I imagined myself as a cinemagoer in 1972 or 1973, looking at the posters, and using the roleplay as a tool to speculate how people must have felt at the time. That's what theatrical posters are designed to do, so could I assess their contemporary effectiveness on myself? The easy answer is 'no'. Of course not! The early 1970s was a different time entirely. A different context, a different culture. I have the benefit of knowing the legacy of Bruce Lee, and the esteem in which he is held to this day. It's an entirely different prism to watch the film through for the first time. Reining in that nonsense idea, I had a rethink. I settled on a simpler plan: to look at the posters as a 2022 Way of the Dragon virgin. I can still look at the material and consider what expectations are generated before I watch the film. When I think of Way of the Dragon, snippets pop into my head. Bruce Lee. Chuck Norris. Third film. 1972. Italy. Colosseum. That dialogue between IT nerd Simon and Gareth in The Office.

Those are slim pickings, though, so it's a relatively clean slate to work from.

Pre-Viewing

Internationally, lots of posters for Way of the Dragon were produced. Some were produced at the time of the theatrical release, but others were created for later distribution after Bruce's passing. Let's look at the contemporaneous Hong Kong poster first, though. It's a fantastic poster, and the hand-drawn art style is right up my street. There are two features which dominate the design: Bruce and the Colosseum. If I didn't already know that the film was set in Italy, this poster leaves me in no doubt. The Colosseum frames a couple of black and white action scenes, indicating that the big showcase fight takes place inside it. Bruce himself seems to be in mid-punch and mid-kick simultaneously. He's the hero and the visceral powerhouse of the movie. There's a love interest, too, by the look of things.

So far, so good. The British quad adds further details. As well as confirming the Italian location, there's a modern car featured in the background, revealing the setting to be the current day. In the same image, there's a fight against a bloke wearing a gi, so it's reasonable to speculate that karate is involved. The quad also trumpets the credentials of Chuck Norris (7 times World Karate Champion) and Bob Wall (1970 No. 1 Karate Professional) to support this supposition. Helpfully, Wong In-Sik's name also reveals that hapkido could feature. I've seen Hapkido, another 1972 Golden Harvest release with Wong In-Sik, and thoroughly enjoyed the martial arts on show, so I'm expecting fireworks from Way of the Dragon! The quad also reveals the (presumably) love interest to be Nora Miao, who played a similar role in Fist of Fury. She appears, in one illustration, to be tied to a post, so Bruce must at one point be rescuing the damsel in distress.

The Italian posters offer more clues about the movie. One of them shows Bruce chopping an adversary in the throat. It seems that the power of the blow has forced his opponent to drop his gun, which suggests that there may be one of those amazing scenes you get in kung fu films where a hero overcomes unfair odds using his superior skills. Guns against fists? No problem!

Both Italian posters that I've seen feature the now-familiar landmark, but the second one adds confusion into the mix. It doesn't

imagery, and even the title of the movie itself, further shore up Bruce Lee's role in the film as that of a symbol of power and righteousness.

Interestingly, the American poster calls it his 'last and best performance', which is both objectively wrong and subjectively questionable. Clearly, it's marketing guff, but it works on a certain level. It adds an extra grain of excitement to the bubbling cauldron of anticipation I'm feeling before watching it.

The Singapore poster is a stunning poster and one of my favourites. It prioritises the fighting, and also reveals the Bob Wall could be a bad guy. Now that I look closer, Bruce seems to be fighting him in front of the car in the British quad.

The Thai variant is the poster that seems to throw everything into the mix, tying up all the threads I've unpicked from the other designs so far. Bruce is positioned protectively in front of Nora Miao, fists blurred by speed. His look is angry and defiant. The Colosseum setting looms in the background. He wields his nunchaku, fights Chuck Norris, kicks Bob Wall, and – new reveal alert! – strikes Wong In-Sik. Three quality screenfighters, all fighting

and Mexican variants, although the latter does feature a strange lack of a connecting chain. It makes sense to show nunchakus – they were a standout moment in Fist of Fury, and a great selling point for the film.

The Mexican entry also shows a gun being fired, but nothing to indicate a shootout. I'm guessing that there'll be a mismatched exchange between Bruce and a hoodlum, with only one winner!

just feature the Colosseum. It reveals a number of different global landmarks. The Eiffel Tower in Paris, the Taj Mahal in Agra, and (unless I've mistaken) Tower Bridge in London. Could Way of the Dragon be more globetrotting than I first thought? I'm getting the feeling that it's more of a cosmopolitan entry than his other films.

The Lebanese poster expands the breadth of my expectations. The fight against Chuck Norris takes up most of the image, so I presume that it's the major fight in the film. Norris must be the villain of the piece. Bruce is also shown holding weapons, so the action scenes must have a fair amount of variety. This focus on weaponry – specifically, nunchakus – is present on several other posters, such as the Japanese

The dragon motif is prominent in this design, as it is in the American and French posters. It presumably symbolises strength, as well as being a callback to Lee's traditional screen name of Little Dragon, and even the year of his birth. This

Bruce. That's just ramped the expectation level up another notch!

Conclusions

So, using these posters, what can I expect?

1) It mostly takes place in Italy, with some other major locations featured.
2) It's a 1970s setting.
3) Bruce fights Chuck Norris, Bob Wall and Wong In-Sik.
4) The main showpiece fight is against Chuck Norris in the Colosseum of Rome.
5) Karate, hapkido and nunchakus are used.
6) There's a scene involving fists versus firearms.
7) Nora Miao is a kidnapped love interest.
8) The film plays a lot on the 'Bruce is the symbol of strength and honour' angle (which is perhaps the most obvious statement ever typed).

They've done a good job of giving me some insight into the content of the film. Bruce looks formidable in most of the images, promising amazing fights and a not-insignificant amount of brooding. Look at the image used on the poster from Turkey. His bloodied lip doesn't make him look vulnerable. It makes him look even more kick-ass. He's the embodiment of power. I'm stoked to watch this film, and these posters have done a stand-up job at hyping me up.

Post-Viewing

Wow. What a great film. So much to digest, and so much to enjoy. I'll address my poster-fuelled predictions first.
1) No surprises that it's set in Italy! However, it's set entirely in Italy. I've no idea what that Italian poster is going on about.
2) The setting is contemporary for the year the film was made.
3) Bruce does fight Chuck Norris, Bob Wall and Wong In-Sik. What I didn't expect was that none of them present the slightest challenge to Bruce, apart from the opening exchanges of the Norris fight. He absolutely destroys them, in the same manner that despatches of the standard minions. In retrospect, it's not unexpected. Bruce is the star, and presents himself as the near-untouchable powerhouse. He is the dragon, and uncorruptible in this tale of bullying oppressors.
4) The main showpiece fight is indeed against Chuck Norris in the Colosseum of Rome. It's a great scene, and merits its prominence on many posters. The stark backdrop in the corridors of the iconic landmark is perfect for the fight. It's distraction-free, and allows the viewer to focus entirely on the combatants.
5) Karate, hapkido and nunchakus are used in the film. I didn't expect the film to hit similar beats to Fist of Fury, with the position of kung fu as a viable martial art, that could stand shoulder to shoulder with Japanese karate, being a central story theme, embodied in Bruce's jeet kune do-esque explanations. The nunchaku work is excellent – the posters sell it well, but the reality still surpasses the expectation.
6) There's several scenes involving fists versus firearms. This was more central to the story than the posters suggested. Early on, Bruce asks about the availability of firearms in the country, and fashions darts to nullify the threat. There are several scenes involving guns, and Bruce is shown as a person who isn't fazed by them. It comes across as an East vs West action aesthetic.

7) Nora Miao is kidnapped, but isn't really a love interest. In the British quad, I thought she was tied to a wooden pole, but she's probably just clinging to a curtain. One of those moments where one feels rather stupid. Bruce seems more of a big brother to her, although the sightseeing tour bubbled with some tension, and her huff at one point is indicative of something extra.

8) The film does play a lot on the 'Bruce is the symbol of strength and honour' angle – to the point where he's pretty much indestructible! He's the country bumpkin with a sense of justice, who refuses to back down to threats and bullies. It's a commanding performance and he eats up the screen every second he features.

What I wasn't expecting was the focus on comedy. The first third of the movie is full of humorous moments, showing a side to Bruce that it's a tragedy we didn't see more of. None of the posters suggest that there's comedy in the film. It took me completely by surprise. I would have also thought that the posters would make more of the cameo by Malisa Longo! For all their prominence on the promotional material, the three main villains barely feature. They were evidently seen as the main additional selling points, regardless of screentime. I liked the 'dial a hard bastard' plot point, even if it meant that they weren't featured as much as I'd have liked.

In conclusion, after watching the film for the first time, I'd say that the posters did their job rather well. Some of the minutiae were wrong, but that's to be expected. There was a greater focus on guns than I expected, and the fights were more one-sided than I predicted, but most other details were round about the ballpark. One notable contrast is that the posters don't really suggest any comedy elements to the film. They are scenes that are deftly written, performed and directed by Bruce, especially during his character's 'fish out of water' circumstances. Having said that, how could they present this on a poster? Goofy caricatures? No thanks. People don't watch a Bruce Lee film for comedy, but it was a nice addition to his repertoire. It's a great film. It doesn't top the emotional intensity of Fist of Fury's ending, but I love the fade-out suggested that Bruce gravitates towards fighting injustice wherever he finds it. The posters of the film support its strengths, and draw the 'virgin' viewer towards the majority of its qualities and details.

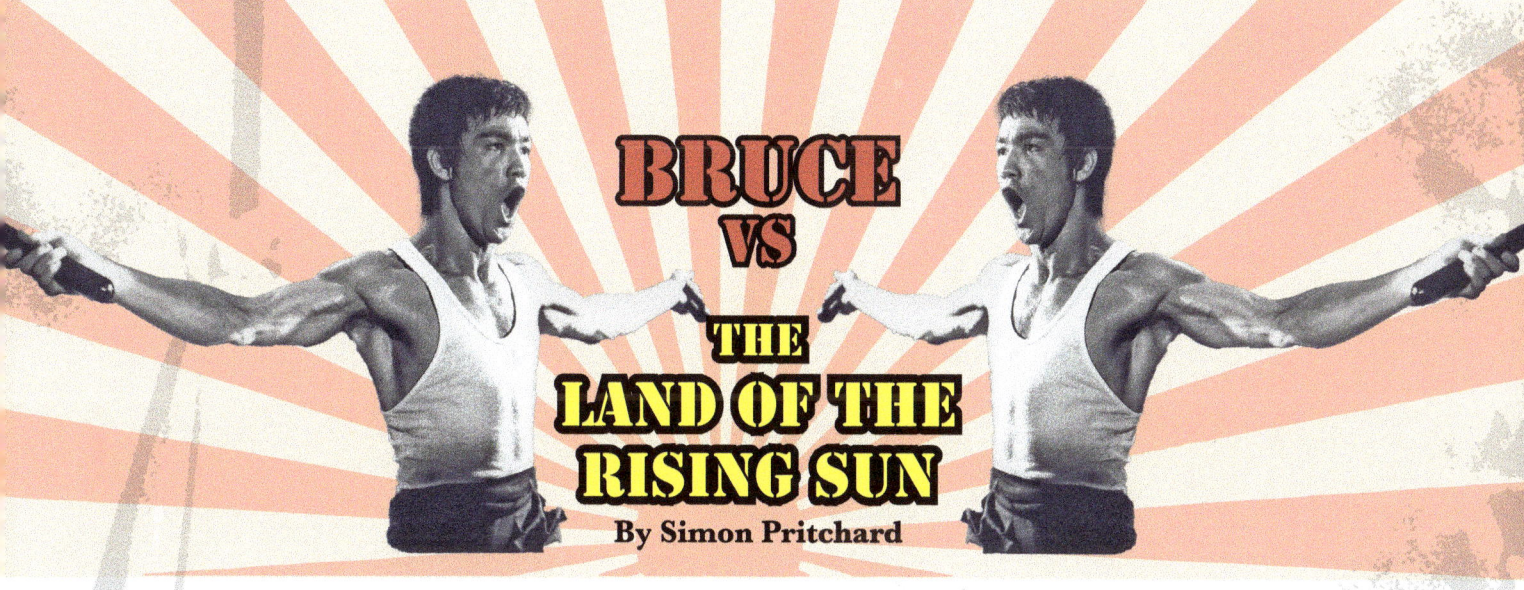

BRUCE VS THE LAND OF THE RISING SUN

By Simon Pritchard

Bruce Lee starred in his first and last directorial film fifty years ago, The Way of the Dragon. The Way of the Dragon was written by Bruce and his third Golden Harvest film, co-produced with Raymond Chow.

China and Japan's relationship throughout history has been one from allies to enemies and everything in-between. In 1854 the treaty of the "Convention of Kanagawa" was agreed between Japan and America; opening up the East to Westernisation and causing many conflicts with China. This conflict between China and Japan officially ended in 1945, but continued until Japan normalised relations with the People's Republic of China in 1972; the same year as the film was made.

In The Way of the Dragon, Bruce continues to go against the traditional and popular Qing dynasty kung fu films. The rivalry between Chinese and Japanese martial arts mixed with the political climate at this time, made this one of the most successful Hong Kong films until Enter the Dragon. Bruce originally wanted for the film to be set in America and for him to fight Western actors. But Bruce was inspired by Spartacus (1960) and wished to film in the Colosseum. The production was then written to take place in Italy.

The Way of the Dragon starts with Chen Ching-Hua (Nora Miao) and her Uncle Wang (Huang Chung-Hsin) being bullied to give up their restaurant by local gangsters. They reach out to their uncle in Hong Kong who sends Tang Lung (Bruce Lee) to help.

Uncle Wang taught the restaurant staff Karate and the staff just made light of Chinese Boxing. The thugs return and threaten the staff in an alley. The first

member of staff, Jimmy, tries to attack the leader of the thugs and is easily knocked out. Lung then defeats the thugs. Whilst Lung is happy with himself, he is told "Thugs are happiest at home and we're on their territory"

"Jimmy" is played by one of Bruce's closest friends, Unicorn Chan. It was after a chance meeting with Unicorn Chan's friend, Yukio Sameno, Bruce was introduced to Raymond Chow and Golden Harvest. More on this story in the previous episode of Eastern Heroes; Vol 1. Ep 3 (December 2021).

The Crime Boss's second in command, a rather flamboyant straight-up gangster, Ho (Wei Ping-Ou) returns with the thugs armed and takes the restaurant staff hostage. Lung is given a ticket back to Hong Kong and escorted out of the restaurant....

This leads to one of the most famous nunchaku fight scenes ever filmed. This scene is frequently seen in popular culture from modern art and branding to cartoons and films, to inspiring people to learn or to master nunchucks from my children, Michael and Amber Pritchard, to experts in martial arts.

Lung at first takes down three thugs with a pole. They return stronger with seven men and that's when Lung brings out two nunchakus. As they attack, Lung uses power strikes with the nunchakus taking them down. As they attack again, Lung parries the attacks with one nunchaku whilst striking with another and attacks again.
Throughout the fight, the thugs are constantly trying to surround Lung and close the distance. Lung uses speed of the nunchakus, constant change in direction

and stance to confuse the thugs, creating space and opportunities to attack.

Lung throws a nunchaku to one side with confidence and proceeds to intimidate the thugs. Their confidence is gone and they attack Lung one at a time, as Lung finishes them. In a rare moment of wit, the last thug picks up Lung's nunchaku and tries to use it, only hitting himself in the face.

Fast forward more threats, an assassination attempt, a presumed kidnapping of the female interest Ching-Hua, pressure for Lung to return to Hong Kong; Ho hires Bob Wall and Hwang In-Shik to defeat Lung. Bob Wall was referred to as 'Tom' within the film and 'Fred' within the credits. Hwang In-Shik was just referred to as 'Japanese Karateka'. "Karateka" is a generic term for a Karate practitioner. The term does not define rank such as "Kyu", "Senpai", "Sensei" etc. does within Japanese forms.
Bob Wall sadly passed on 30th January 2022 aged 82 and left a true legacy for others to follow. Bob was an 8th Dan in Kyokushin Budokai (Karate) and 9th Dan in Tang Soo Do. Bob co-founded World Black Belt Inc. with Chuck Norris. Bob is best known for playing O'Hara in Enter the Dragon but was first and foremost a martial artist. Bob also trained with "Judo Gene" LeBell, Benny Urquidez, Richard Norton and many others.

Hwang In-Shik's appearance, although short, is a real treat for kung fu fans to see the man fighting Bruce. Born in Sunch'ŏn, North Korea, In-Shik's family moved to Seoul, South Korea, as a young child and started to learn martial arts. In-Shik earned his black belt in Hapkido at the age of sixteen and went to study at the Korea Hapkido Association under Ji Han-Jae, the founder of Sin Moo Hapkido and also an actor on Game of Death.

Also in 1972, the director and writer Huang Feng brought Jackie Chan, Sammo Hung, Angela Mao, Tang Wei-Cheng and more to Korea looking for new techniques to evolve the Hong Kong skill set. Huang Feng enrolled the actors in Korea Hapkido Association for a little over three months training under Hwang In-Shik and his Master, Ji Han-Jae.

Hwang In-Shik fought Jackie Chan for fifteen minutes in The Young Master and played the main villain in Dragon Lord.

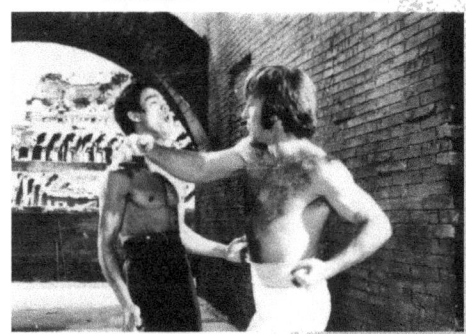

In-Shik also starred in Hapkido, When Taekwondo Strikes & The Association with Angela Mao and in one of the best Wong Fei-Hung films, The Skyhawk. Hwang In-Shik is 10th Dan and one of the most well known teachers and practitioners of Hapkido.

Four of the restaurant staff and Lung are lured away under the pretense of a truce, only to be met by 'Tom' and 'Japanese Karateka'. The first member of staff attacks Tom who overpowers him with Yoko-geri's (roundhouse kicks) and a mae-geri (front kick). Tom reaps and strikes. Another member of staff attacks and Tom uses strikes to close the gap and the kiba-dachi (horse stance) to uki-goshi (floating hip throw) to the ground and strikes and repeats these moves.

The origins of what we consider Karate-do today has only been around since approximately the 1850's. Karate was introduced to mainland Japan by a native of the Okinawan Prefecture, Gichin Funakoshi in 1916. Gichin Funakoshi founded a style called Shotokan. Shotokan became a very popular style of karate due to its focus on a handful of powerful blocks, strikes, and kicks with the aim of finishing the fight in a couple moves. (Footage of Gichin Funakoshi - https://www.youtube.com/watch?v=jH9TDqeAPFA)

Japanese Karateka enters to fight the restaurant staff whilst Lung challenges Tom. Tom tries his Yoko-geri which Lung avoids and side kicks Tom to the ground. Tom gets up and tries attacking. In this scene it shows one of the essential principles of Jeet Kune Do where Lung uses an attack as a defence, in this instance a low kick before using the momentum to attack again.

Bruce created a method within Jeet Kune Do that removes the unnecessary and leaves the purest of movements. In sparring competitions, looking at an opponent's upper torso, rather than their eyes, you can learn quickly the signals the body gives off and where their attack will come from. Bruce has heavily reduced or eliminated these signals. Using his whole body, leading from hips, Bruce moves forward with all attacks, reducing reaction time, like an explosion. With all the power and unpredictability, Jeet Kune Do remains a very effective form still today.

After taking a beating, Tom realises he will not win in a standing position. Tom then tries to reap / throw Lung to the ground which Lung counters and attacks taking Tom down. A dazed Tom gets to his feet, realising his defeat tries one more time to attack and is then finished by Lung.

At this point the Japanese Karateka is defeating the restaurant staff and literally giving a good kicking to brother whilst he's down! In the classic kung-fu production technique, the dramatic music starts and the Japanese Karateka and Lung meet eyes over the open plain and they walk towards each other, knowing one will not make it out alive. The Japanese Karateka is unfortunately easily defeated by Lung and restaurant staff drag him off to continue the beating.

Whilst arranging for Tom and the Japanese Karateka to finish Lung off once and for all, the crime boss tells Ho that money is no object. Ho takes this opportunity and also employs a world class Karate expert, Colt (Chuck Norris), to defeat Lung. After the defeat of Tom and the Japanese Karateka, Ho lures Lung away to face Colt.

There are also key scenes in regard to the storyline within these sequences. I will avoid 'spoilers' for anyone who has not seen the film in its entirety. That said, if you do not know or cannot guess Bruce beats Chuck, sorry.

Bruce wanted to film in the Colosseum, Italy, but even the films that inspired him had to recreate the scenery in Hollywood studios as filming inside the Colosseum is illegal. The film team bribed Officials to sneak cameras in and film for a few hours. This did not give enough time to film the whole sequence there but they managed to get usable footage from inside the amphitheater. The rest of the sequence was filmed in the Golden Harvest studios.

Lung and Colt meet in the Colosseum and without words, remove their jackets and "warm-up". The scene also introduces a calico kitten who oversees the fight. The camera flicks to the kitten throughout the fight and shows the kitten's reactions, from curiosity to hissing anger. With Bruce's philosophy, is the kitten a representation of innocence against evil and the defensive skills of a natural predator? Or was Bruce just trying to inspire Carl Thomas to write a song about "cats that are as fast as lightning" two years later? Who knows!?

As they warm-up, Colt performs kata movements that are stronger and more fluid than Tom's previously. Lung is performing Chinese boxing techniques. The kitten 'meows' and the fight is on.

Lung attacks with the same roundhouse kicks that defeated Tom. Colt blocks these and returns his own kicks. They kick and block each other until Colt catches Lung and knocks him over. Lung is clearly not impressed. Lung returns to his feet and attacks, Colt blocks these and strikes Lung several times finishing with an elbow. Taking this opportunity Colt performs a hip throw taking Lung to the ground. Lung blocks the proceeding strikes and grabs Colt's chest hair. Lung returns to his feet blowing the chest hair out of his hand but takes another beating.

Colt at this point is getting cocky and Lung reconsiders his strategy. Colt attacks with

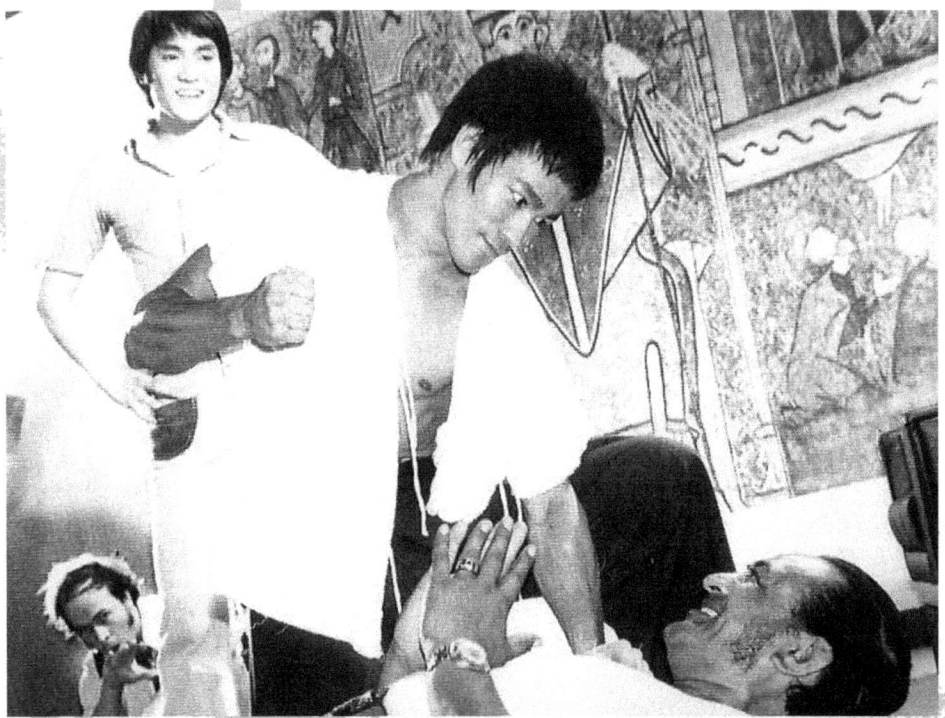

multiple kicks which Lung evades. Colt who has been dominating the fight so far starts to get more cautious and frustrated. They front up again and Colt looks concerned over Lung's foot work and he is caught off guard by a multitude of kicks, knocking him off his feet.

Colt now attacks harder with a combination containing a beautiful Uraken (spinning backfist) and Mawashi-geri (spinning roundhouse kick) to no avail. Lung starts to mix body shoots and facial strikes with his kicks, confusing Colt, giving Lung the opportunity to land some strong strikes.

As they face off again, Colt is clearly injured as Lung reaps his legs, dazing him further. Colt will never give up despite his injuries, leading Lung to end the fight by breaking Colt's arm and then an "oblique kick". This is a stomp kick made to keep an opponent at bay which focuses its impact a little above the knee or at the shin. A move famously used by the MMA fighter Jon Jones. This can cause long-standing damage to the joints and ligaments but as Bruce shows, can break bones easily as well.

As a true martial artist, Colt struggles to his feet, falling and struggling from the injuries he has sustained, refusing to give up; Colt tries to kick, only falling flat on his face. Struggling to his feet again, they make eye contact and they both know how it will end. Lung subtly shakes his head telling Colt it is over. Colt refuses to lose and lunges at Lung resulting in his neck being broken.

Lung looks visibly distressed after taking the life of a fellow martial artist and shows respect by humbly placing Colt's Gi jacket and belt over his body. The film then concludes with more key scenes in relation to the storyline ending with Lung speaking with Chen. With Bruce's inspiration from Hollywood movies, he could have ended it with "Frankly my dear, I don't give a damn!"

Bruce's writing and directing skills were cut far too short, along with many other things in his life. Bruce's spirit will always live on.

A Chance Meeting with the Big Boss
By Michael Nesbitt

"I get what I want and I want that restaurant"
Jon Benn – Way of the Dragon

In April 2000, like so many before me, I decided to have my own little pilgrimage to Hong Kong in search of anything Bruce Lee. At the time, I had been a fan of Bruce and Asian cinema for around 15 years, and so the anticipation of visiting the motherland where all my heroes lived and worked, left me highly excited for what I was about to experience. Unfortunately for me, the journey didn't turn out to be quite what I hoped for.

At the start of the millennium, the Internet was in its infancy, so I couldn't research the places I wanted to go visit. In reality, I expected Bruce Lee to be found on every street corner in Hong Kong. Looking back on the trip over 20 years later, I feel a little disheartened by the lack of research I did before carrying out my so-called pilgrimage. I didn't know the addresses of anywhere I wanted to visit, not even Bruce Lee's home on Cumberland Road… The closest I got to Bruce, was visiting Aberdeen Harbour which was seen at the beginning of Enter the Dragon. I was hoping the shops would have an abundance of magazines, books, Posters, and a host of rare memorabilia. In fact, I couldn't find anything. Even when I visited one of the most famous martial art shops in the world, Kung Fu Supplies on 188 Johnston Road, Wanchai, unfortunately, it had nothing Bruce Lee related for sale, the only thing I came away with was a Kung Fu Supplies carrier bag.

Three days had passed, and still nothing. That was until one of the tour guides mentioned The Puzzle Café in Kowloon, which housed Bruce Lee exhibits. Holding the vague directions on how to get there in my hands, given to me by the tour guide, I set off with high hopes. By the time I got to the area where the Puzzle Cafe was supposed to be, it took me over an hour to find it, and when I did, it was mid-afternoon, and it wasn't even open. One of the people working there told me to come back after an hour. As I waited, I was thinking about the three hours it took me, just so I could visit, and thought to myself, it better be worth it. I can't describe what it was, it was sort of a cafe/museum, and as I wandered around, I found a few bits and pieces relating to Bruce Lee, some posters, lobby cards, and photos, however, they were not the exhibits I was hoping to find.

My girlfriend at the time must've been sick to death of me complaining about the lack of Bruce Lee things to see in Hong Kong, and blurted out: "Why don't you just look in the phonebook". To me, that sounded like a great idea, but to her, it was a sarcastic joke. It took me only a few minutes to come across a little ad for The Bruce Lee Cafe. I quickly wrote the address on a piece of paper and jumped into a taxi. It must have been the shortest taxi ride ever; we literally got in, and got out, as the Bruce Lee Cafe was only a two-minute walk from our hotel. As soon as I saw the entrance, I remembered reading about it in Impact magazine a few months previous. I wouldn't say the café itself was anything spectacular, however, it did feel special to me, as it was solely dedicated to Bruce, and the walls were adorned with posters, lobby cards, photos and other kinds of memorabilia of him. The Cafe itself was empty, but Bruce was everywhere, on the walls, above the counters, on the tables, and as I made my way downstairs, there

was even more stuff to see.

We had been there for about half an hour, slowly walking around, taking footage with my trusty camcorder, and using the last few photos left on my camera roll. Having seen everything I thought there was to see, we decided to sit and have a well-deserved cold beverage, while we decided where to go next, whereupon an older gentleman, with a big white goatee, and even whiter bushy eyebrows, came over to our table and said hello. There was of course something very familiar about him, but I just couldn't place him at all. As he carried on chatting with us, he asked us if we had liked the Cafe and if we were fans of Bruce Lee. He told us that he had transformed his restaurant just so that he could dedicate it to Bruce, as there wasn't much in Hong Kong as any kind of memorial to him. I knew that I knew him from somewhere but just didn't know where, so I asked him if he knew Bruce or had ever met him. He glanced at me with a surprised look on his face, and then started to laugh…

"You could say I'm the boss!" he told me. "Do you mean you're the boss of the cafe?" I asked back. Another hearty laugh filled

the air… "I thought you were a Bruce Lee fan?" he asked. I must've looked at him quite quizzically, because he didn't wait for me to answer, and said: "my name is Jon Benn, and I played the Mafia Boss in Way of the Dragon". As soon as he said that, it clicked in my brain. Even though I only remembered Jon from The Way of the Dragon, which had been filmed nearly 30 years previously, I still felt stupid for not realising sooner, as he still had the same look, just older. We must have sat there talking for around thirty minutes, as Jon regaled his memories of working with Bruce. Only in hindsight, do I wish I had turned my camcorder on to film him, but I was so engrossed in his tales that it didn't even cross my mind. As we were about to leave, I mentioned to Jon, that I wished that I had brought a photo for him to sign, Jon replied by saying: "Hold on one second". He then walked behind the counter and brought back one of the paper table mats with an image of Bruce on the front,

which he kindly signed for me. We said our goodbyes, and as I left The Bruce Lee Cafe, I had a feeling of accomplishment, as my pilgrimage to Hong Kong wasn't a complete failure.

The next day, we decided to go to Planet Hollywood for lunch, I had already been to a number of those restaurants in other countries, and always loved the movie memorabilia that surrounded the tables. I was in for a treat when I finally got there. Bruce's original suit from Enter the Dragon was hanging high up on the wall, but it was difficult to take a photo of it as it was hidden behind a large projection screen. There was also what was left of his original three-section staff, with one of the sections missing. And there was also the jacket and sunglasses Jason Scott Lee wore in Dragon: The Bruce Lee Story. There were other bits of legendary memorabilia housed in there, such as the sword Nora Miao uses in the 1971 classic movie, The Blade Spares None. There was also a Cobra Kai uniform from the Karate Kid, and a wine pot from Drunken Master 2. But the highlight of my trip to Hong Kong will always be the day I met the Big Boss from Way of the Dragon.

Jon Benn at his jazz club in Central, Hong Kong, which he renamed The Bruce Lee Cafe in honour of his late co-star in 1972 film The Way of the Dragon. Photo: C.Y. Yu

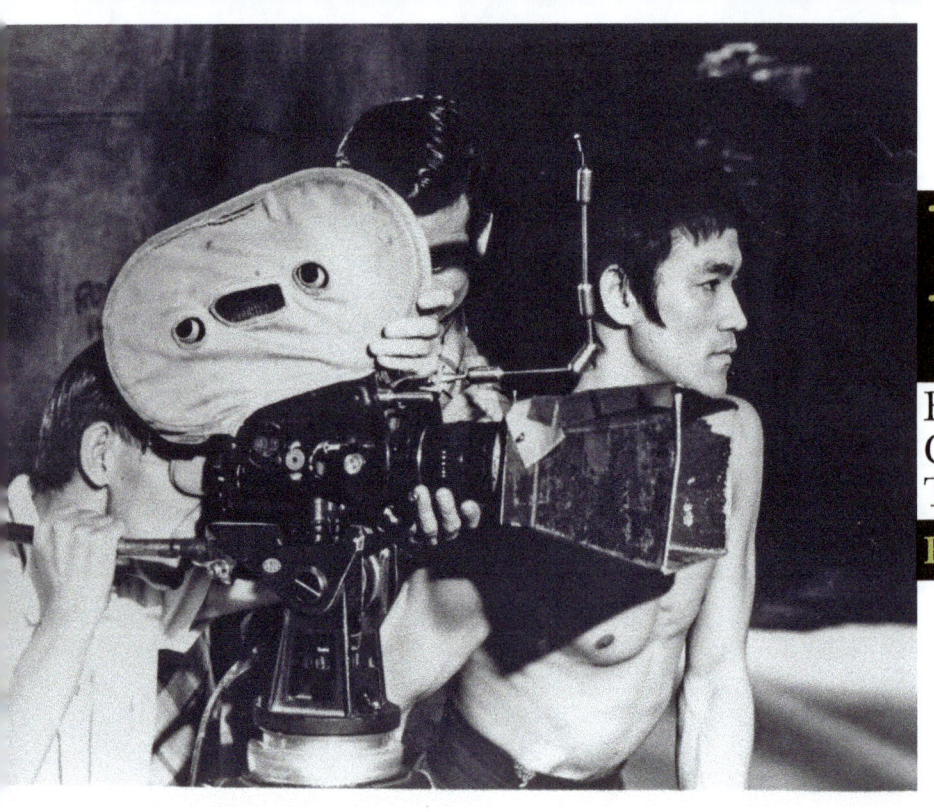

THE WAY OF THE CAMERA

Bruce Lee and his Cinematographer Tadashi Nishimoto

By Michael Worth

There are few collaborations quite as important on a film production as that of the director and the cinematographer. There are cases where they are one and the same, but most often they are a duo of creators whose discussion, decisions and debates will form the view from which you experience their story. When Bruce Lee, after completing two feature films as an actor for Golden Harvest, was given the reins to direct his own film, his cinematographer was one of the first hires he would make. This cinematic team is rarely discussed in Lee's history, but his choice of Japanese director of photography Tadashi Nishimoto actually created one of the most historical pairing of artists in Hong Kong history. Lee as the industry's fastest rising stars and Nishimoto as possibly the most influential cameramen in Hong Kong cinema working together has been a glaring omission from the record.

Way of the Dragon's most identifiable participant is certainly its director and star, but his choice of cameraman would be one of the most important innovators in Kung Fu movie history without whom the now famous words "Shawscope" may never have existed. By the mid 1950s, the dominant Shaw Brothers studio was already actively exchanging technicians and performers with others from Japan and with studios like the famous Toho Studios (of Godzilla fame). One of these men, Japanese cinematographer Tadashi Nishimoto, would become an instructive partner in the evolution of their cinema through his influence in Shaw's adopting anamorphic widescreen in 1961 (with the musical Les Belles). Like many notable Japanese directors that would follow him over to Shaw Brothers, Nishimoto would adopt a Chinese name that he would often use when working for the productions (including Way of the Dragon): Ho Lan Shan.

Nishimoto literally carried a camera over from Japan which the Shaws then purchased. By using the process of Tohoscope, they developed their own version of anamorphic widescreen, and inserted into the now-familiar introductory fanfare of the Shaw Brothers' "glass shield" opening logo the proprietary title "Shawscope." In fact many may not know that prior to Way, Nishimoto worked alongside another celebrated director, King Hu, Hu Jinquan, to create one of the tentpole classics of martial arts cinema, Come Drink with Me (1966). Legendary director Chang Cheh revealed in his memoir that the Japanese filmmakers had "nurtured" a number of the talent at Shaw Brothers, noting that "renowned auteur director" Li Han-hsiang (The Love Eterne, Beyond The Great Wall) "had used Nishimoto as his long-term cinematographer, and was greatly influenced by him".

By the time 1972 rolled around and Golden Harvest was about to give their star talent his first directing duty, Nishimoto was semi-retired working for his commercial advertising company. Raymond Chow called to meet with him at the Hong Kong Island where he asked Nishimoto: " 'Do you know Bruce Lee?' I replied, 'Sure, I do.' ", Nishimoto recalled in his biography. " 'Actually, this is the first time he is going to direct and play in the movie and he personally hopes that you could be the cameraman.' " That's a hard request to turn down. Initially, Nishimoto was asked to shoot the exterior Rome locations (which the production scheduled first) but it would turn into a full term job as cinematographer after a screening in Rome, where the look of the Techniscope footage surprised even Nishimotio. "That was why Bruce didn't want to let me go.", he said.

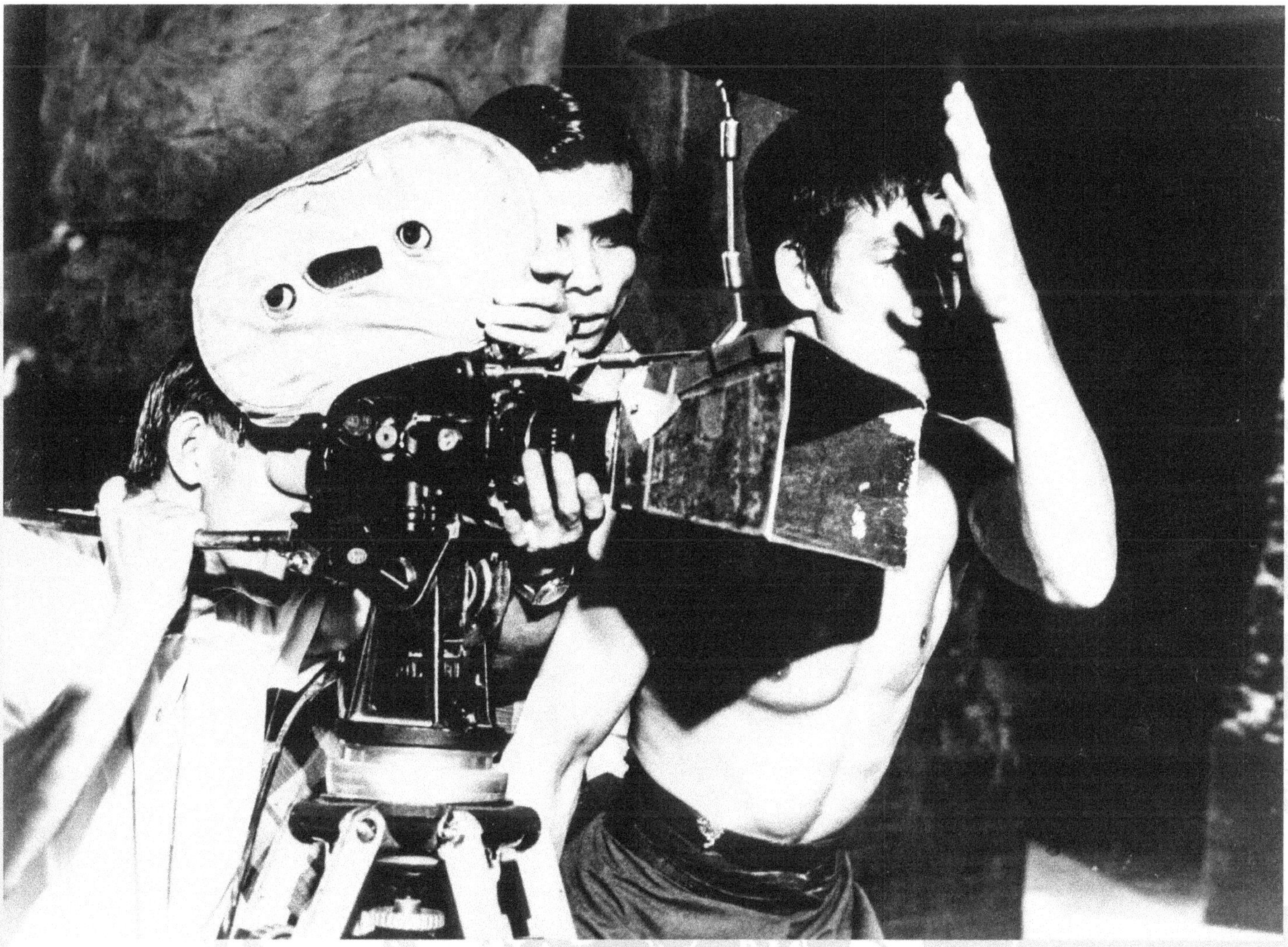

One of the aspects of Way that differentiates it from former Golden Harvest productions was the use of the Italian developed Techniscope format by Technicolor. Where ShawScope was the Shaw Brother's trademark shooting system, GH had partnered with the French-developed anamorphic Dylascope, which name is featured as part of the logo at the opening of almost every Golden Harvest film. Andre Morgan, Raymond Chow's chief assistant, explained that the inclusion of the logo gave them a financially beneficial partnership to use the format in trade for the advertising. But with Way, Nishimoto had seen the Italian made "Yesterday, Today, Tomorrow" (Ieri, oggi, domain -1963) from director Vittorio De Sica and he "found it to be a great film. It was filmed with Techniscope." Although both systems shoot in a 2.35 widescreen aspect ratio, Dylascope and Shawscope are anamorphic formats while Techniscope relies on spherical lenses. It was also a technology embraced by lower budget productions at the time, since it required half the shooting footage of a normal anamorphic shoot, as the frames were

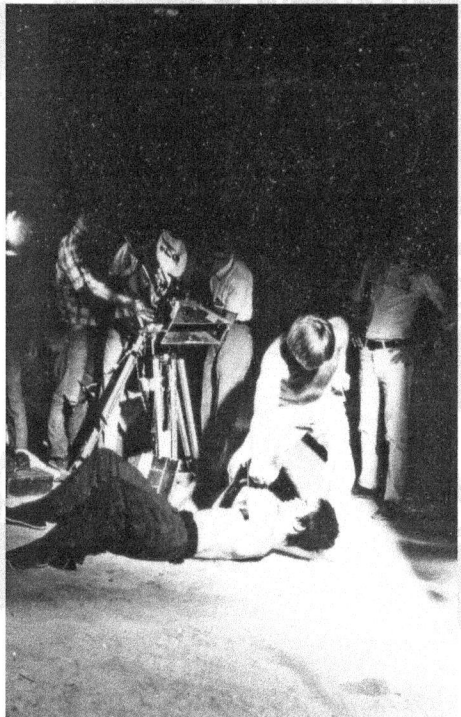

enlarged later in the process. However, this procedure would also enlarge any imperfections in the film, including focus issues, which are at times very noticable in the location shooting. The initial wide-shot, in example, where Lee approaches the child in the airport, or the tracking shot once he moves through the airport restaurant are examples of soft focus and the learning curve of the format for the cinematographer.

The film's look, though it may not be immediately apparent, is distinct and immediately gave Way a different tone and color palette from Lee's prior two films. (As an aside, Enter The Dragon was also anamorphic but would be the first time a Hong Kong produced film would use Panavision lenses, which later became known to Hong Kong filmmakers as the "Enter the Dragon lens"). Nishimoto would eventually run into issues with the local Golden Harvest processing company in trying to reproduce the technicolor look they were all so happy with in Rome. Eventually he would (through some added "muscle" provided by Lee) get the result corrected with the transfers, and all was good.

There were some challenges to face, particularly in the early Rome exterior footage, where the crew amounted to Nishimoto, Lee, Nora Miao and a handful of others. One aspect was the use of handheld photography which Lee wanted to include in his production. Nishimoto was a slight man and the strength it took to hold their camera for any length of time was not an easy task. There are moments in the "travelogue" sequences as well as one specific move as Lee walks through the columns towards Norris where handheld work is employed, but the shot becomes noticeably unsteady at times as a result. Way of the Dragon does contain a brief effective use in the final Chuck Norris fight filmed when they were back in the Hong Kong studio (using a local cameraman), where Lee is kicking into the lens as a Point of View shot for Norris' character "Colt".

In the initial Rome trip, Nishimoto took specific photos of the coliseum where the classic final fight would take place. The photos were meant to be blown up and used as a backdrop for the set to be constructed at Golden Harvest. This was another example of Nishimoto's problem-solving, as the photos taken in the glaring overexposed sun had to be corrected with paint and lighting techniques on the set to match the staged version in Hong Kong. But to see the film, the results are beautiful, and his experience shines through.

One of Lee's personal issues with his prior action sequences were the more fantasy-like jumping and "flying" that took place in them (a familiar trope to the choreography of Han Yin Chieh and his many errant knight style battle sequences). Lee had noted to Golden Harvest's Andre Morgan he was not happy with all the purposeless "leaping" he was being asked to do. To watch his own directorial work (including his sequences in Game of Death save for one or two shots) you see where Lee stayed away from wires and trampolines in the action,

preferring to rely on skill and technique. He wanted Nishimoto to create dynamic frames to hold the action and show the audience they were all trained martial artists and not relying on the camera to hide any inexperience. In many ways, this approach in Way gives it the most realistic and practical display of his fighting skills on camera. When Lee does jump in the air (to destroy the lamp in John Benn's office) it is sans a trampoline, using his actual athleticism to make the jump with a designed purpose (ie: destroy a lamp to scare off a thug he can't communicate with) and not just in effort to fly to the other side of the room for effect.

The movie opens with an interesting choice; a tight close up of Lee that could indicate in his gaze that he is about to take on an opponent. But with an uneasy wipe across his face with his hand (also to cue Nishimoto's camera zoom out) we see he is actually pushed into a corner of the Rome airport being stared at by other travelers (in my own teenage-made super 8mm film, Fists of the Toad, a Way of the Dragon parody, I replicated the exact scene with my mother in place of the staring woman). Immediately Lee and Nishimoto were setting up that this film would break some molds from Lee's prior two features with the very first shot. Playing against type, this took Lee through a series of awkward moments that seem more appropriate for a soon-to-be-known Jackie Chan than a Bruce Lee. The tracking camera shot was one Nishimoto was very familiar with and is used in beautiful and effective fashion in Hu's Come Drink with Me. Noting one example, its use in the saloon fight as the camera tracks back through the opponents moving into position to fight Pei Pei, landing on a wide frame holding an exceptionally staged image. These uses are minimized in the action scenes of Way but an economical use of diagonal tracking during the Lee/Bob Wall fight (the exact same track is used several times) contains similar attributes from Nishimoto's earlier work. There are dynamics worth noting in several of the fight scenes crafted by the pair of artists. For instance, again n the Lee vs. Wall fight towards the climax, there are some illustrious uses of "snap zooms". The opening reveal of their face-off moment features a snap-zoom back from both of their close ups into a wide shot as they prepare to fight each

other. The fight sequence then concludes on the well-known groin punch, using the exact reverse camera move that opened the sequence to end it as the camera now snaps close into Lee's face in punctuation. It is a subtle visual opener and a closer to the story of this short but entertaining fight. The tracking camera also plays a small role in the more comedic but tension filled beats between falling opponents as Lee dismantles them in the alley fight with his nunchaku. Lee chose to give each opponent a "finisher" suiting their personalities and ckosen means of attack which showcased Lee's fight creativity.

Nishimoto has crafted some memorable snapshots in several well-known and not so well-known features especially from Shaw Brothers. These moments would certainly have weighed in on Lee's decision to go after the cinematographer. You watch his dynamic use of color and tone in films like The Blue and The Black Parts 1 and 2 (1966) or Hong Kong Nocturne (1966) and can see how anyone would be affected by his camera work and lighting. Way features a few memorable action scenes, but between the obvious stand-out fights, Way also presents several spectacular select framed images representing the photography craft At about an hour in, when Tang Lung (Lee) pursues the hitman outside of the apartment, there is a close up of his face peering out from the wall looking to the rooftops. Lee's face is lit with such a subtle profile light that it looks like green marble in the night glow creating a striking portrait of the young star. The wide shot where Lee runs through the coliseum columns on his way to meet Colt is bathed in natural light and architecture almost like an Edward Hopper painting. No one film survives on a single shot, but good filmmakers always leave a pattern of them through their work to linger in an audience's mind.

Way of the Dragon has another distinction in the oeuvre of Lee as it would be the only time his production company Concord's opening logo would appear on screen (The simple text of Concord survives in all the opening credits). The unique animated 1970s-1980s Hong Kong introductions have always been a personal fascination for me with their many fanfares and creative text animations, and with the Concord logo it actually offers us another glimpse into a form of Lee's personal artistic creativity. It would only be available on some of the most early release prints of the film (most likely before his passing) and several later Japanese releases but is a simple and rare showcase of Lee's artistic expression. Two circles, yellow and gold, begin to

move across a black screen. It is quickly apparent they are sparring, in combat, as they bounce in and out of each other, circling like two opponents. Finally they settle along side one another and a larger circle forms around them, manifesting into the gold and red Yin and Yang symbol Lee used often as the core symbol for his martial art; Jeet Kune Do. In a Eurostile Bold Extended font, the name "A Concord Production" appears to signal a new production company had arrived. This is a small but interesting relic of the martial artist's vision for his unfulfilled future filmmaking career.

Nishimoto's work with Lee would not end with Way of the Dragon as Lee was quick to request him once again for his meant to be follow up feature, Game of Death (1972). These filmed sequences would evolve into some of martial arts cinema's greatest lore and legends, in no small part to the unfinished and spontaneous nature of the shoot. Game would up the pairs "game" in not only the choreography but their framing and camera staging within the action. Filmmaker Alan Canvan notes about one of the final sequences where Lee and Kareen Abdul Jabbar are carried through a long complicated shot ending on Jabbar's death grip on a cushion: "not only do I consider it one of the most beautifully composed (shots) in cinema history, but it's a perfect illustration of an entire story encapsulated in a single image". There is no doubt that the creative relationship between the two men was only beginning to flourish and Game of Death showcased the direction their influential collaboration was headed. It did not unfortunately see its course through, as Nishimoto recalled: "It was planned to film the fights in the pagoda of Game of Death and that pagoda was in Korea. Bruce said to me, "Mr. Tadashi, after this, I'm going to tour Europe and the whole world and then spar with the first class martial artists. I hope to film all the fighting arts in the world and make them into series." This is the last time I talked to him over the phone."

Way of the Dragon becomes the one and only completed project from a pair of Hong Kong cinema's most cherished contributors. Though each fan has their own distinct order of these filmmakers' best films there is no doubt that wherever Way of the Dragon rests in your own list, the collaboration of these men is not only historical but also gave martial arts cinema some of it's most iconic sequences and memorable frames that will last throughout its history.

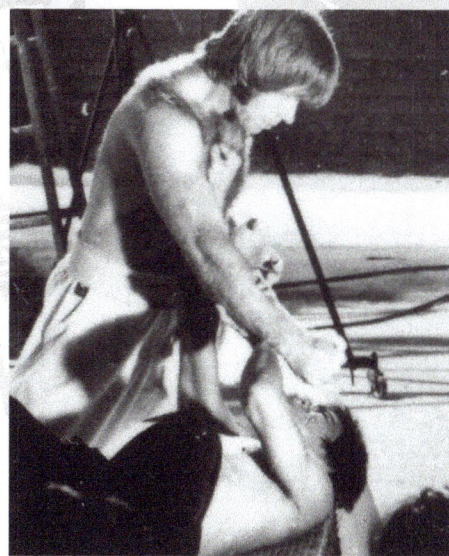

Nunchaku Sequence Photo Gallery

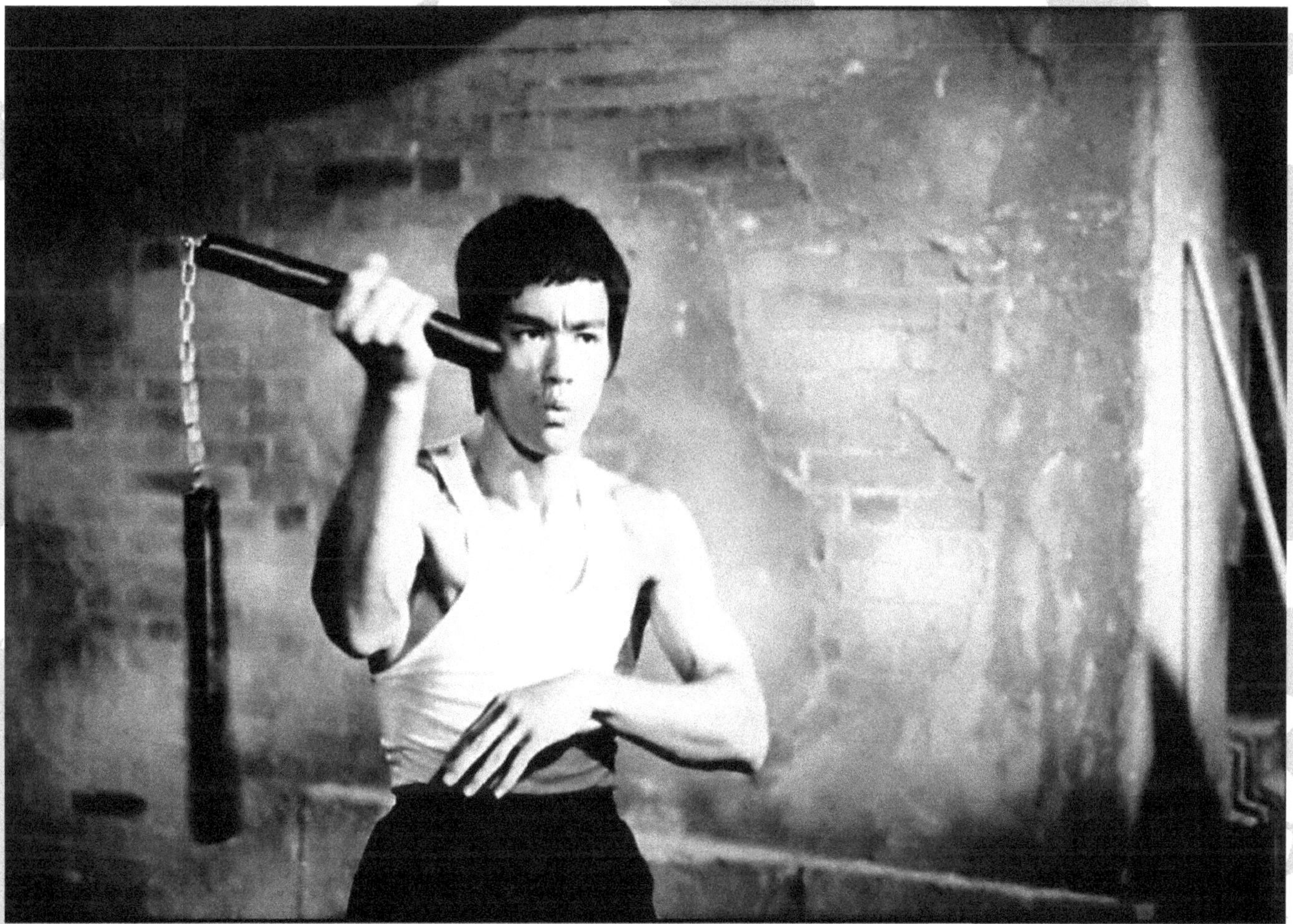

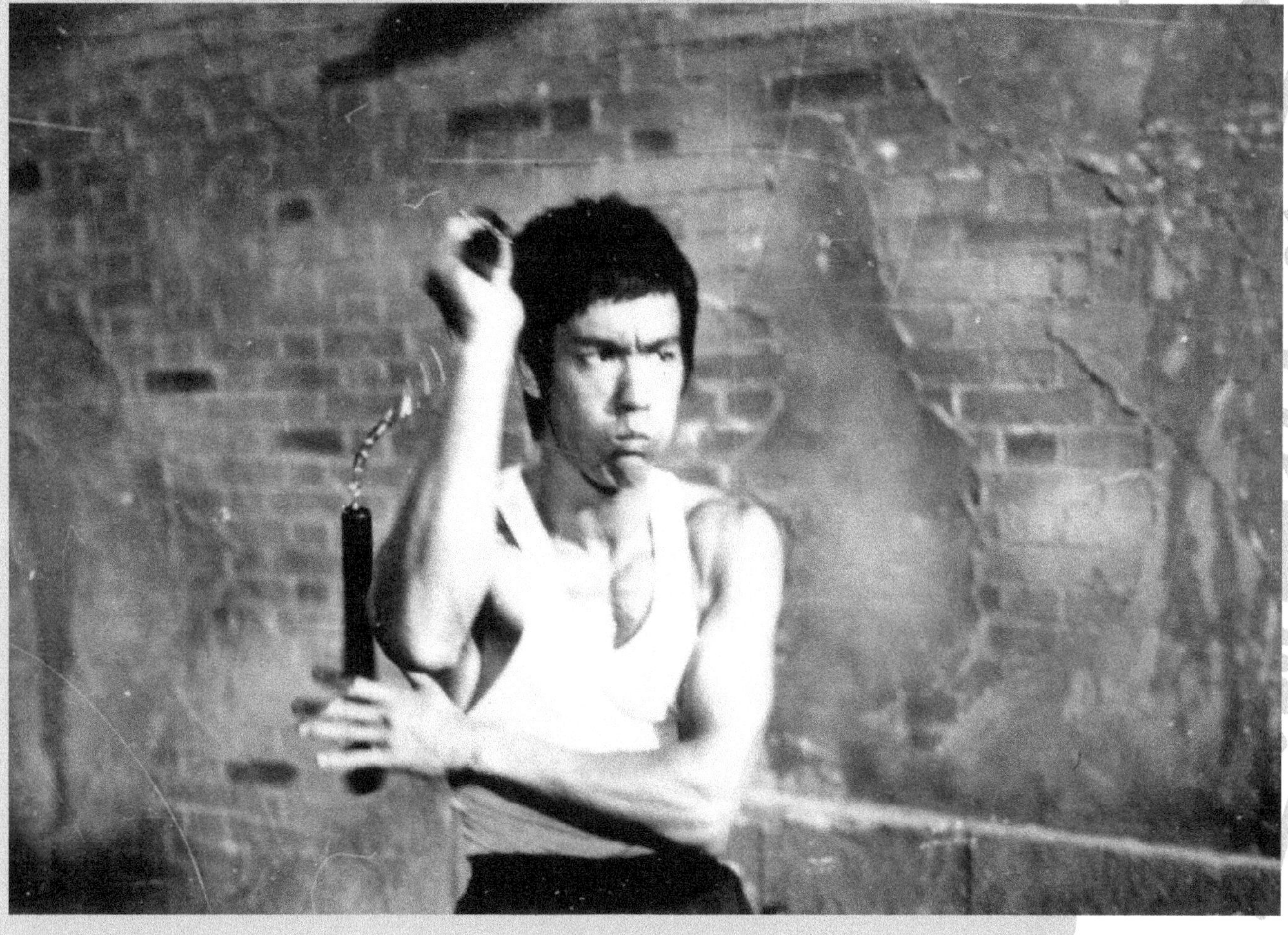

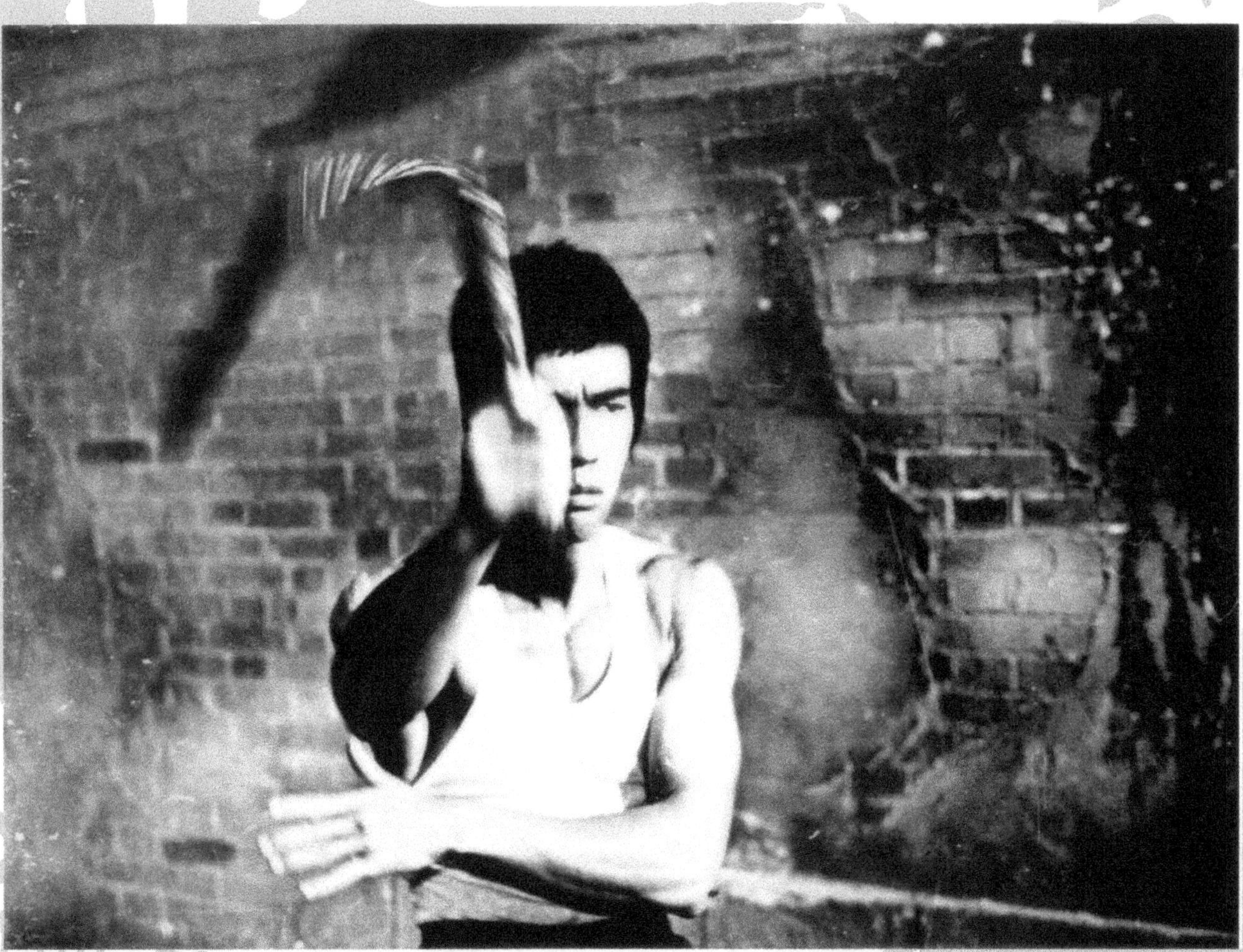

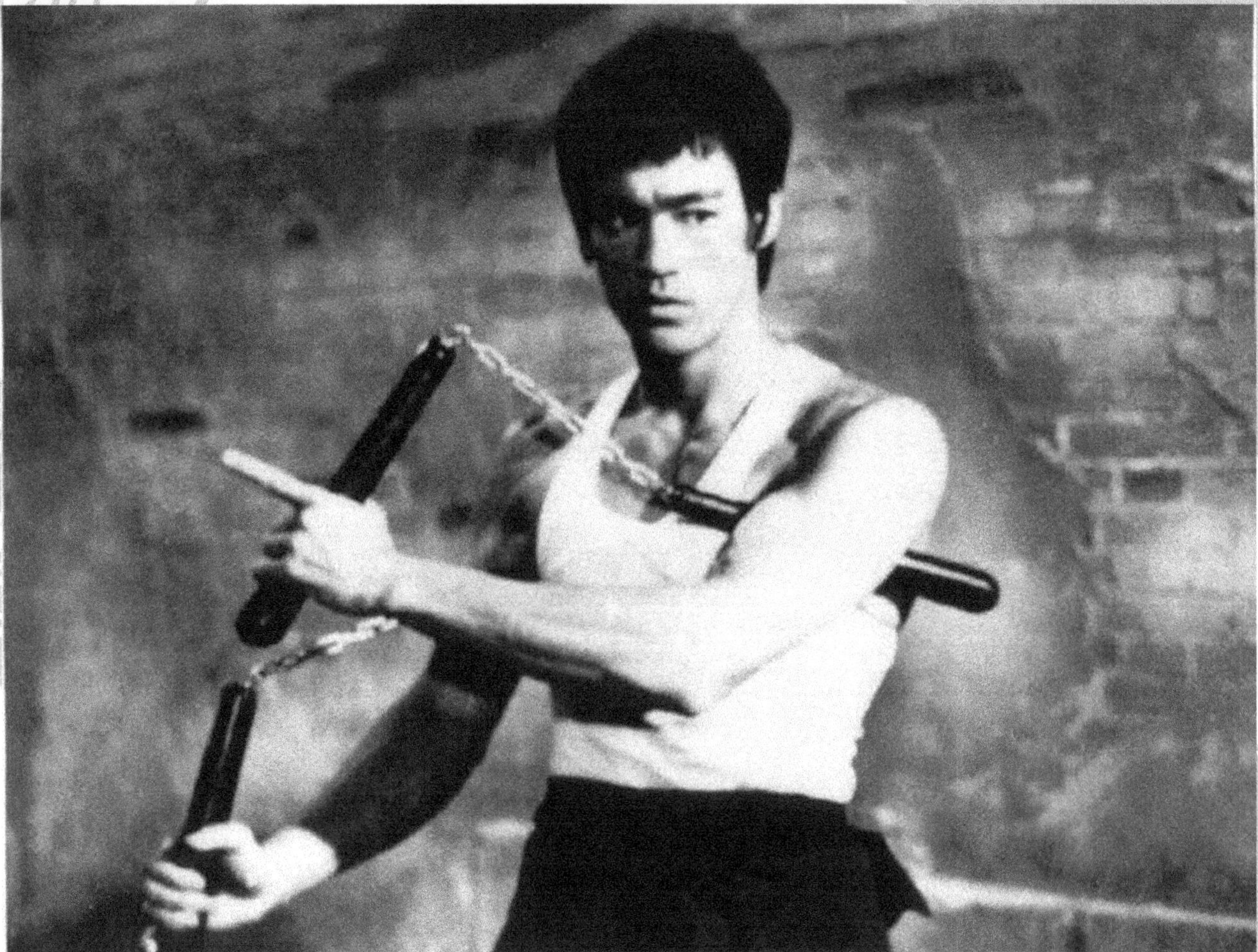

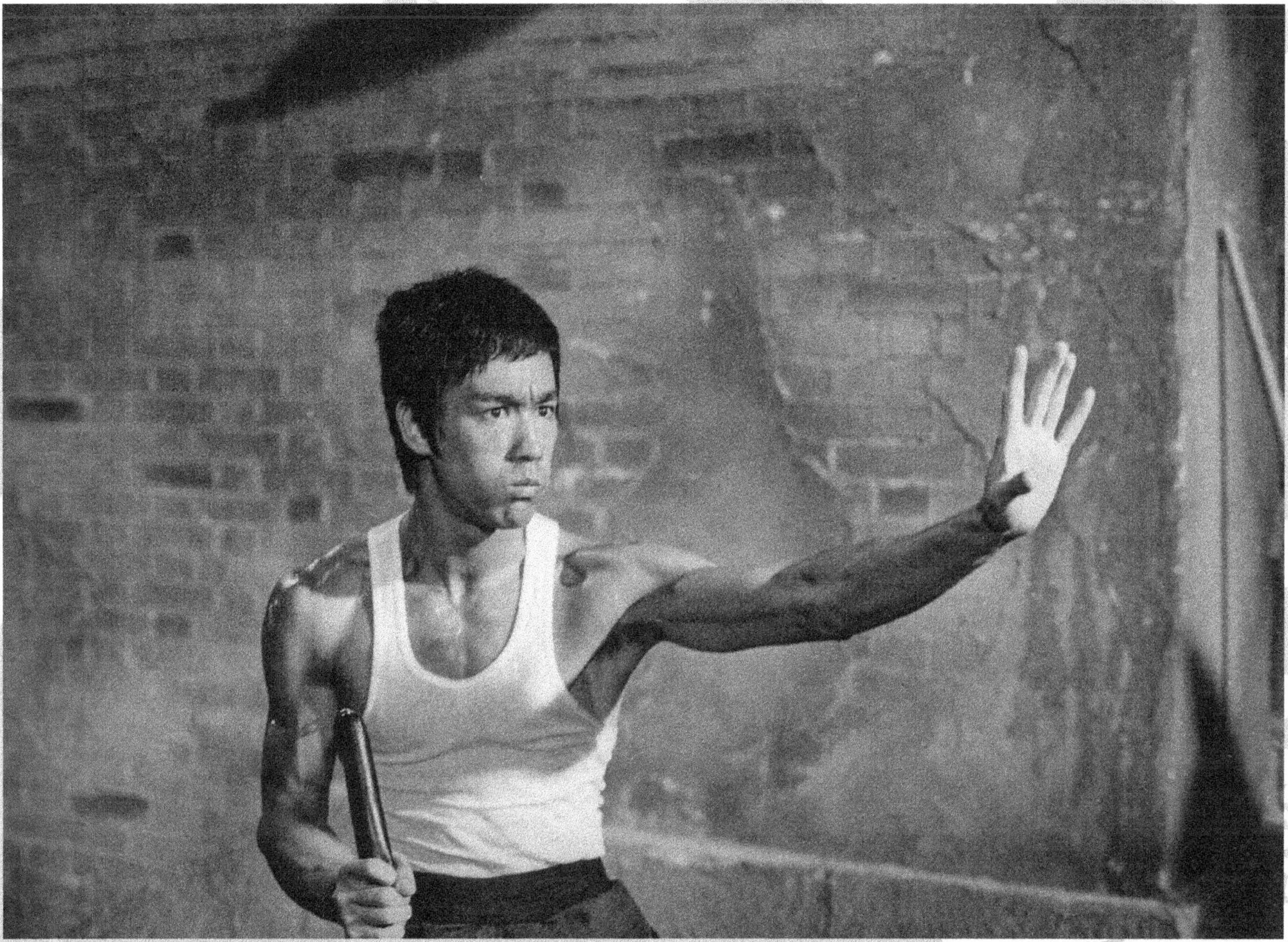

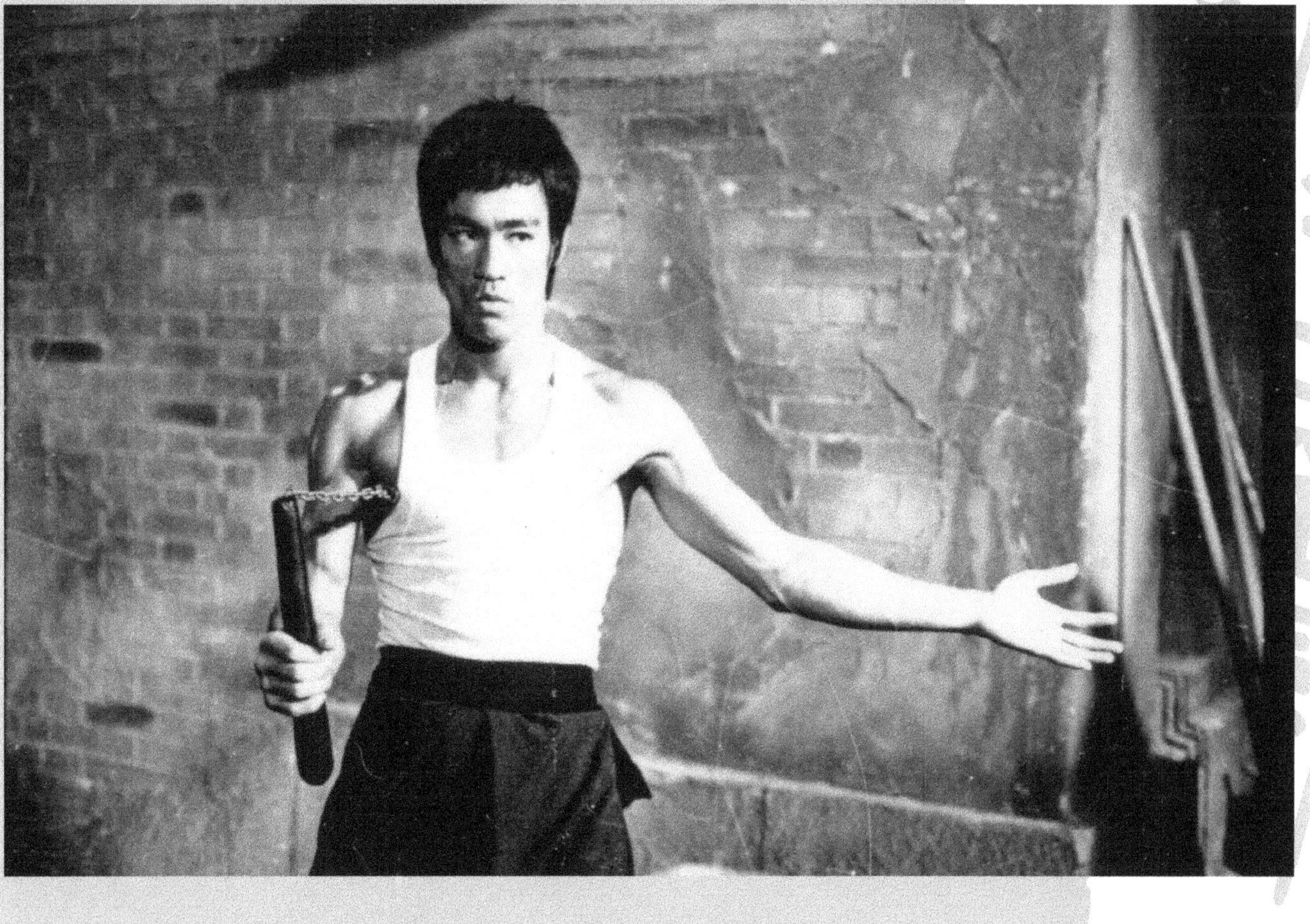

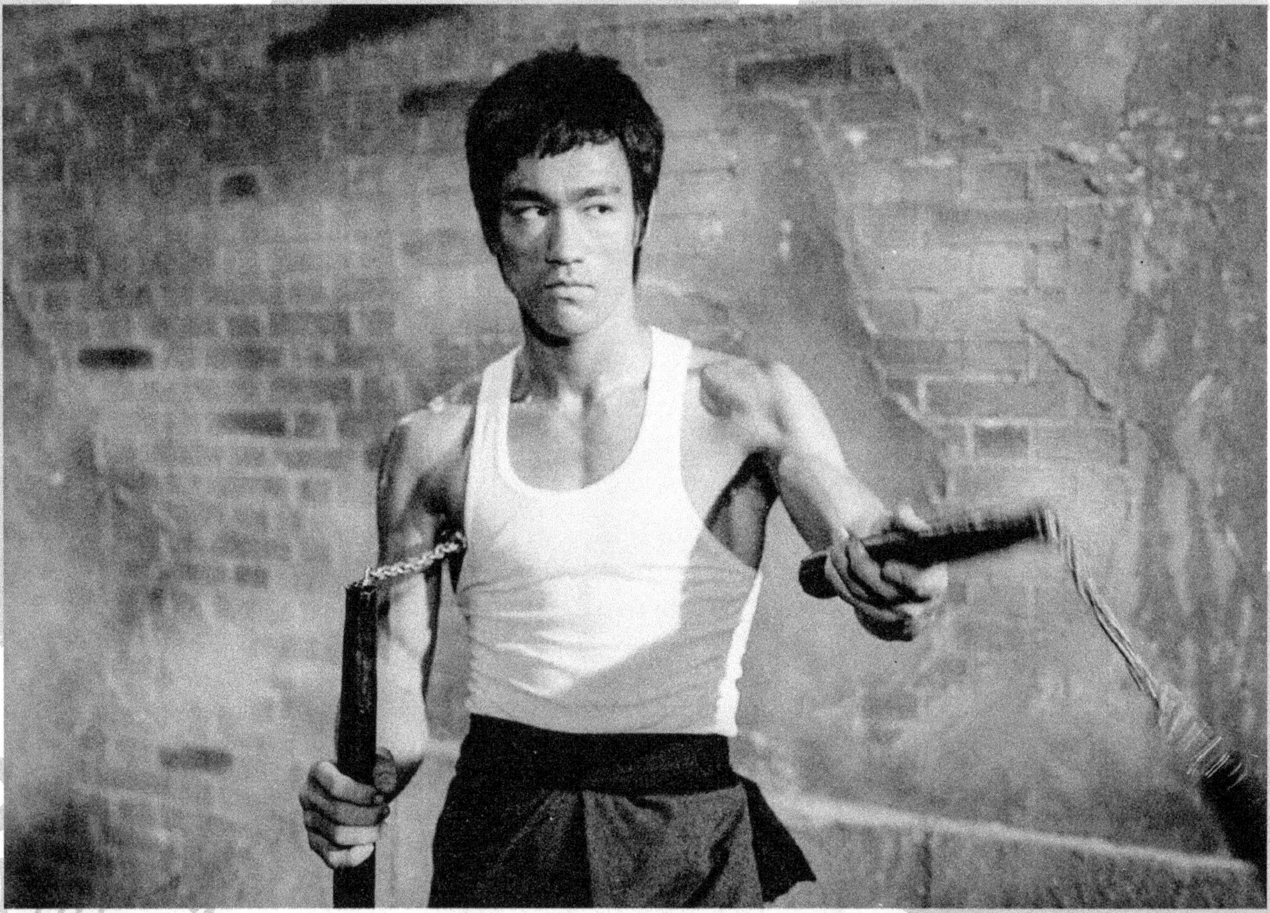

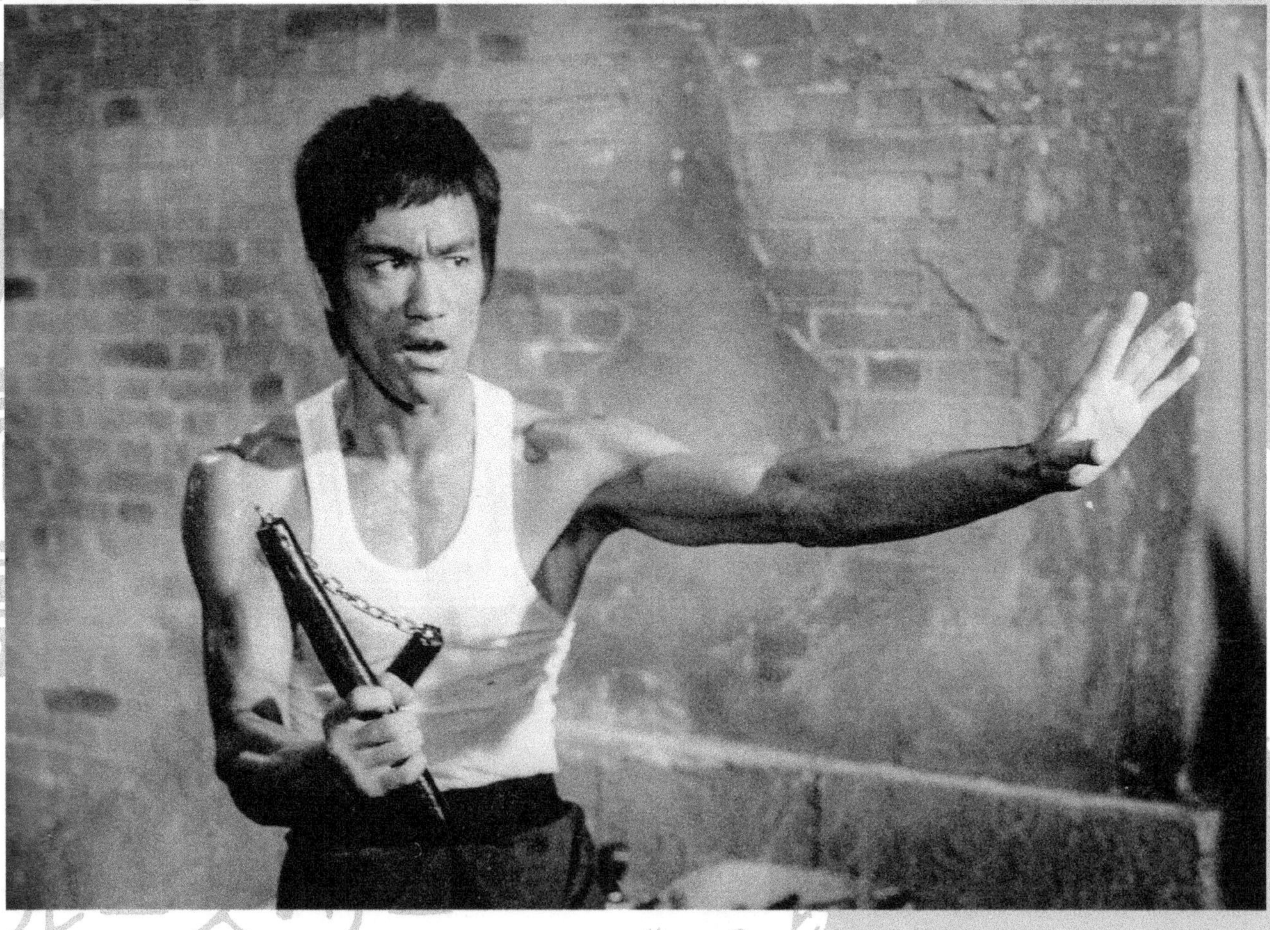

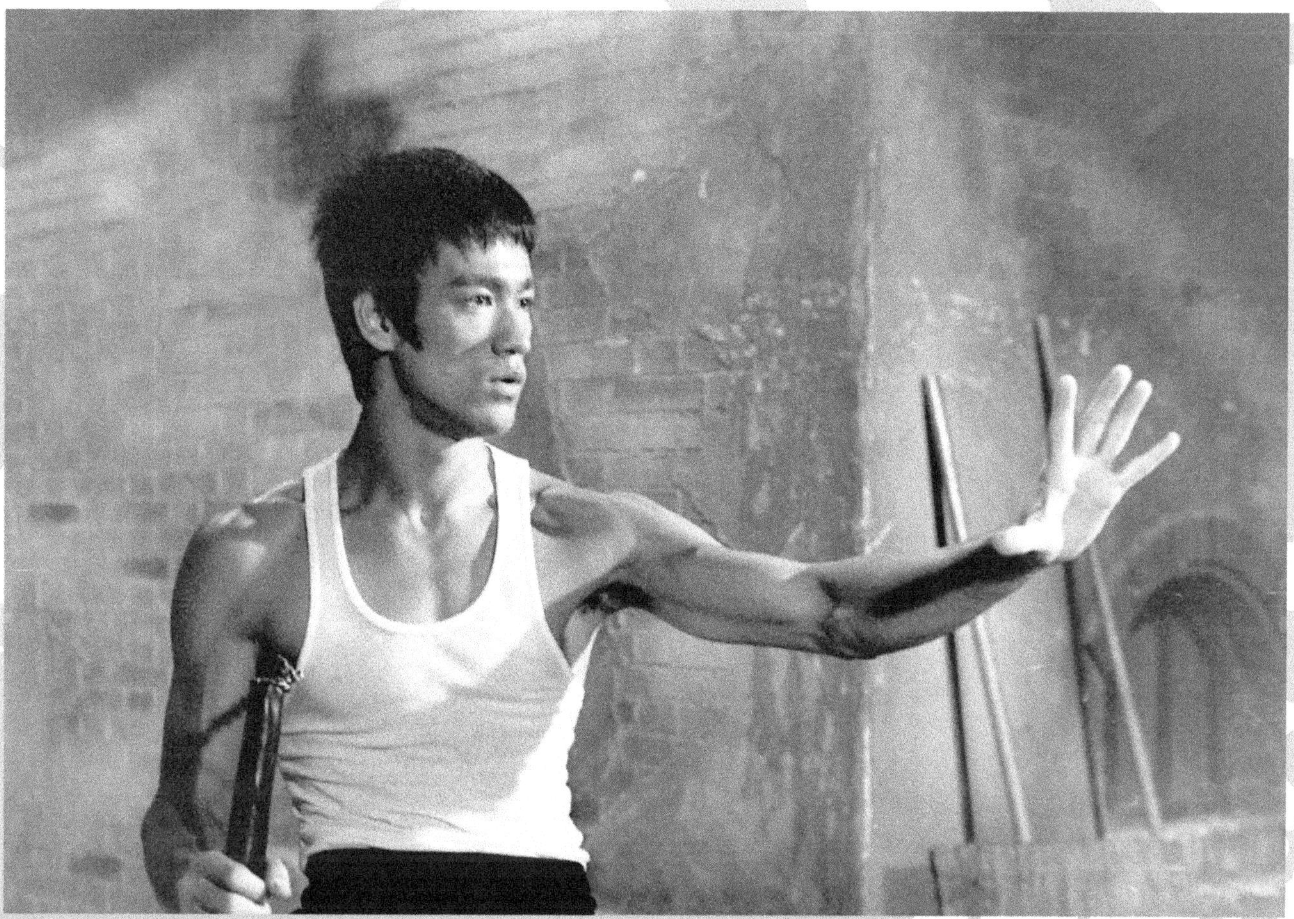

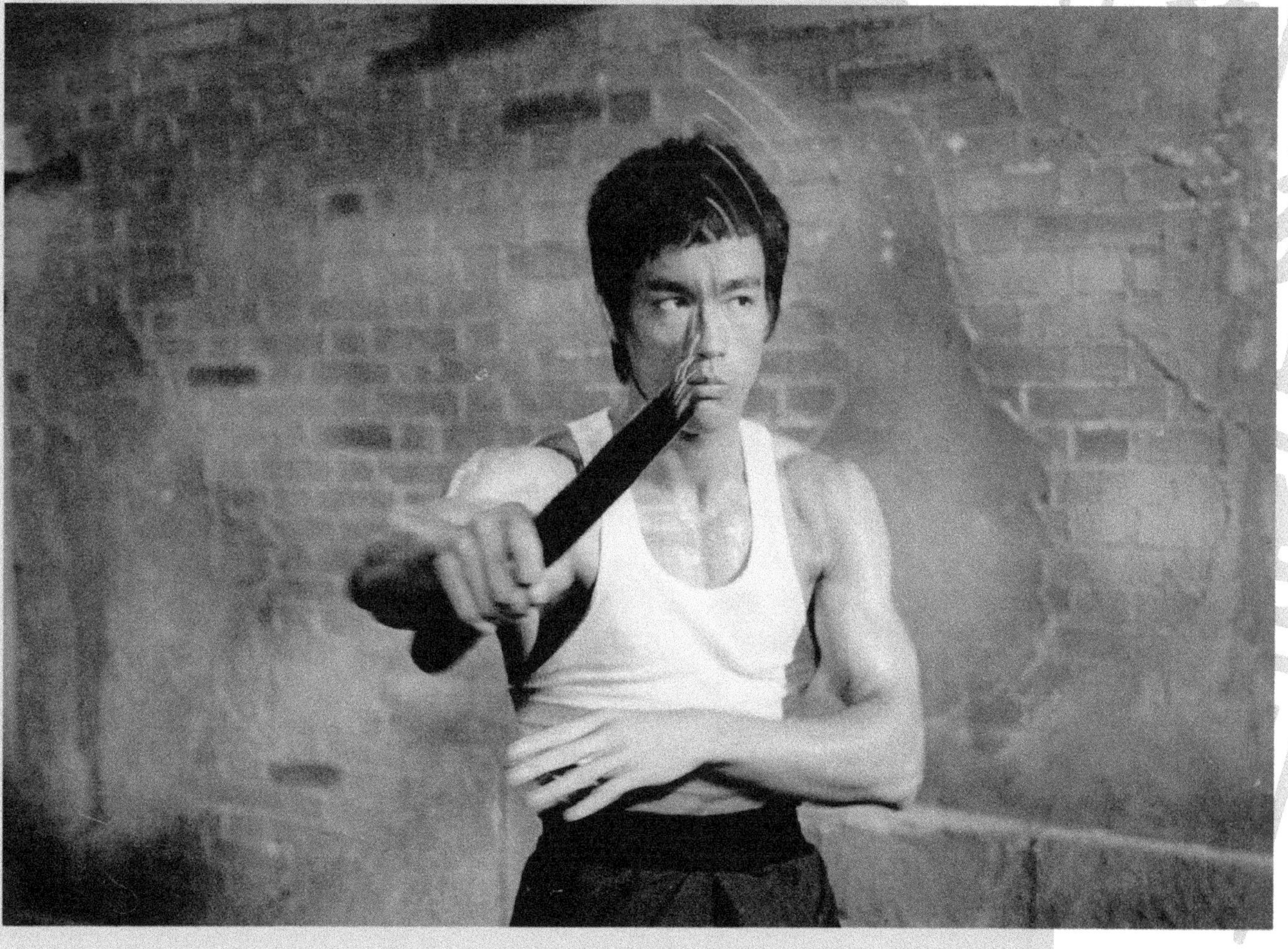

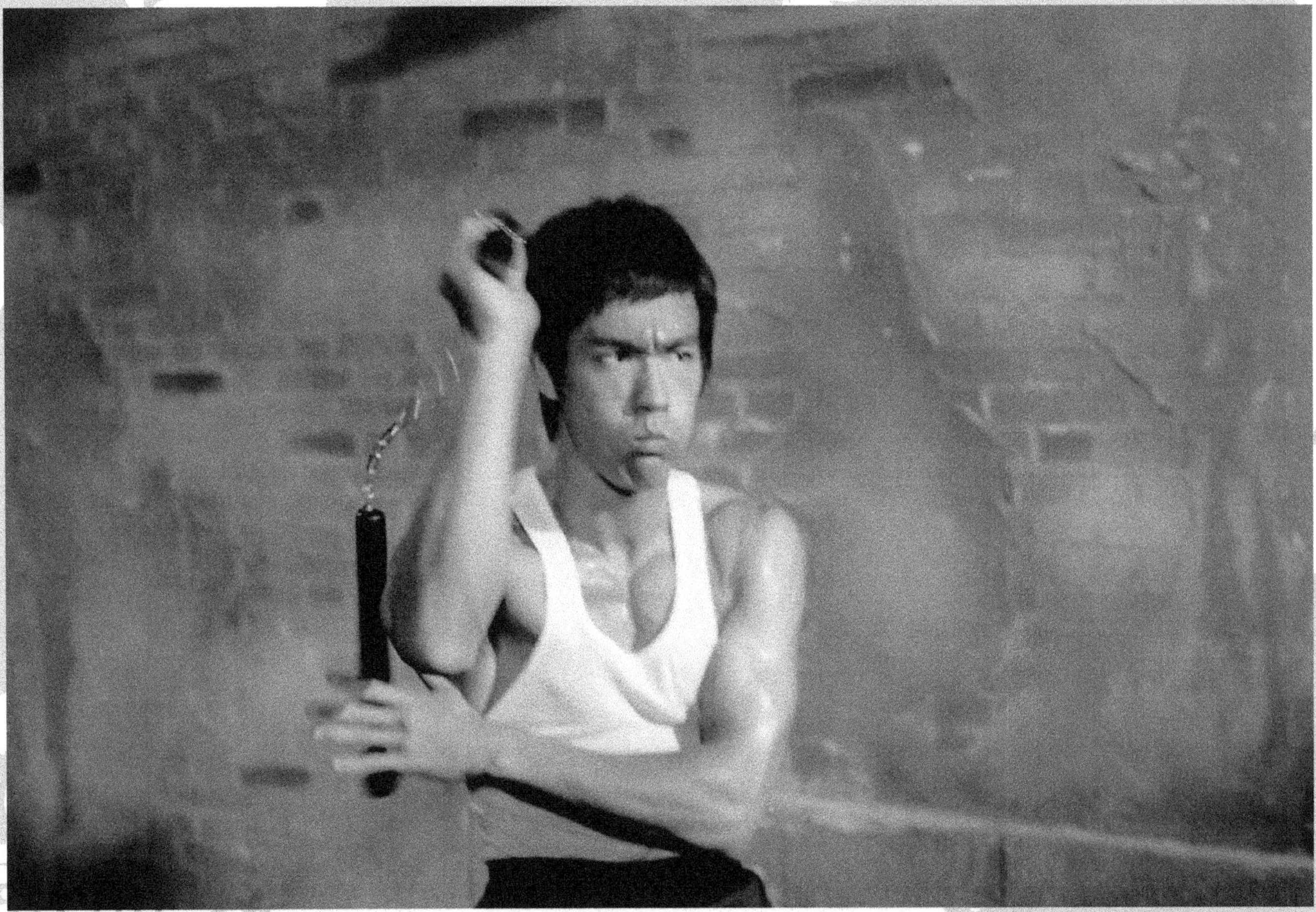

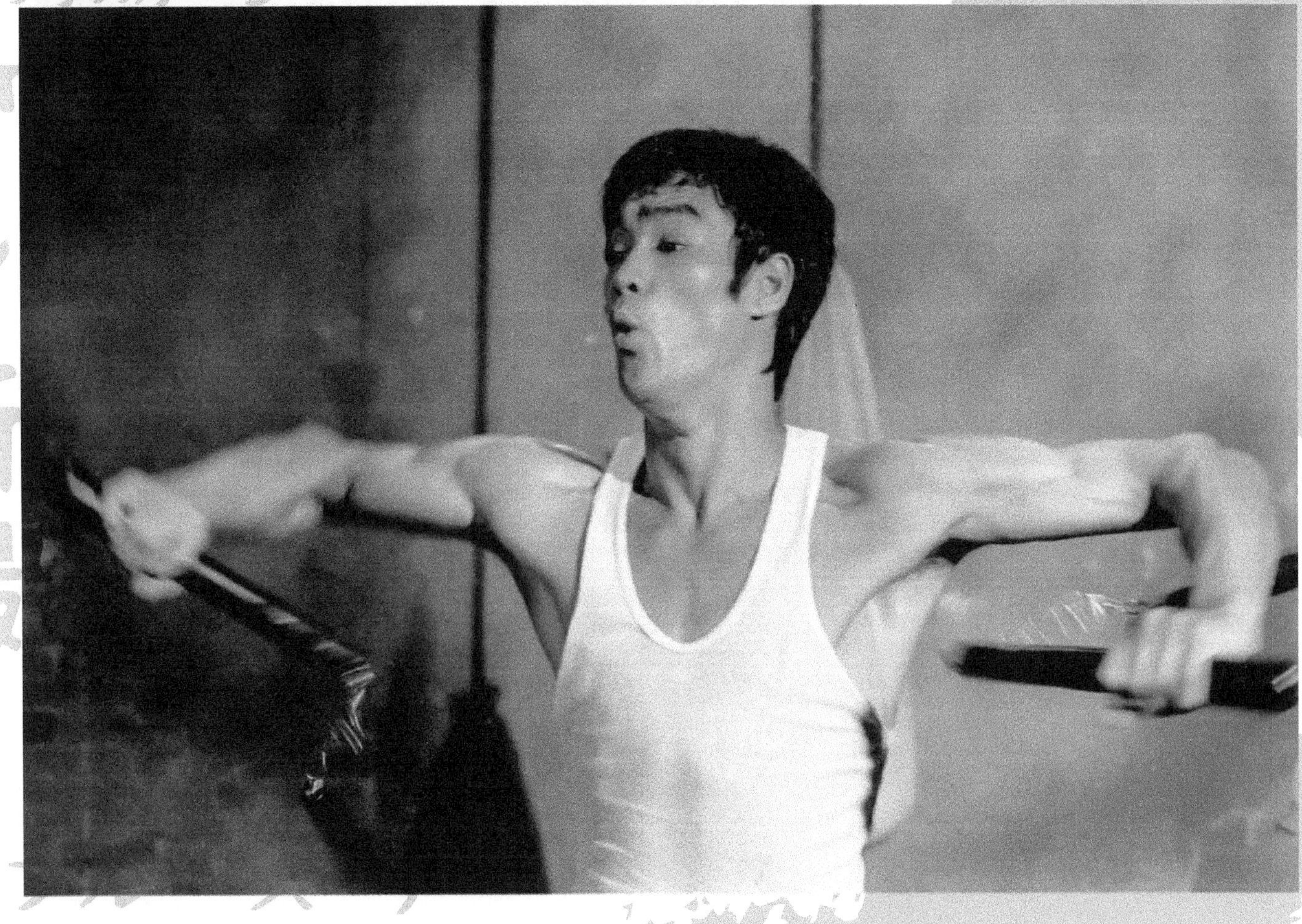

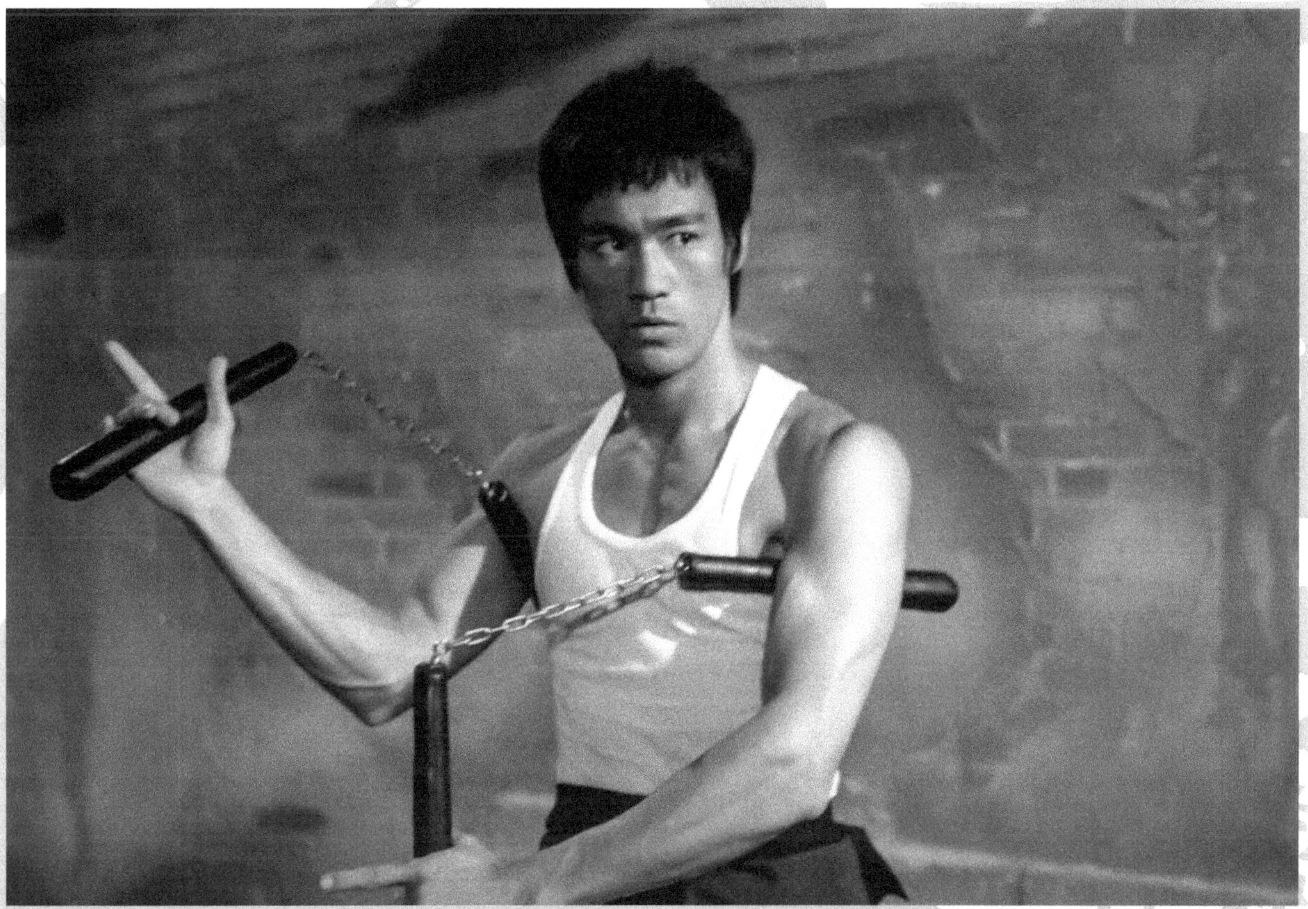

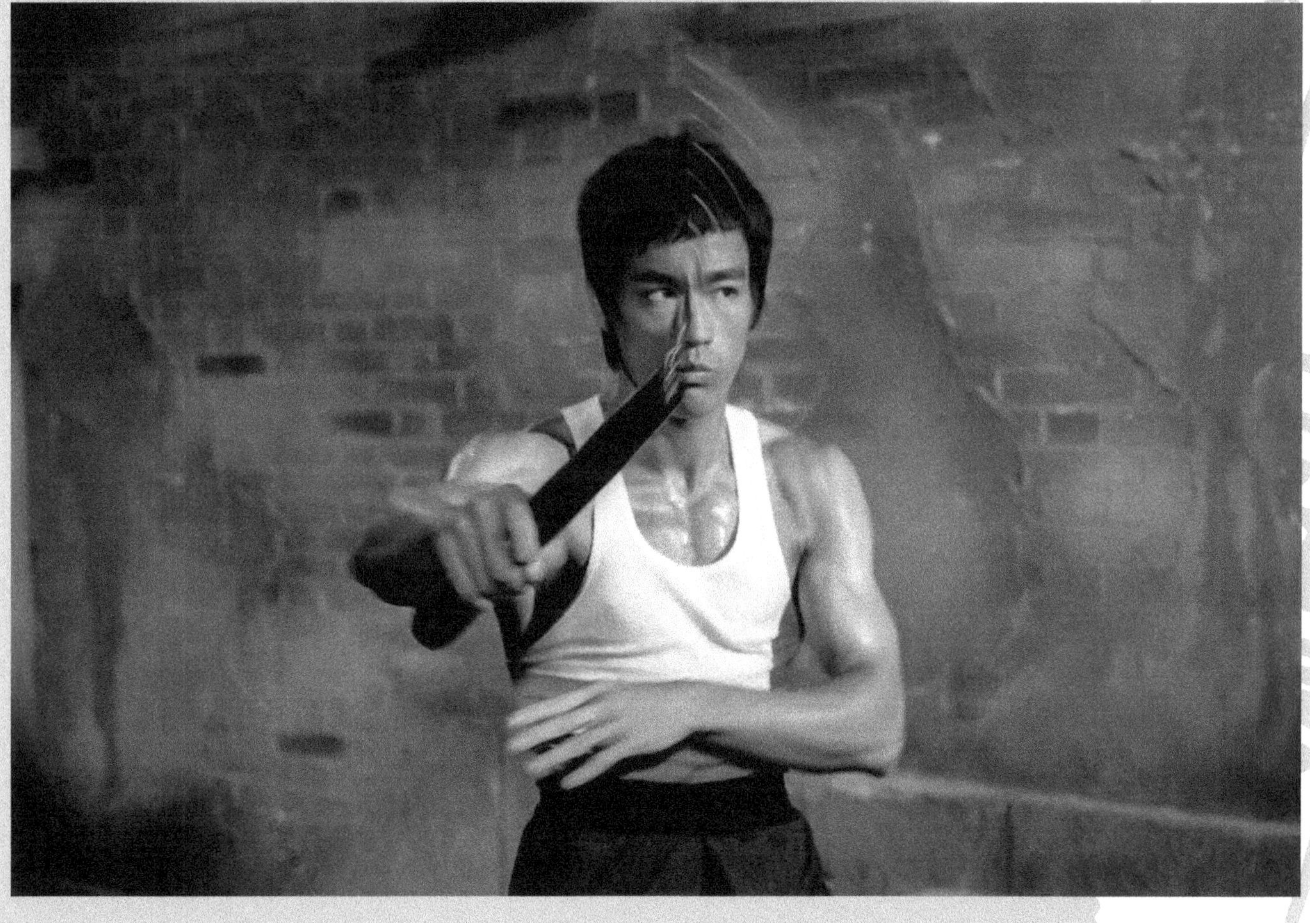

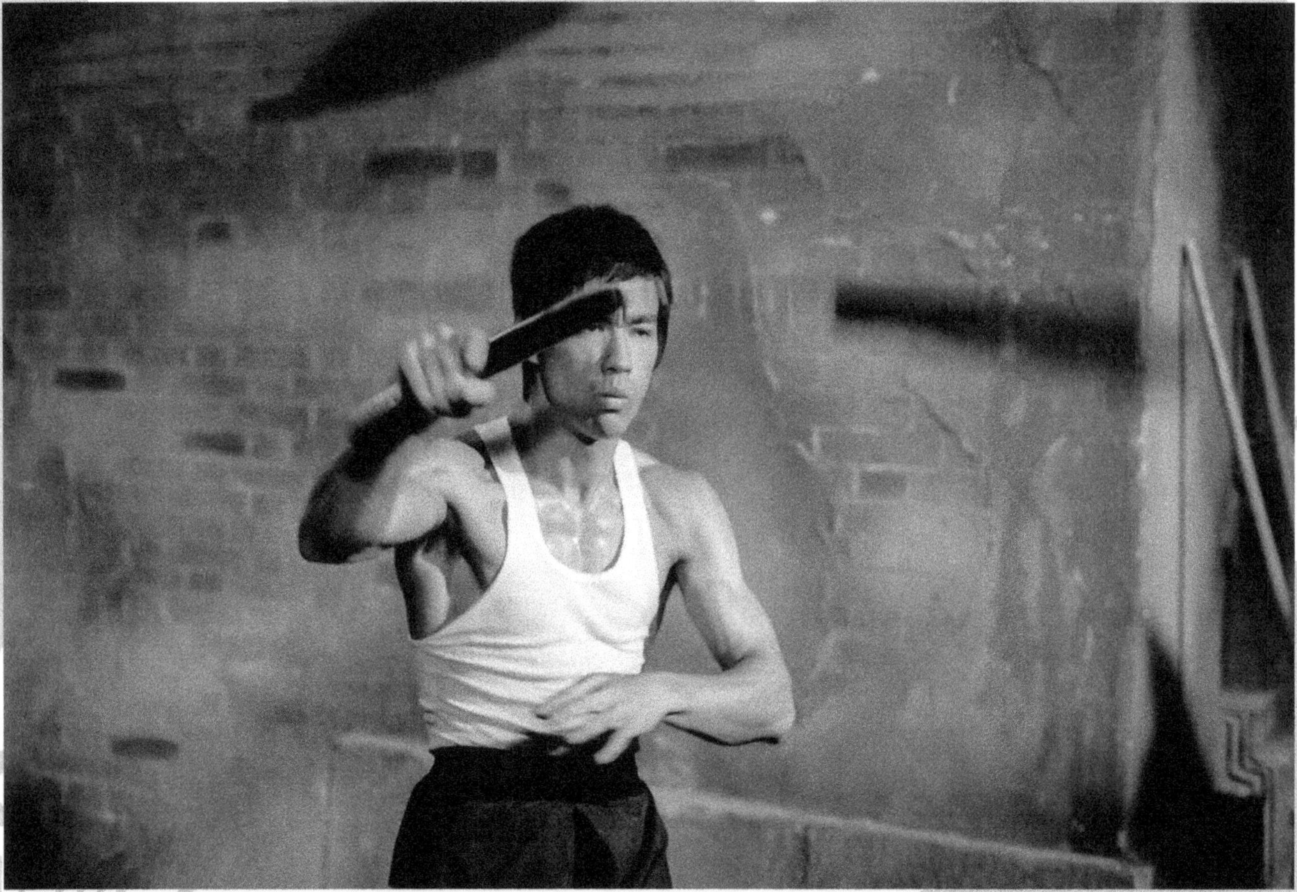

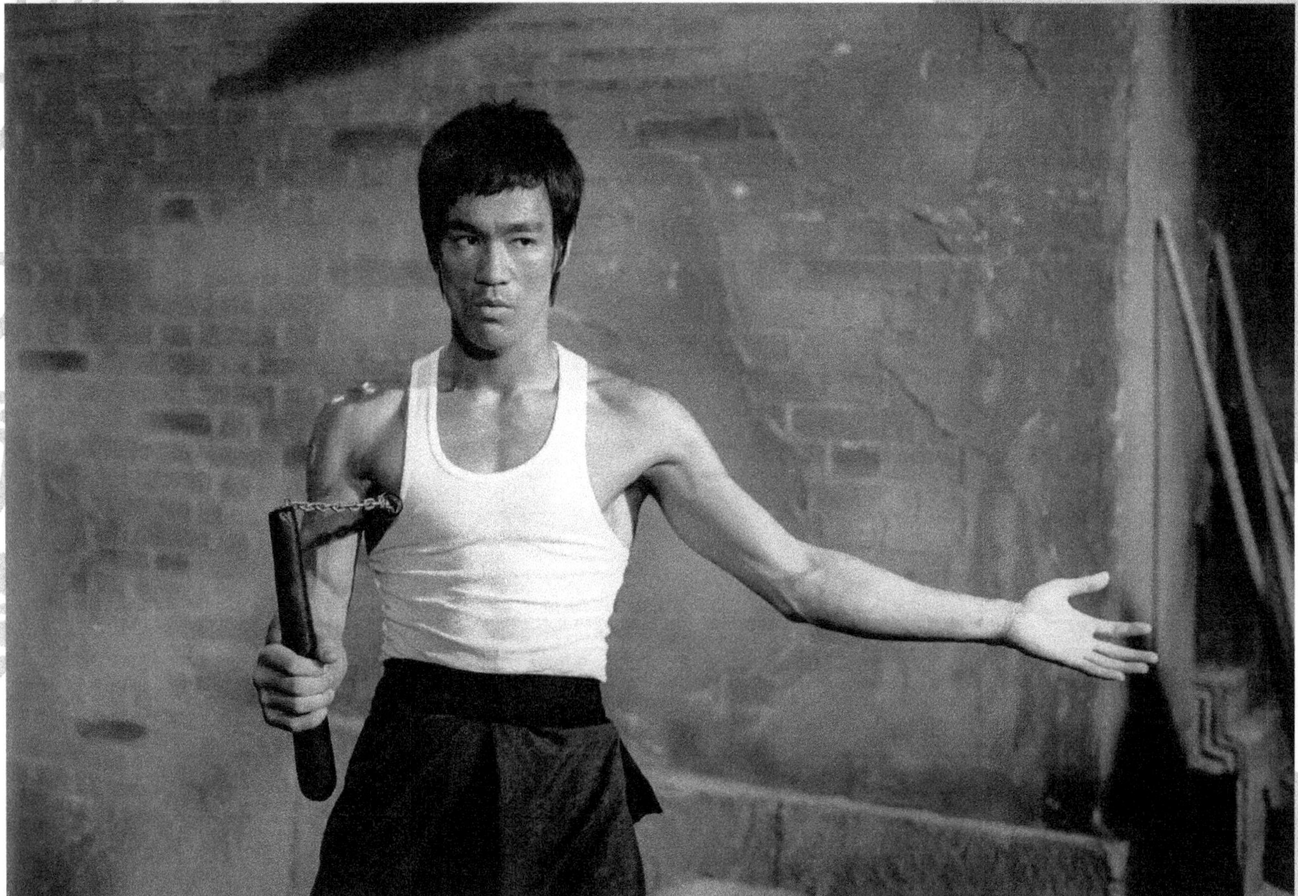

FANATICAL DRAGON PRESENTS
5 FINGERS OF DISCS — THE RAY OF THE DRAGON

Greetings Dear friends, your friendly neighbourhood Dragon here once again, celebrating the 50th Anniversary of Bruce Lee's Way of The Dragon (aka Return of the Dragon for our US friends) with this quick overview of the various different Blu-Ray (and one DVD) editions available of Bruce's 1972 classic, his one and only fully completed movie as Director.

As we go to print, rumours are circulating about a 4K release of not just Way of The Dragon, but of all 5 of Bruce Lee's movies, coming later this year as part of a special 4K boxset, no firm details have emerged thus far. For the time being, the options presented below represent the key notable releases of the film world-wide on Blu-Ray.

Grab your best white vest, rip off some of Chuck Norris's chest hair and let's take these Blu-ray's to the Coliseum and see which one will be the last disc standing.

1) Hong Kong Legends 2 Disc Platinum Edition DVD Region 2 - (UK PAL)

Long in the tooth now, but rarely bested in terms of special features, the good old Hong Kong Legends Platinum Edition DVD is still widely available second hand and very cheaply too,
You can pick up the 2 disc set for a couple of quid and it houses over 4 hours of extra features.

The quality of the transfer may not be up to Blu-ray standards, but most modern Blu-ray players will upscale a DVD to 1080p quite effectively.
The extra features of note include:
A Dragon Remembered - interview with Bruce Lee's brother Robert, Double Edged Sword, an interview with Bob Wall, Memories of the Master featurette featuring Lee's friend and training partner Pat Johnson, Dragon Rising, a remastered transfer of Bruce's only remaining screen-test,
Inside Way of The Dragon, interviews with the production manager Chaplin Chang and Louis Sit, interview with Tony Lau Wing, Warrior Immortal featurette featuring co-star Wong In-Sik, trailer archives, photo gallery and a commentary track from HKL regular Bey Logan.

This same two disc set can also be found on the (also excellent) Bruce Lee 30th Anniversary DVD boxset also from Hong Kong Legends, and also available cheaply, about £10 secondhand usually.
It includes all four of Bruce's HK movies (no Enter the Dragon on this set as back then Warner's wouldn't let it be included or asked for too much money, or both ;))

2) MediumRare UK Blu-ray Region B

The best UK Blu-ray currently available, this can be found either as a part of MediumRare's Bruce Lee Master Collection Boxset (including Enter The Dragon) but can also be tracked down as a standalone disc. This is the only Blu-ray release to port over all the extra features from the old Hong Kong Legend DVD listed above as well as adding an extra commentary track by Big Mike Leeder taken from the US shout select release. English, Cantonese and Mandarin Audio options for the movie.

3) Shout Select US Blu-ray Region A

This US release (presented under its US title of Return of the Dragon) has had a few different incarnations from Shout Select, previously in a glorious 11 disc Blu-ray/DVD Legacy Collection Boxset, sadly now out of print and selling for insane prices, thankfully, you can still find the standalone versions. initially released as a

Blu-Ray/DVD combo pack, now also out of print, but currently available as a single blu-ray release. Extras wise, we get Mike Leeder's commentary track, an alternate title sequence, interviews with Sammo Hung, Simon Yam and Wong Jing as well as the 'Kung Fu - Jon Benn remembers Return of the Dragon' featurette. a TV spot and
Stills gallery round out the disc.
Audio wise here you also get Cantonese, Mandarin and English Tracks.

4) Umbrella Australian Blu-Ray Region B

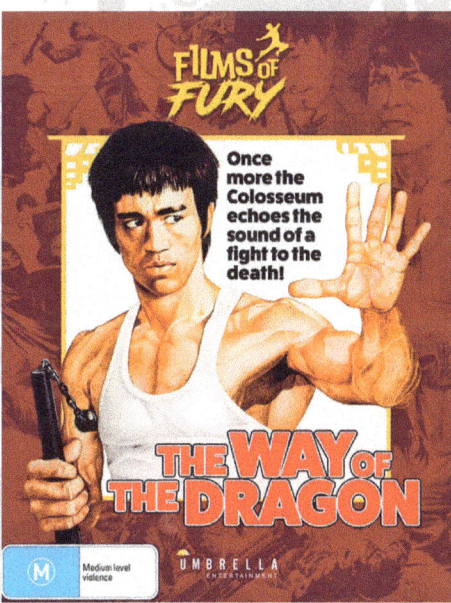

From the good folks down under over at Umbrella Films (who previously released the best version of Jimmy Wang Yu's The Man From Hong Kong currently available) comes the Australian release of the movie, no commentary track on this one, but the disc does also feature the celebrity interviews found on the Shout Select release and adds the fantastic 'Iron Fists and Kung Fu Kicks' documentary. This doc which runs for almost 2 hours, makes this release pretty attractive, though Netflix subscribers may well find that the documentary can be viewed online depending on which region you're based in. The Umbrella release also adds an interview with Brian Trenchard Smith (Director of the Man From Hong Kong) speaking about the Way of The Dragon along with a stills gallery and a trailer. As with the Shout Select version, you get Cantonese, Mandarin and English Tracks.

5) Kam & Ronson HK Blu-Ray Region A

The HK release of the movie houses a 4K restoration of the movie (on a 2K disc) but on a pretty bare bones disc extras wise, you just get a short interview with Anthony Liu and an extra titled 'Celebrity interviews' which whilst unconfirmed at the time of going to print, is very likely the same series of interviews found on the Shout Select and Umbrella releases.
No English dub on this release though, just Cantonese and Mandarin audio options.

6) Nova Media Korean Blu-ray Region A

The Korean release is virtually identical to the HK release in terms of extras and audio/video presentation (also a 4K scan presented on a standard Blu-ray disc)
But this release does have a slipcover with different quite striking artwork, a full Scanavo case
and includes a short interview with Tsui Hark on the disc too.

7) Criterion Collection US Blu-Ray Region A

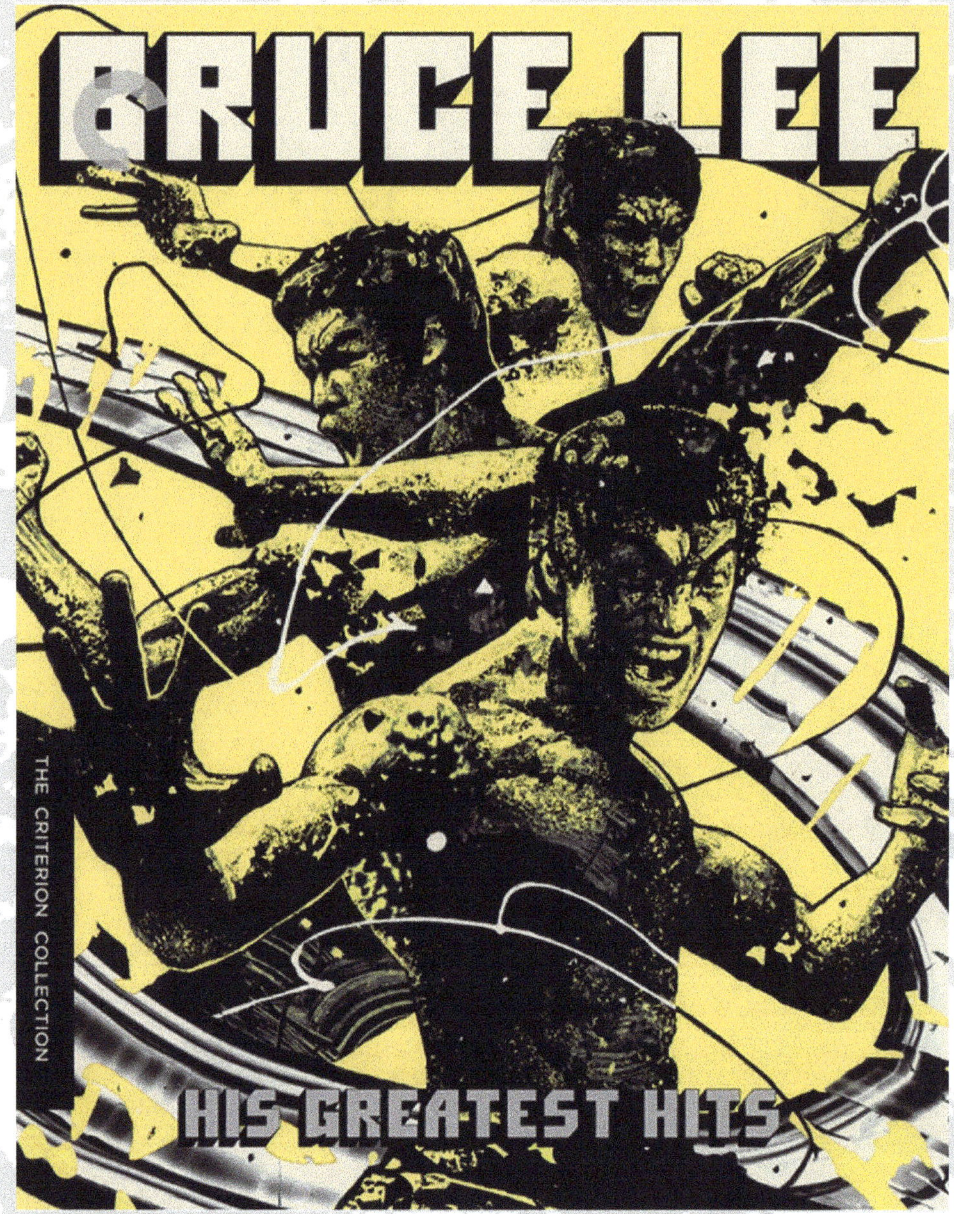

For my money still the best overall single Bruce Lee Boxset presently available anywhere in the world comes from the Criterion Collection, their fantastic Bruce Lee - His Greatest Hits boxset.
This set houses all 5 of Bruce's movies as well as a stack of exclusive extras and includes Mike Leeder's commentaries ported over from the Shout Select releases as well as the Celebrity Interviews found on the Shout, HK and Umbrella releases along with multiple documentaries.
English dubs of all the movies including Way of the Dragon and it even adds in Game of Death 2 as an extra feature. If you only track down one single release, make it this one.
It is region A locked, so UK friends will need a multi-region player to access this one,
No plans are in place for Criterion UK to release this, this US release is easily the best boxset and the best overall showcase for Bruce's filmography available anywhere…. so far.

As previously hinted at in my introduction, we may well see a new UK Boxset coming in 4k from a very well known UK boutique Blu-Ray label this year, if I was a betting man, my money would be on Arrow Video. Watch this space, as soon as any more information becomes available you can be sure we'll cover it in the pages here and I'll be all over it over on my youtube channel, please stop on by there and subscribe to the channel if you don't already!

Be Water My Friends!

https://www.youtube.com/c/TheFanaticalDragon

Return of The Dragon
A PIECE OF CINEMATIC EXCELLENCE
ドラゴンへの道
THE WAY OF THE DRAGON
By John Negron

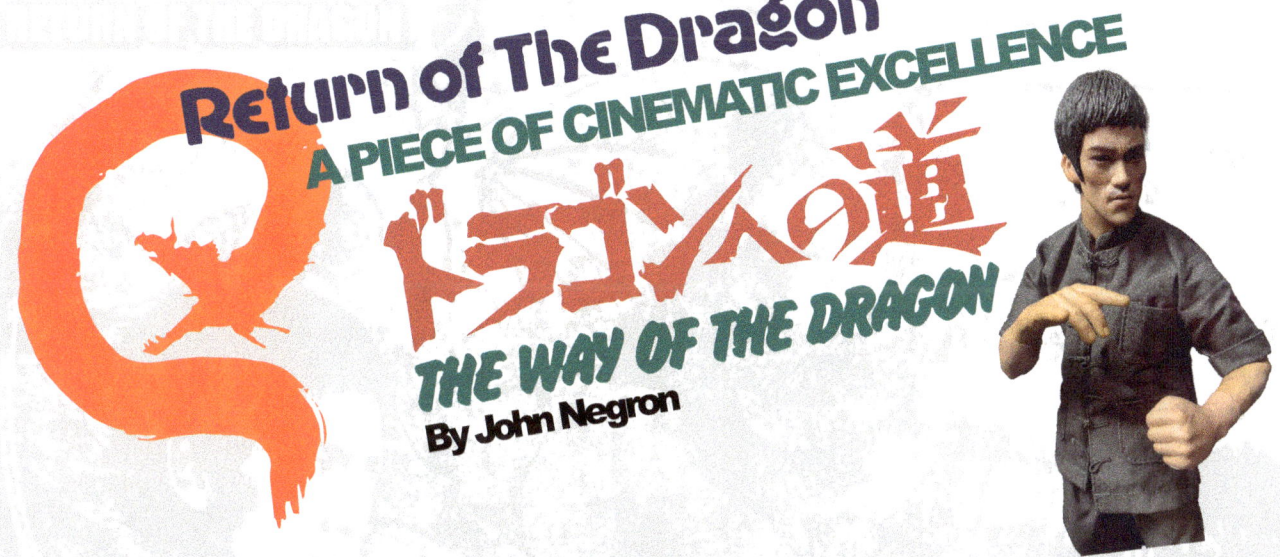

I would like to start this article with a little background on my early experience with Bruce Lee I was first introduced to Bruce Lee as Kato on the Green Hornet T.V series opposite of Batman series as a young lad of 6 years old in 1966. Although at this time, I had no known knowledge of who, he was or Martial Arts. My fascination with Bruce Lee came watching him as Kato walk into a room an within seconds clearing it and eliminating the threat of the bad guys whereas watching Batman it was so campy they walked into a room and the bad guys would be dealt with crash, Bam, Boom and they would get beat up and then finally at some point get captured which would lead up to a 2 part episode to determine their fate. Let's fast forward to 1971 and here comes Fists of Fury AKA The Big Boss. Oddly enough by this point in 1971 I still had a lot of my early Christmas presents which were Batman & Green Hornet toys. In1971 I still had my original gum cards, Corgi Car and several other GH toys of which most did not feature my future

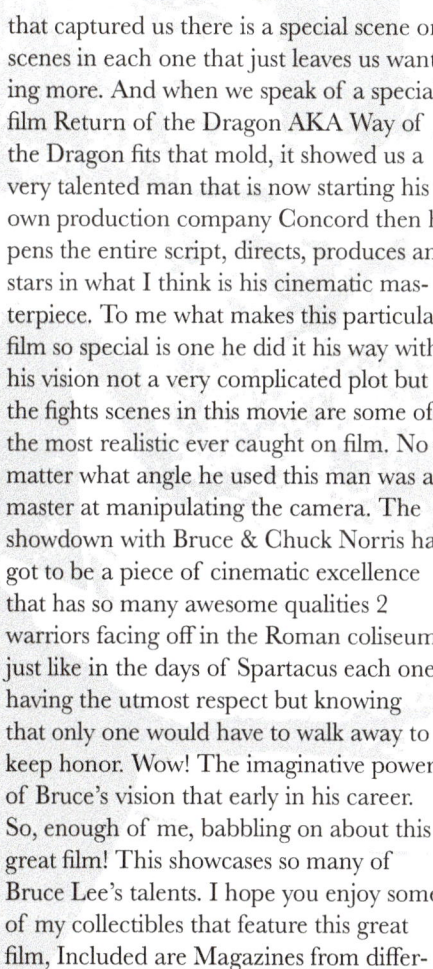

idol Kato/Bruce Lee. So now sometime in 1971 I caught the Bruce Lee bug which I have had for almost 50 years now. After seeing Bruce on the big screen and the excitement it caused watching other movie goers amazed at what he was doing on the screen, you got it I WAS HOOKED and here I am about 50 years later still mesmerized by the impression I saw on the screen. It's hard for a true die-hard Bruce Lee fan to pick a favorite Movie. WHY? well, each one is so unique and shows us a side of Bruce Lee that captured us there is a special scene or scenes in each one that just leaves us wanting more. And when we speak of a special film Return of the Dragon AKA Way of the Dragon fits that mold, it showed us a very talented man that is now starting his own production company Concord then he pens the entire script, directs, produces and stars in what I think is his cinematic masterpiece. To me what makes this particular film so special is one he did it his way with his vision not a very complicated plot but the fights scenes in this movie are some of the most realistic ever caught on film. No matter what angle he used this man was a master at manipulating the camera. The showdown with Bruce & Chuck Norris has got to be a piece of cinematic excellence that has so many awesome qualities 2 warriors facing off in the Roman coliseum just like in the days of Spartacus each one having the utmost respect but knowing that only one would have to walk away to keep honor. Wow! The imaginative power of Bruce's vision that early in his career. So, enough of me, babbling on about this great film! This showcases so many of Bruce Lee's talents. I hope you enjoy some of my collectibles that feature this great film, Included are Magazines from different countries, toys, Lobby cards, I tried to feature a little variety of different items etc.... Enjoy!! and long live the cinematic excellence of the Return of the Dragon!

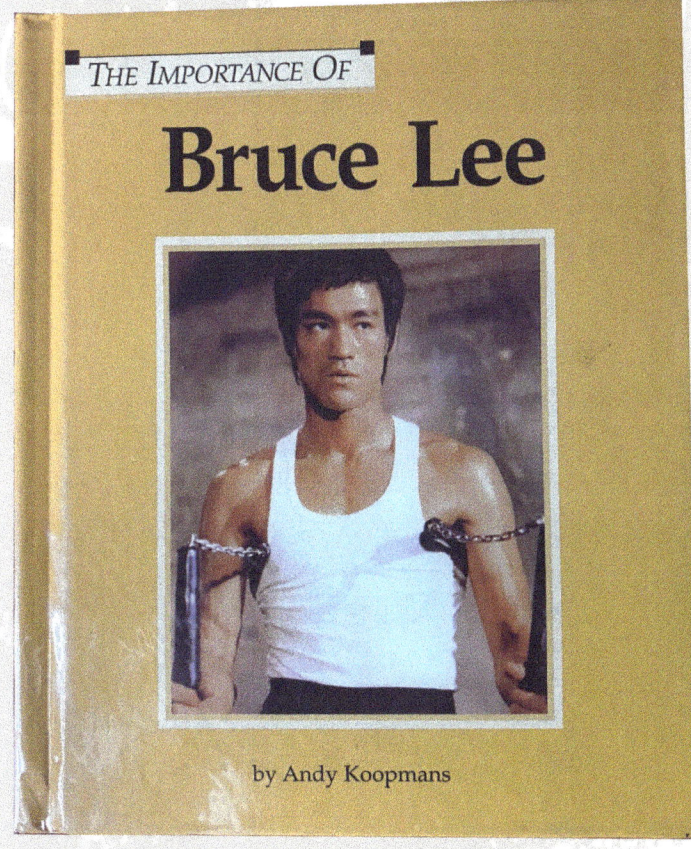

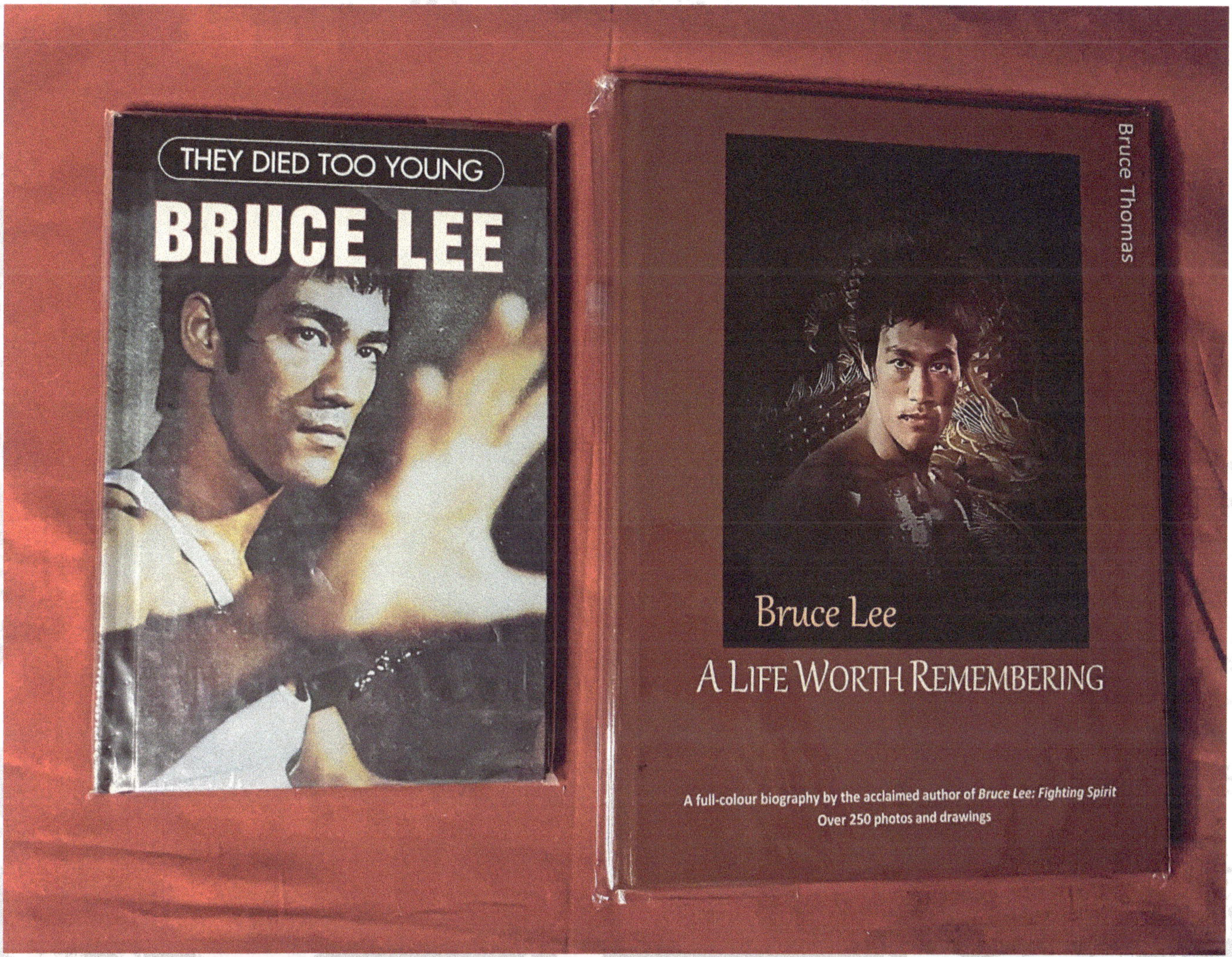
THEY DIED TOO YOUNG
BRUCE LEE
Bruce Thomas
Bruce Lee
A LIFE WORTH REMEMBERING
A full-colour biography by the acclaimed author of *Bruce Lee: Fighting Spirit*
Over 250 photos and drawings

S 比武实录
Q 表演
J 截拳道宗师
F 猛龙过江

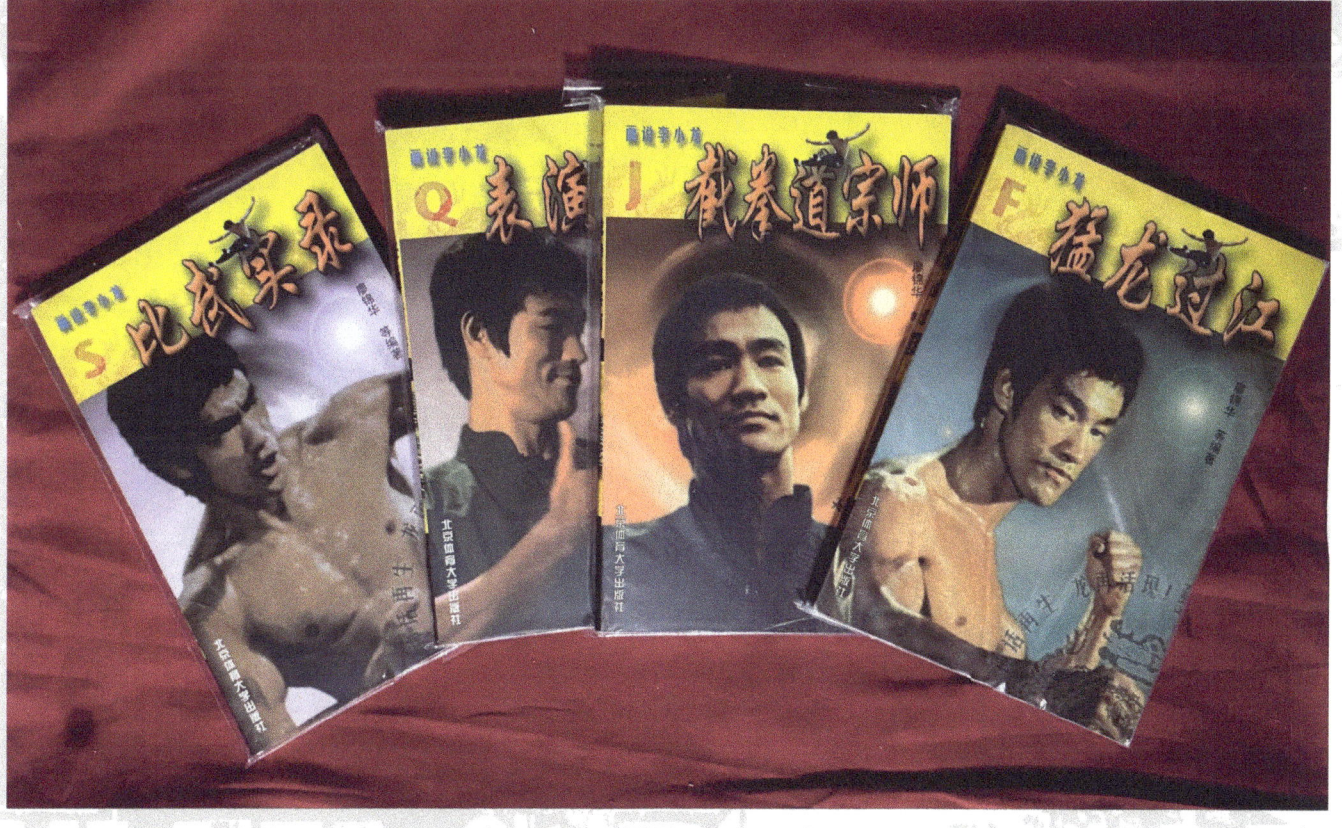

布魯斯
李
5
BRUCE LEE
Rare Images 2
Limited Edition
Collector Issue!
BRUCE LEE
MANÍA
edición limitada
¡¡ 35 AÑOS DE LEGADO !!
BRUCE LEE
MANÍA
edición limitada
1940-2015
75 YEARS
CLUB

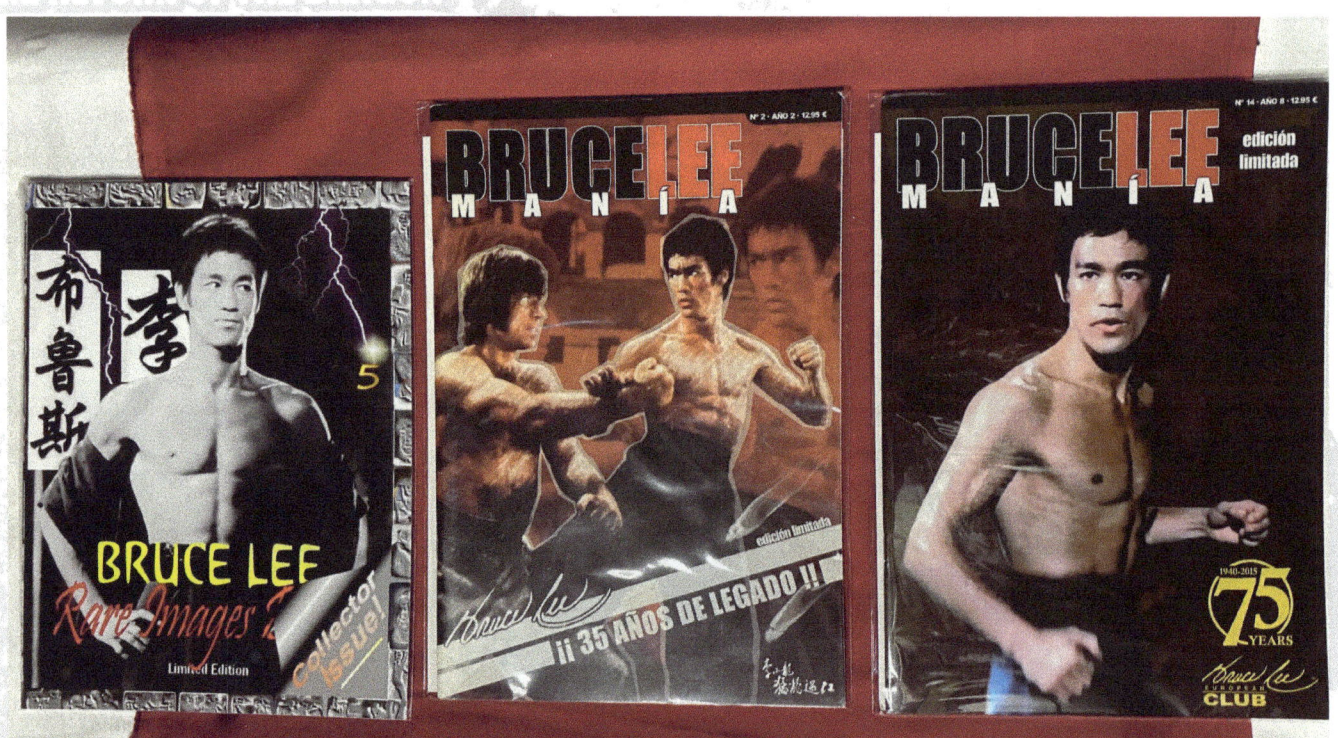

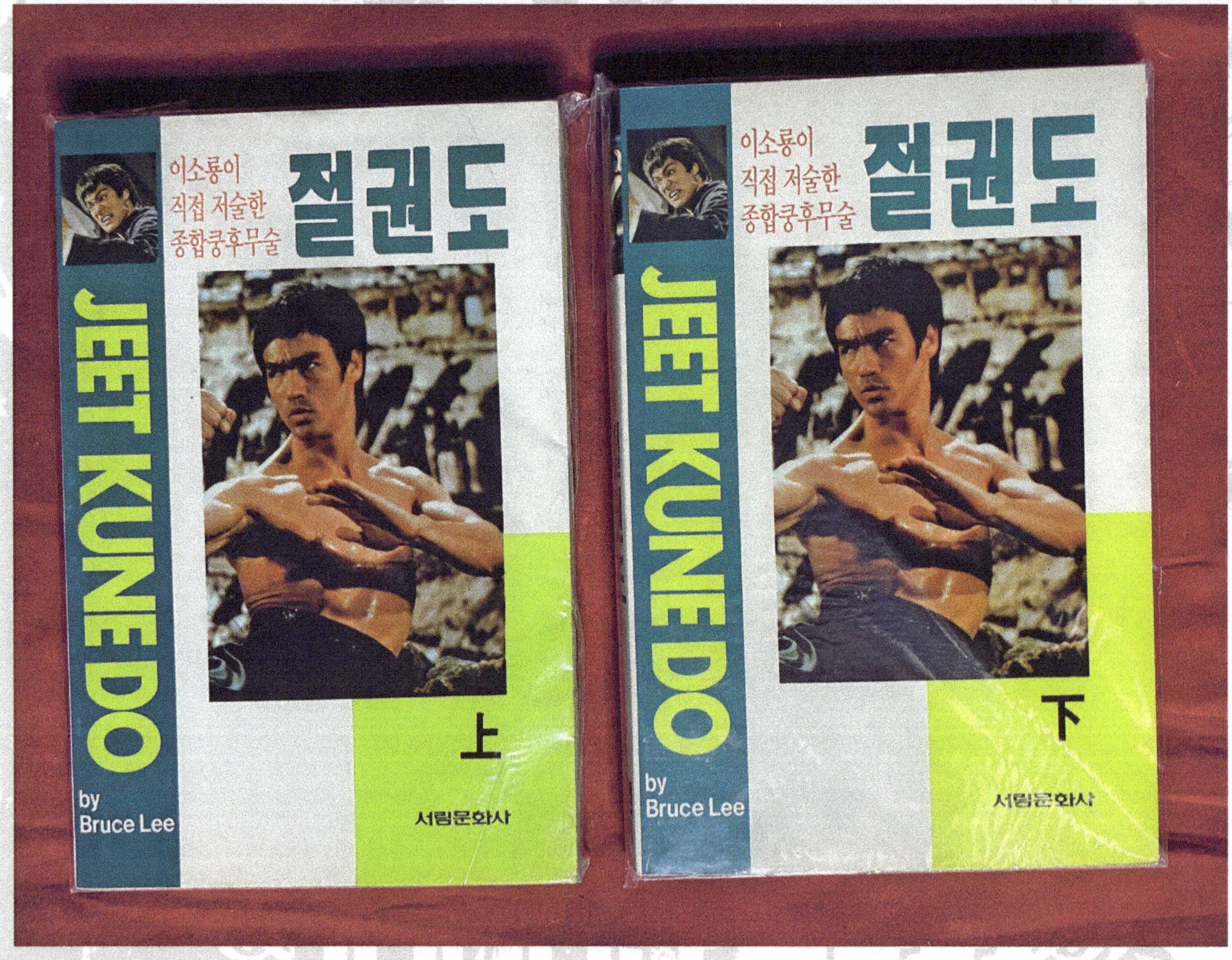
이소룡이
직접 저술한
종합쿵후무술
절권도
JEET KUNE DO
by
Bruce Lee
上
서림문화사
이소룡이
직접 저술한
종합쿵후무술
절권도
JEET KUNE DO
by
Bruce Lee
下
서림문화사

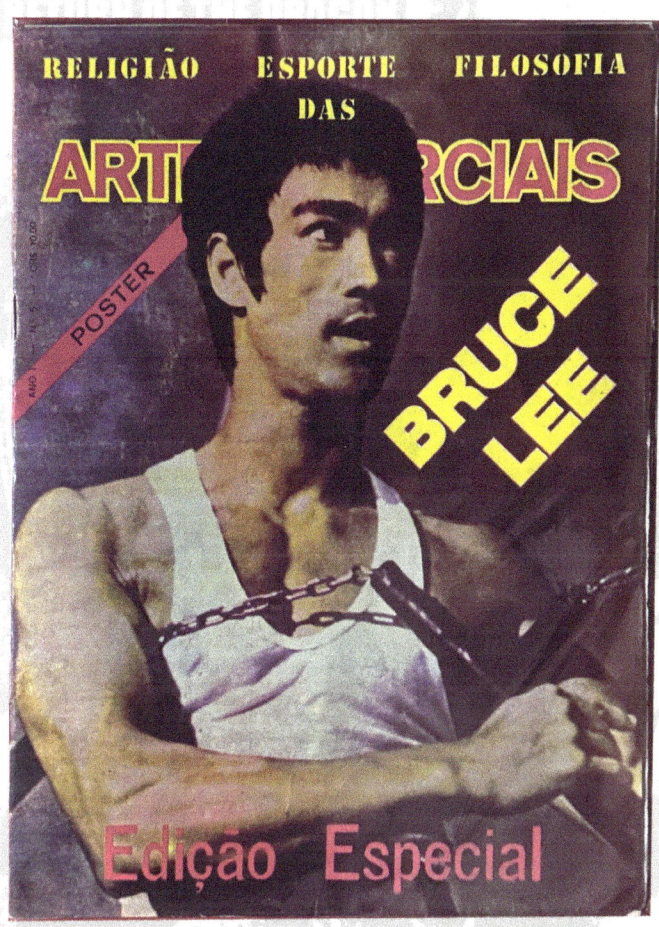
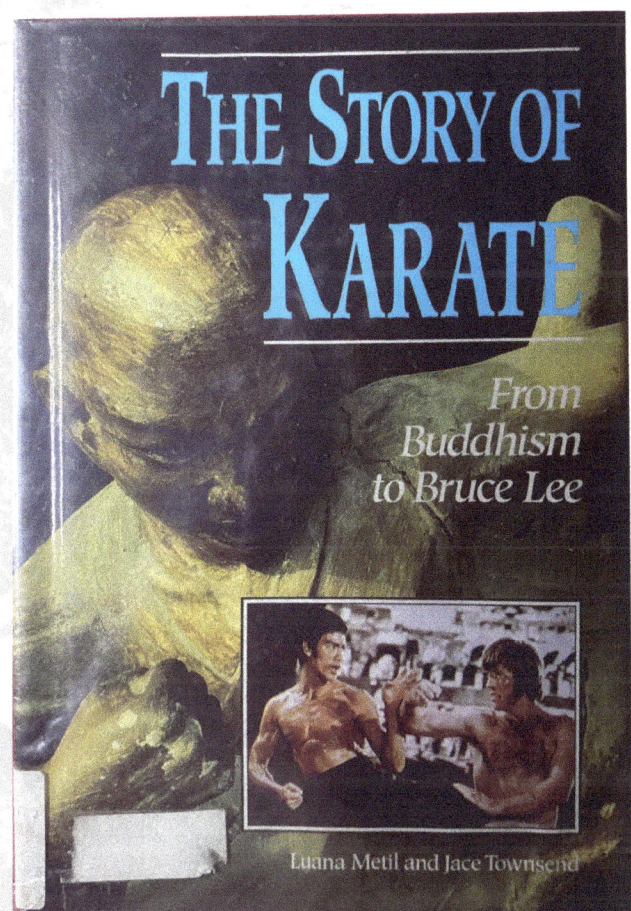

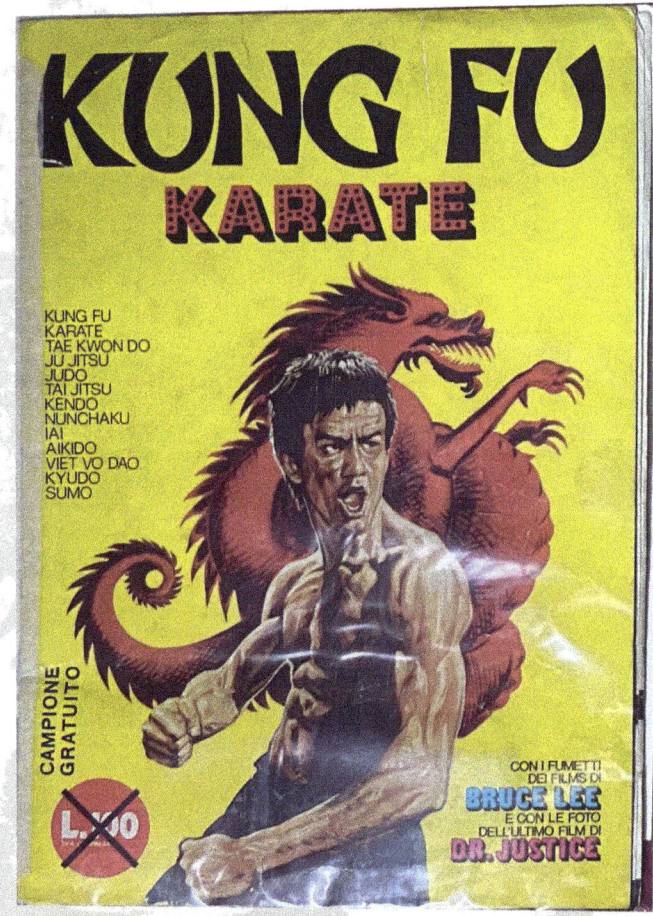
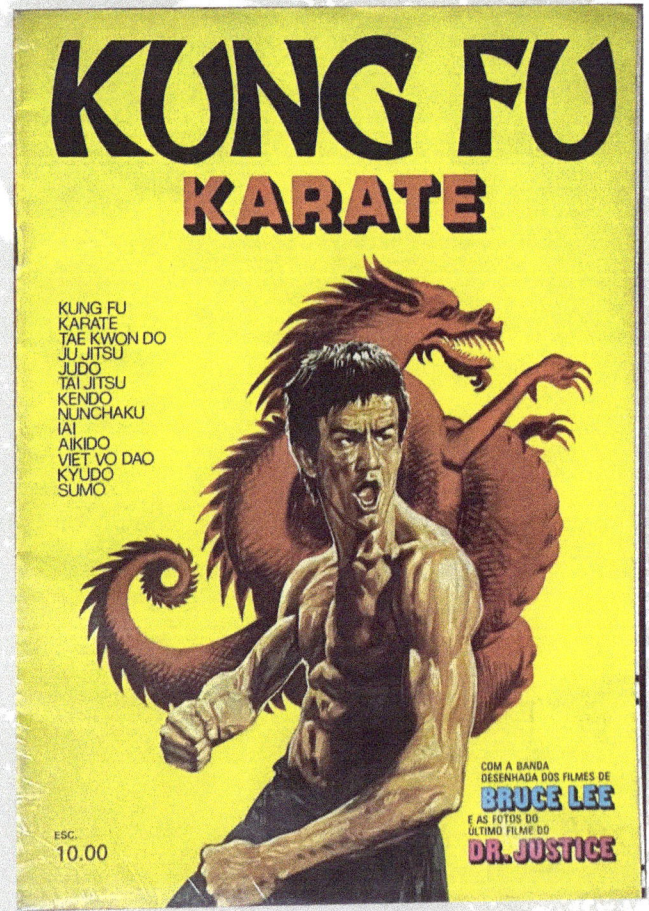
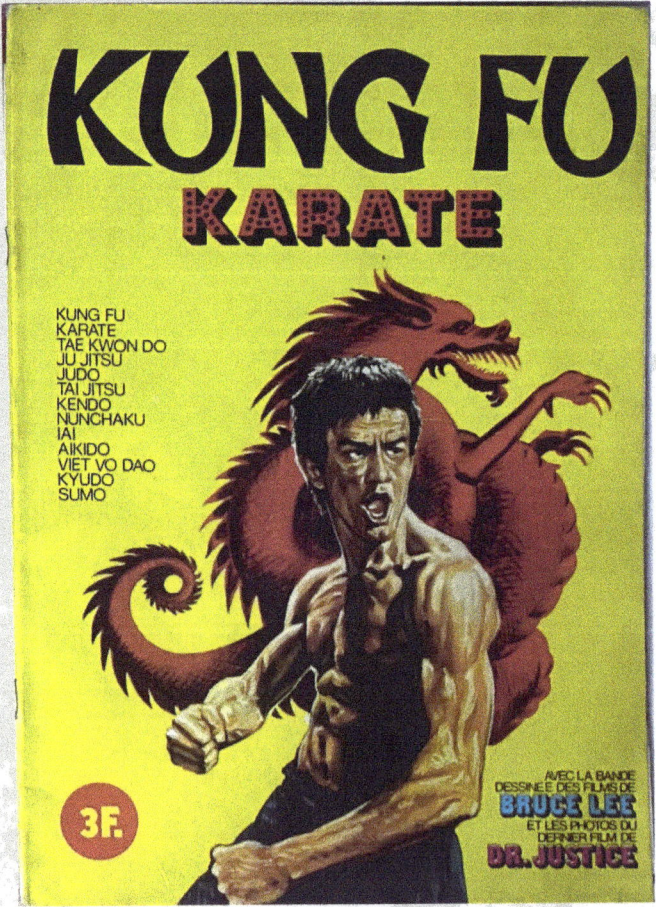

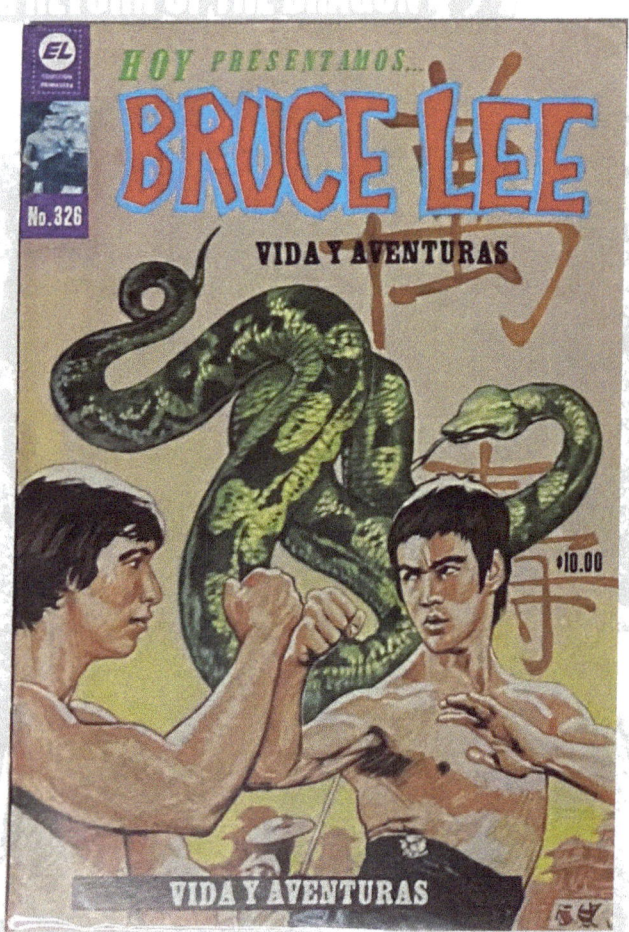

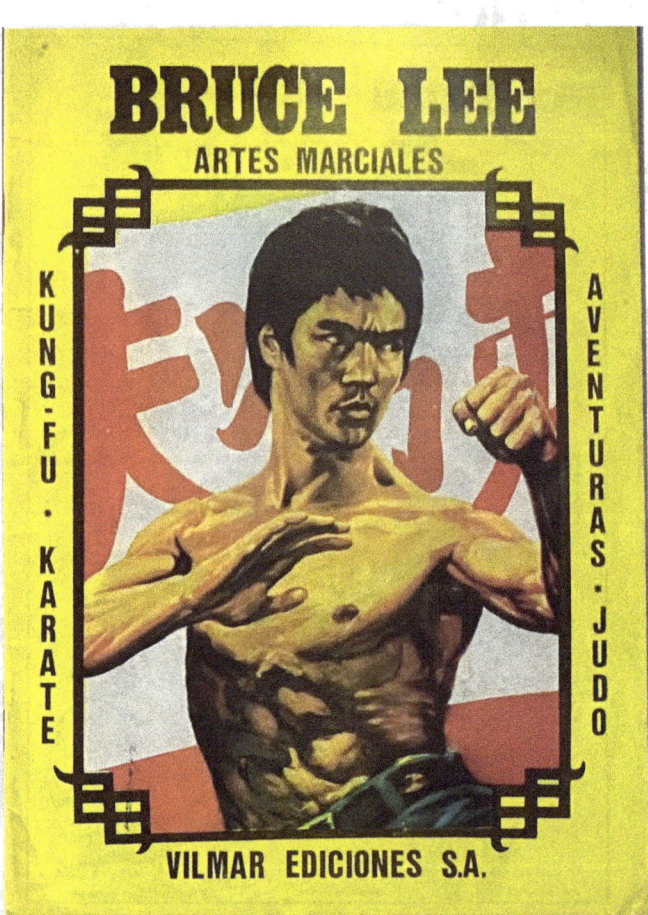

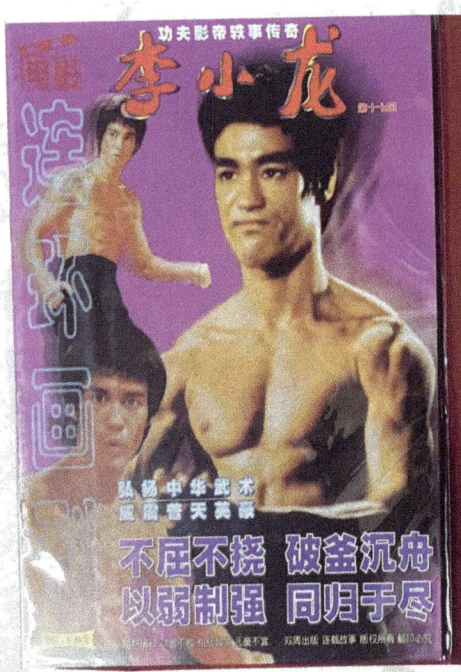
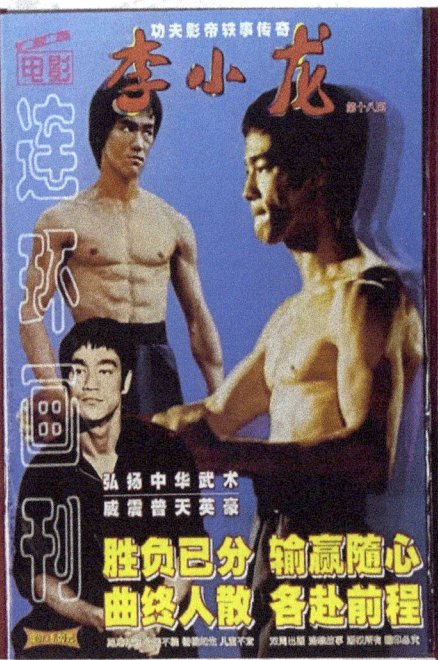
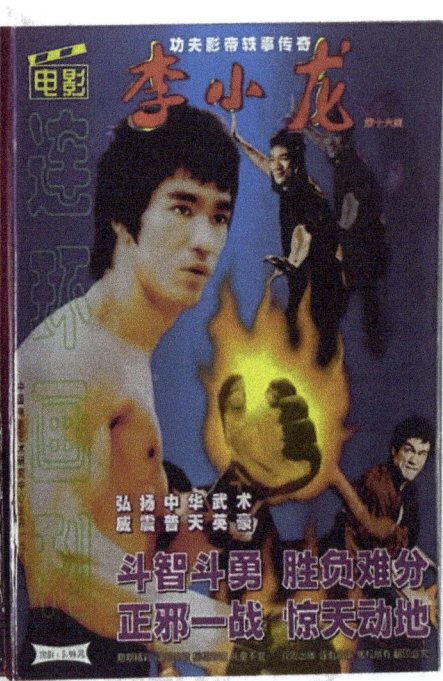

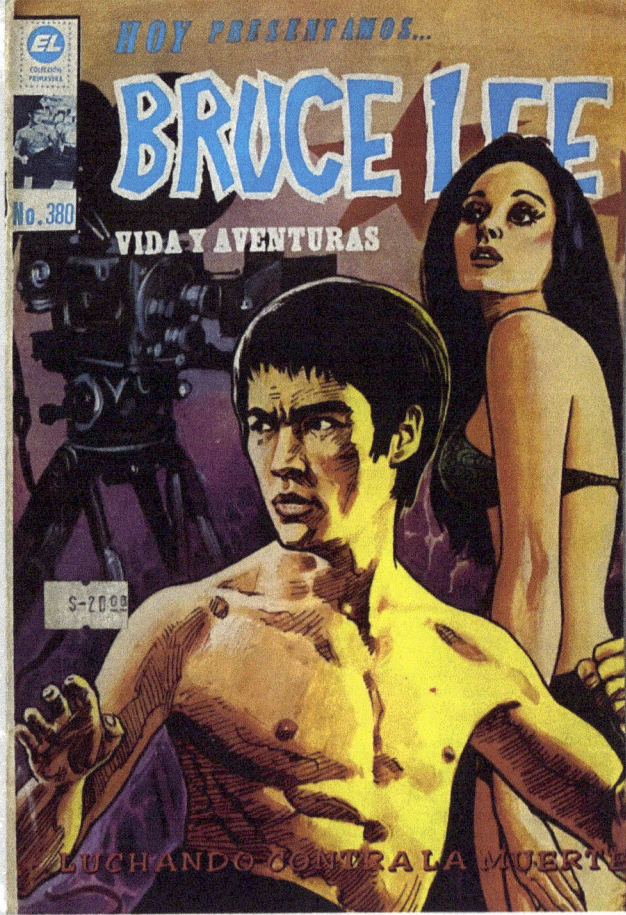

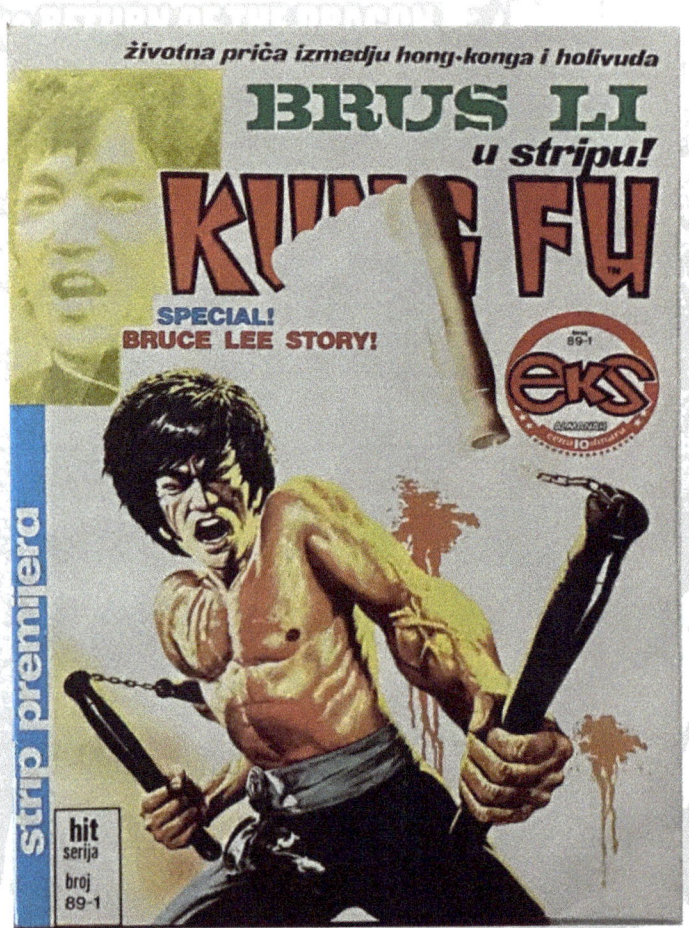

小龍記
hyper off-line meeting 2011
猛龍見聞録III
猛龍争伝説 1972-1973
李小龍生誕70周年記念
チャップリン・チャン来日交流 超オフ会
2011/4/16 at "Saha"
OFFICIAL IMITATION
4.85

fangraphic
original art
poetry
articles
puzzles & prizes
information
feb, 1977
Happy Year of the Serpent!

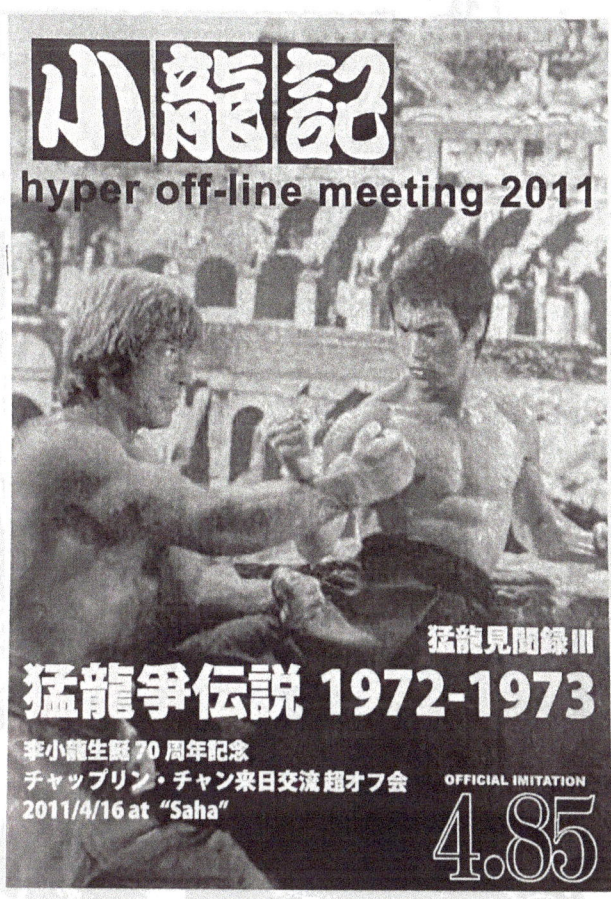

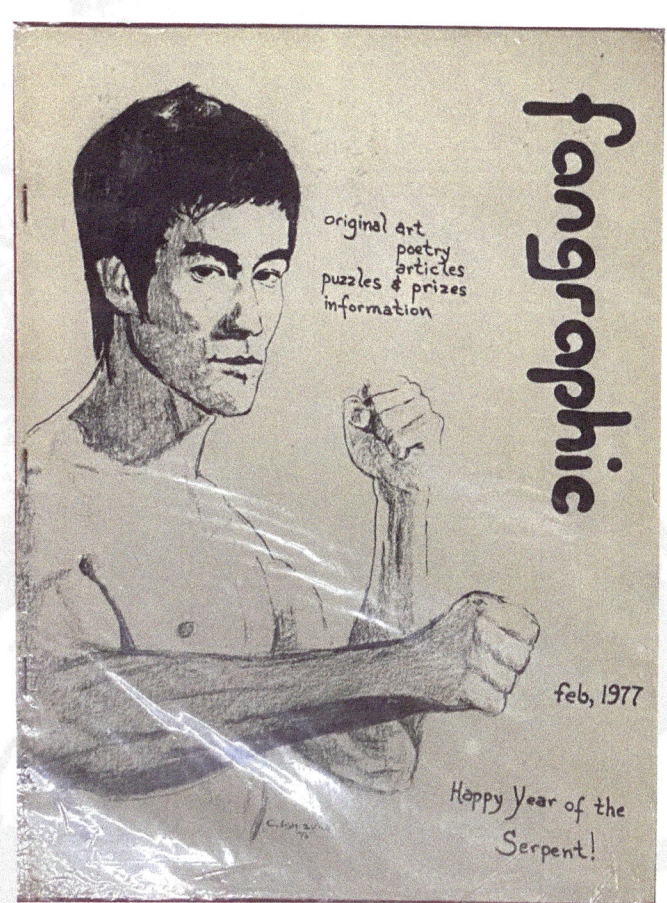

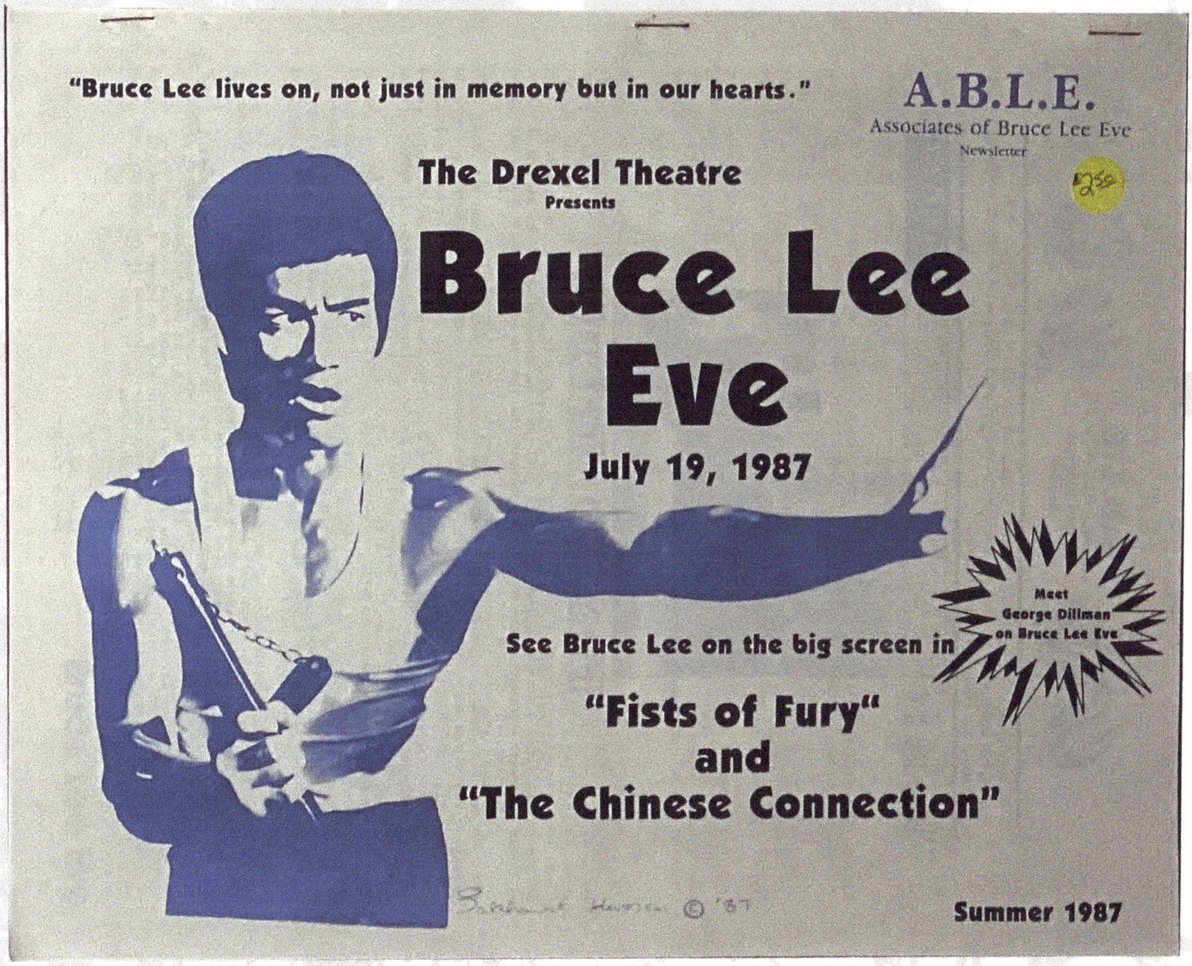
"Bruce Lee lives on, not just in memory but in our hearts."
A.B.L.E.
Associates of Bruce Lee Eve
Newsletter
The Drexel Theatre
Presents
Bruce Lee Eve
July 19, 1987
Meet George Dillman on Bruce Lee Eve
See Bruce Lee on the big screen in
"Fists of Fury"
and
"The Chinese Connection"
Summer 1987

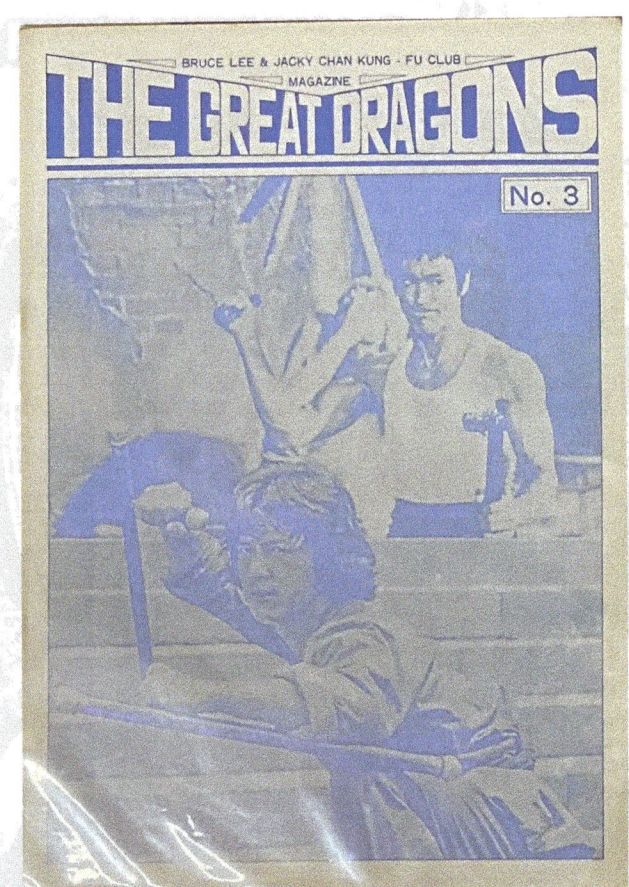

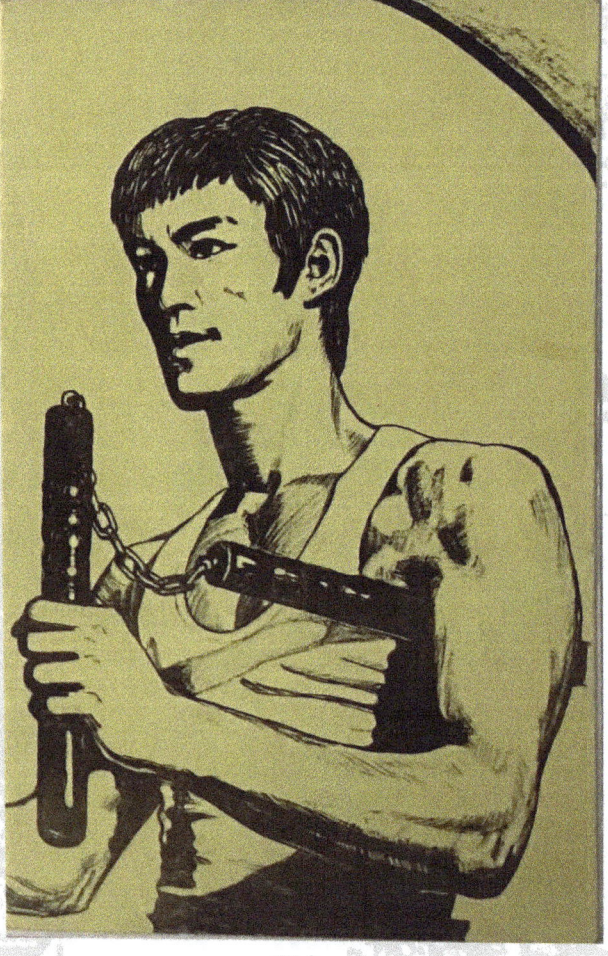

LA MUERTE DE / THE DEATH OF
BRUCE LEE

MARCOS OCAÑA RIZO

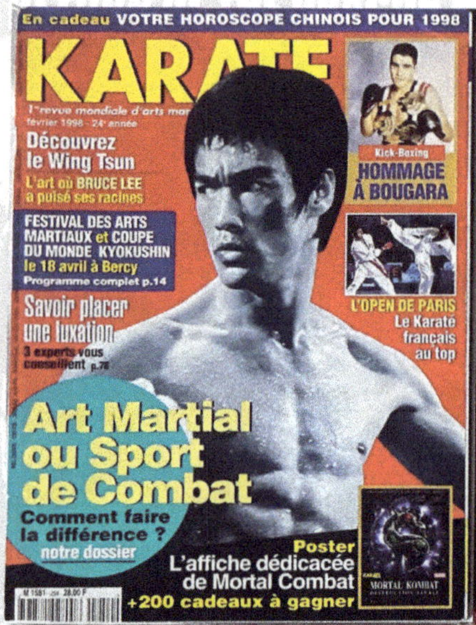

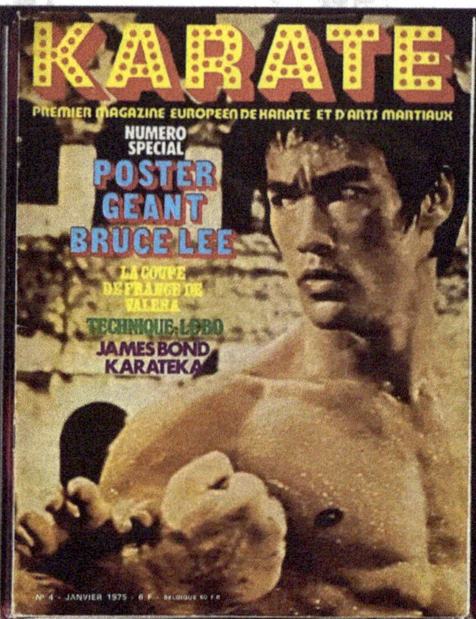

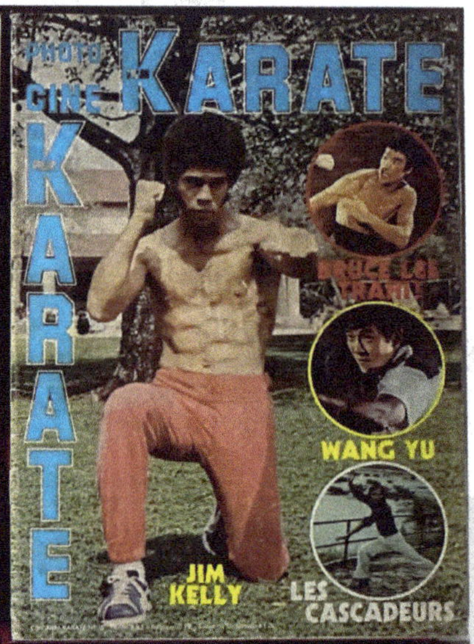

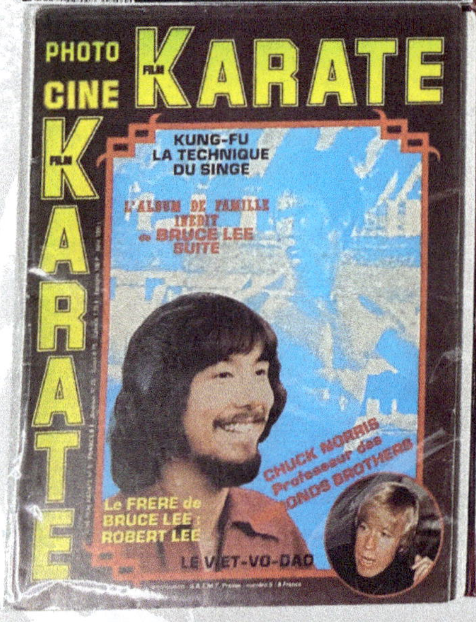

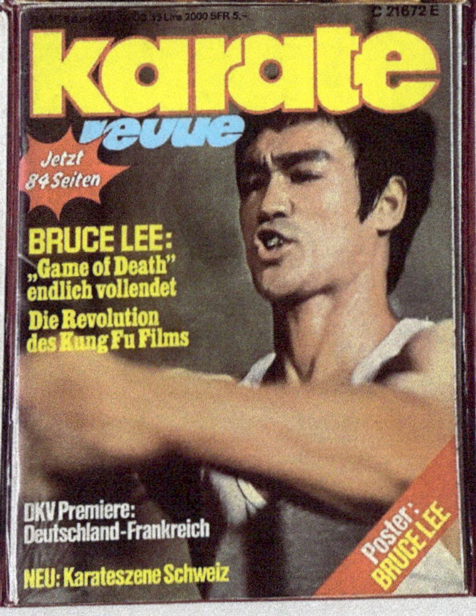

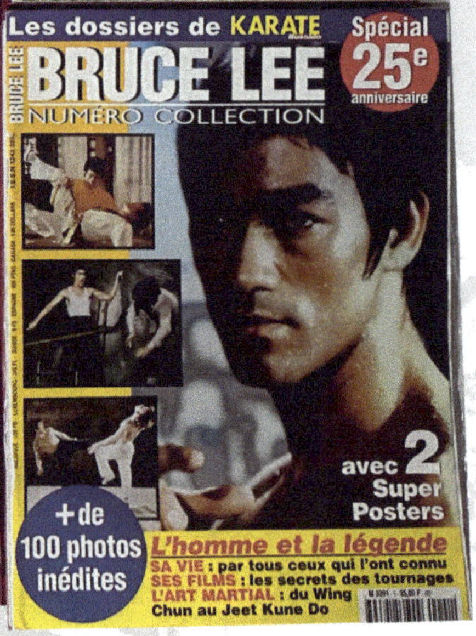

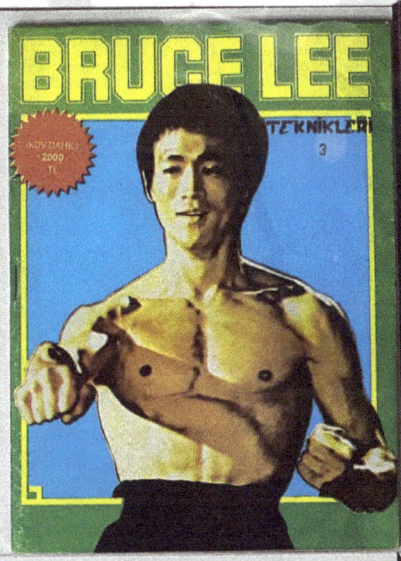

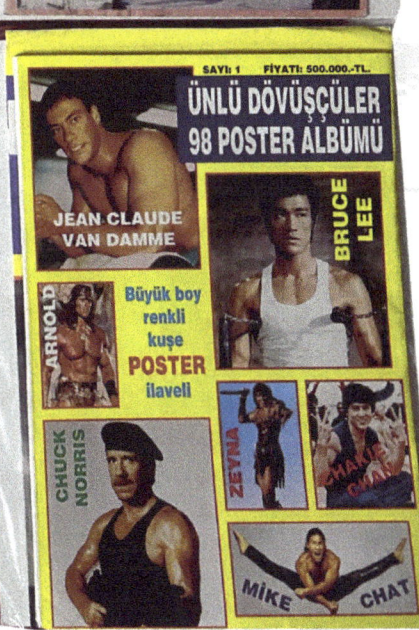

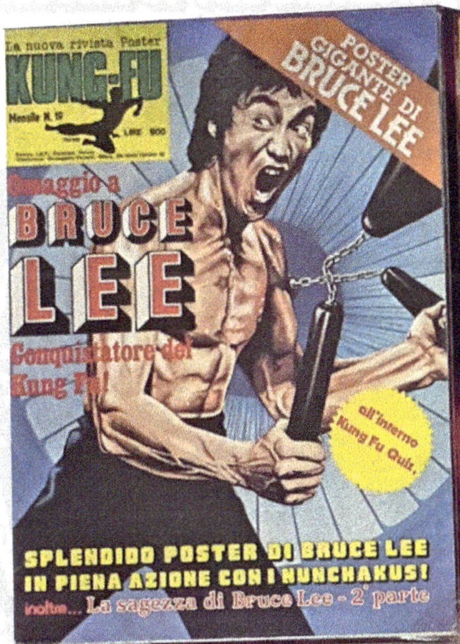
La nuova rivista Poster
KUNG-FU
POSTER GIGANTE DI BRUCE LEE
Omaggio a
BRUCE
LEE
Conquistatore del Kung Fu!
all'interno Kung Fu Quiz
SPLENDIDO POSTER DI BRUCE LEE
IN PIENA AZIONE CON I NUNCHAKUS!
inoltre... La saggezza di Bruce Lee - 2ª parte
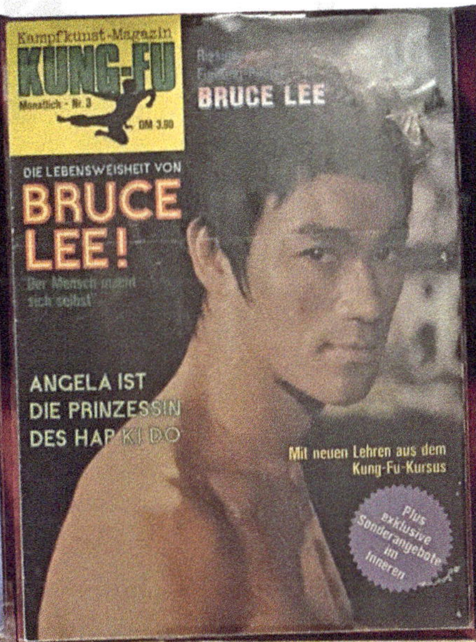
Kampfkunst-Magazin
KUNG-FU
Monatlich - Nr. 3
DM 3.50
BRUCE LEE
DIE LEBENSWEISHEIT VON
BRUCE
LEE!
ANGELA IST
DIE PRINZESSIN
DES HAPKIDO
Mit neuen Lehren aus dem Kung-Fu-Kursus
Plus exklusive Sonderangebote im Inneren
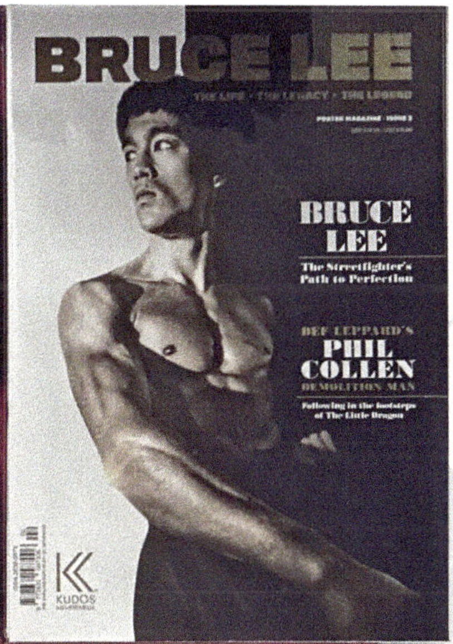
BRUCE LEE
BRUCE
LEE
The Streetfighter's Path to Perfection
DEF LEPPARD'S
PHIL
COLLEN
DEMOLITION MAN
KUDOS
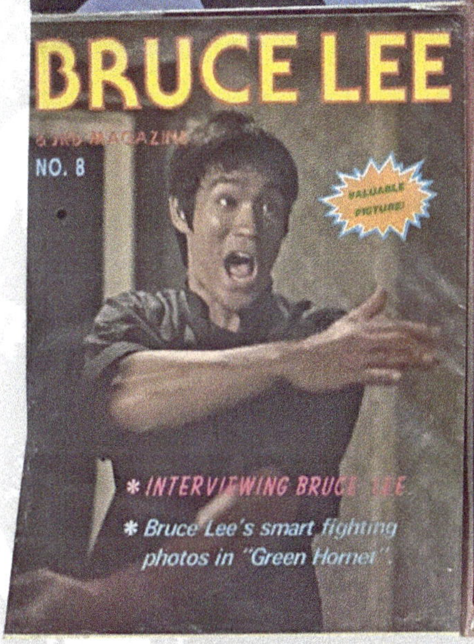
BRUCE LEE
& JKD MAGAZINE
NO. 8
VALUABLE PICTURE!
* INTERVIEWING BRUCE LEE
* Bruce Lee's smart fighting photos in "Green Hornet".
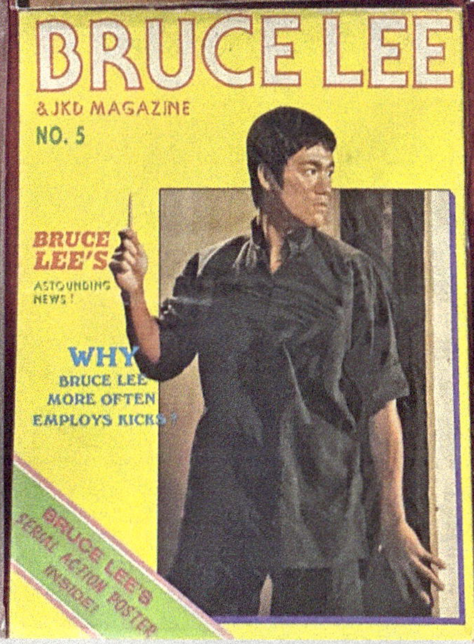
BRUCE LEE
& JKD MAGAZINE
NO. 5
BRUCE LEE'S
ASTOUNDING NEWS!
WHY
BRUCE LEE
MORE OFTEN
EMPLOYS KICKS?
BRUCE LEE'S SERIAL ACTION POSTER INSIDE!
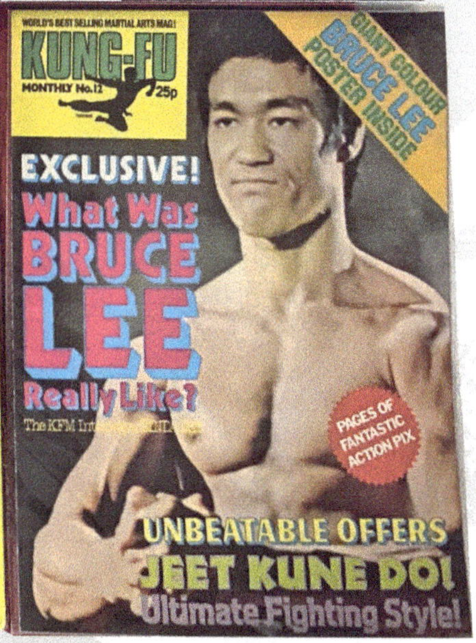
WORLD'S BEST SELLING MARTIAL ARTS MAG!
KUNG-FU
MONTHLY No.12
25p
GIANT COLOUR BRUCE LEE POSTER INSIDE
EXCLUSIVE!
What Was
BRUCE
LEE
Really Like?
PAGES OF FANTASTIC ACTION PIX
UNBEATABLE OFFERS
JEET KUNE DO!
Ultimate Fighting Style!
WORLD'S BEST SELLING MARTIAL ARTS MAG!
KUNG-FU
MONTHLY NO72
70p
DANGER:
BRUCE LEE'S MASTERPIECE THE 'UNCUT'
WAY OF THE DRAGON REVIEWED
WORLD'S BEST SELLING MARTIAL ARTS MAG!
KUNG-FU
MONTHLY No.73
70p
THE
TWENTIETH CENTURY
GLADIATOR
BRUCE LEE
'WAY' PART II CLASSIC LEE/NORRIS BATTLE
ASTOUNDING BOB WALL INTERVIEW
WORLD'S BEST SELLING MARTIAL ARTS MAG!
KUNG-FU
MONTHLY NO. 16
30p
GIANT BRUCE LEE POSTER INSIDE
THE TAO OF
BRUCE
LEE
The Jeet Kune Do Bible!
PAGES OF FAX, PIX AND INFO!
MEET THE MAN WITH
THE GOLDEN TOUCH!

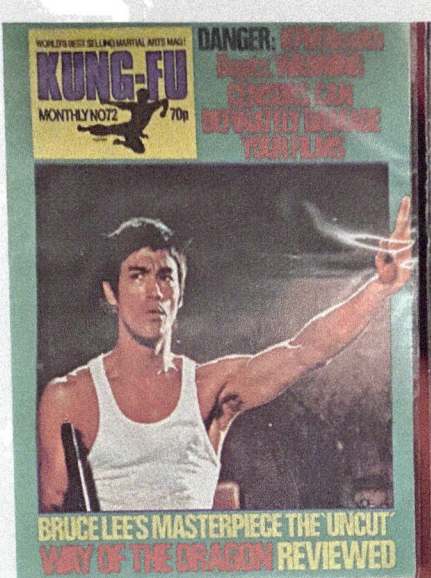

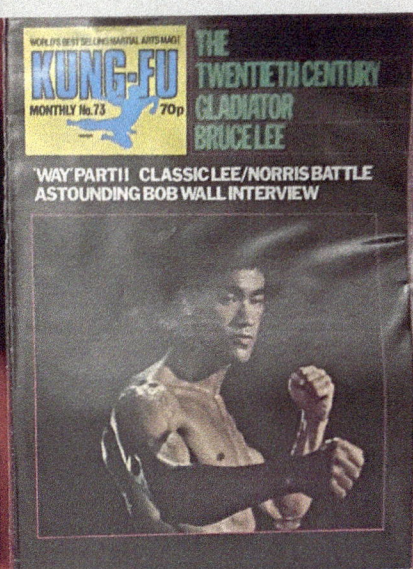

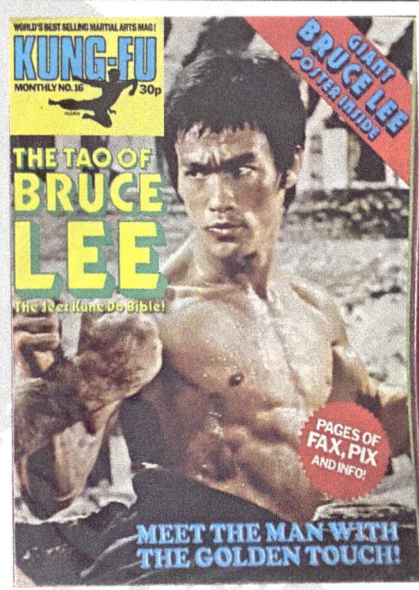

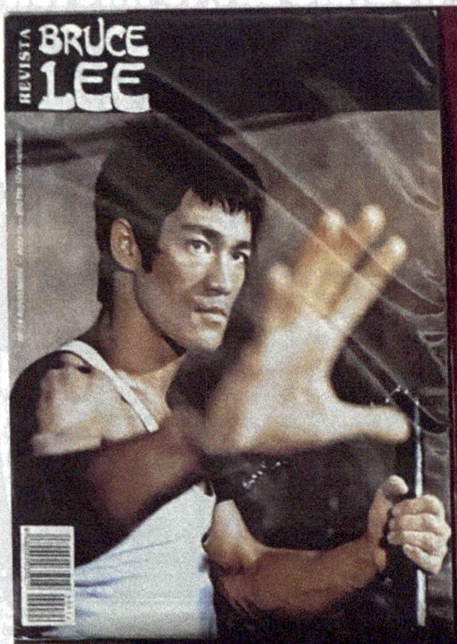
REVISTA
BRUCE LEE

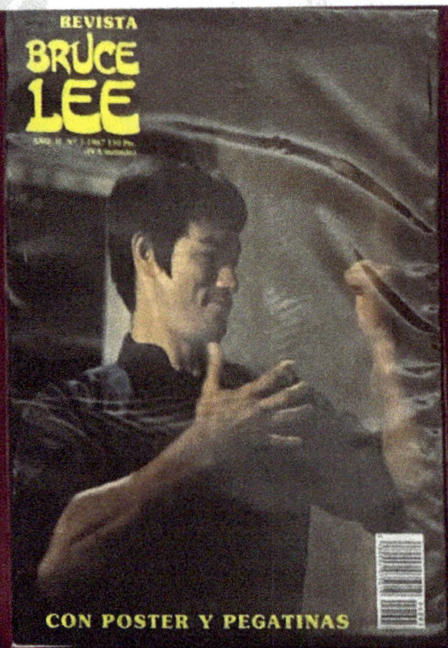
REVISTA
BRUCE LEE
CON POSTER Y PEGATINAS

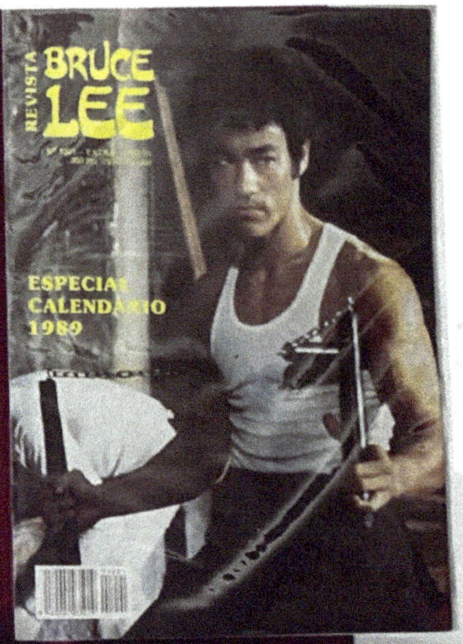
REVISTA
BRUCE LEE
ESPECIAL
CALENDARIO
1989

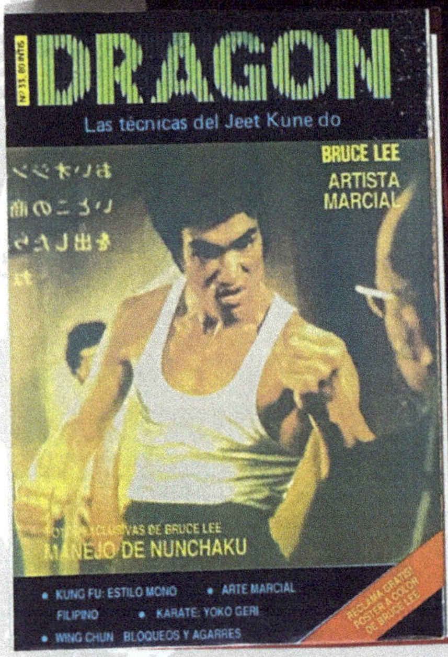
DRAGON
Las técnicas del Jeet Kune do
BRUCE LEE
ARTISTA MARCIAL
MANEJO DE NUNCHAKU
KUNG FU: ESTILO MONO
ARTE MARCIAL FILIPINO
KARATE: YOKO GERI
WING CHUN: BLOQUEOS Y AGARRES

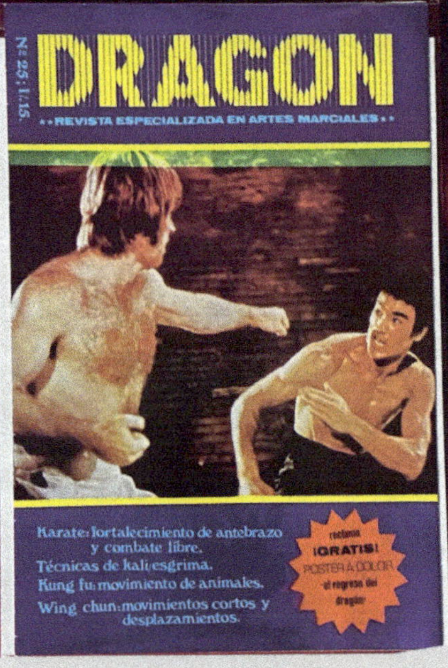
DRAGON
REVISTA ESPECIALIZADA EN ARTES MARCIALES
Karate: fortalecimiento de antebrazo y combate libre.
Técnicas de kali-esgrima.
Kung fu: movimiento de animales.
Wing chun: movimientos cortos y desplazamientos.
¡GRATIS!
POSTER A COLOR

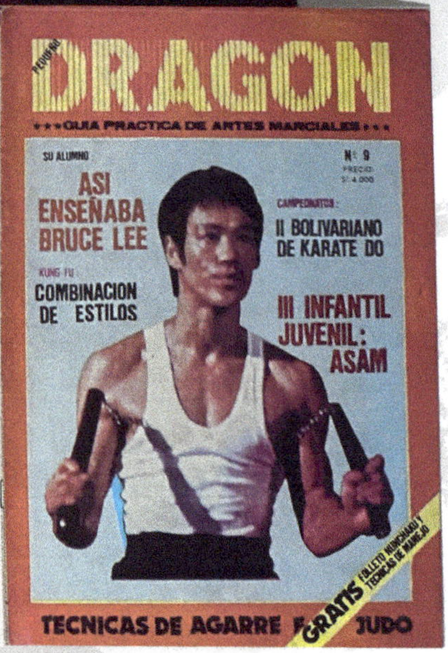
DRAGON
GUIA PRACTICA DE ARTES MARCIALES
ASI ENSEÑABA BRUCE LEE
Nº 9
II BOLIVARIANO DE KARATE DO
COMBINACION DE ESTILOS
III INFANTIL JUVENIL: ASAM
TECNICAS DE AGARRE
JUDO
GRATIS

DRAGON
REVISTA ESPECIALIZADA EN ARTES MARCIALES
SPECIAL DE BRUCE LEE: EL REGRESO DEL DRAGON Y CALENDARIO A COLOR 87
WING CHUN
DEFENSA PERSONAL CONTRA DOS...

BASES CIENTIFICAS DEL TAEKWONDO
Nº 6
TECNICAS DE JEET KUNE DO
KUNG FU:
LA DANZA DEL NANQUAN
DEFENSA PERSONAL
POSTER EL REGRESO DEL DRAGON
ESTILOS EN EL KARATE JAPONES
DRAGON

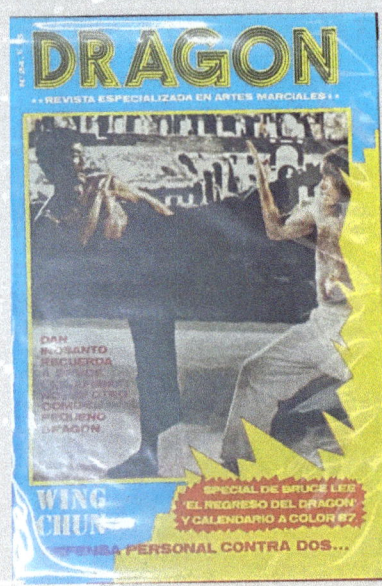

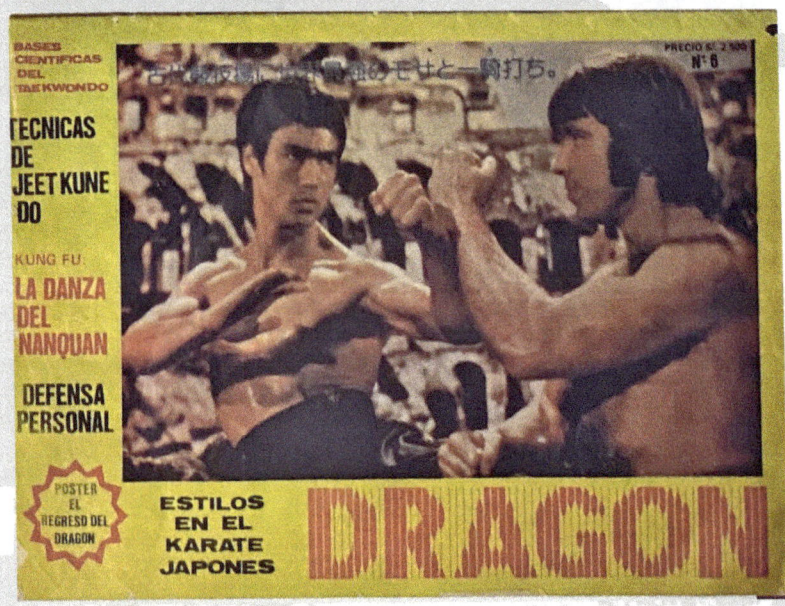

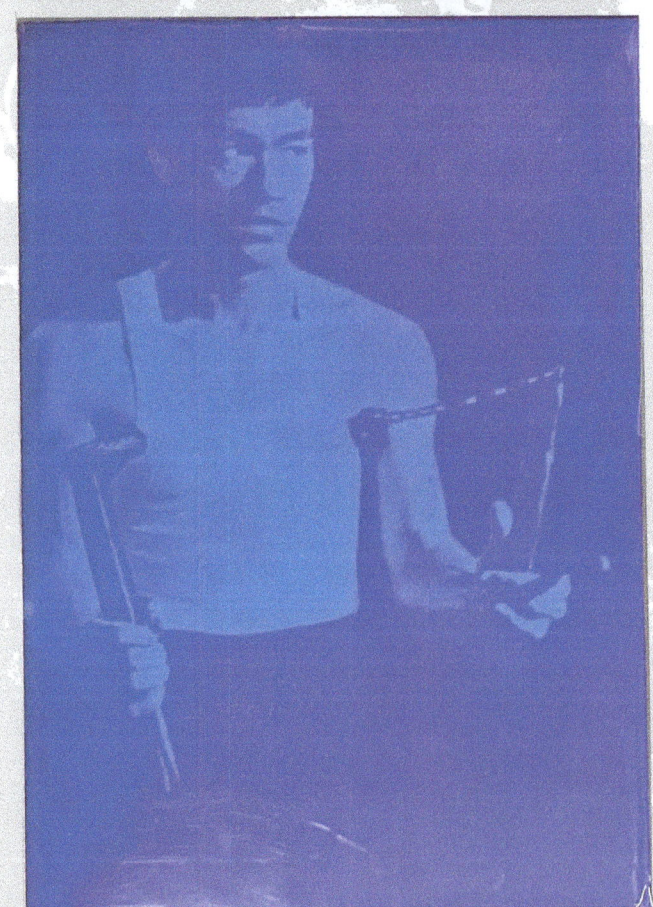
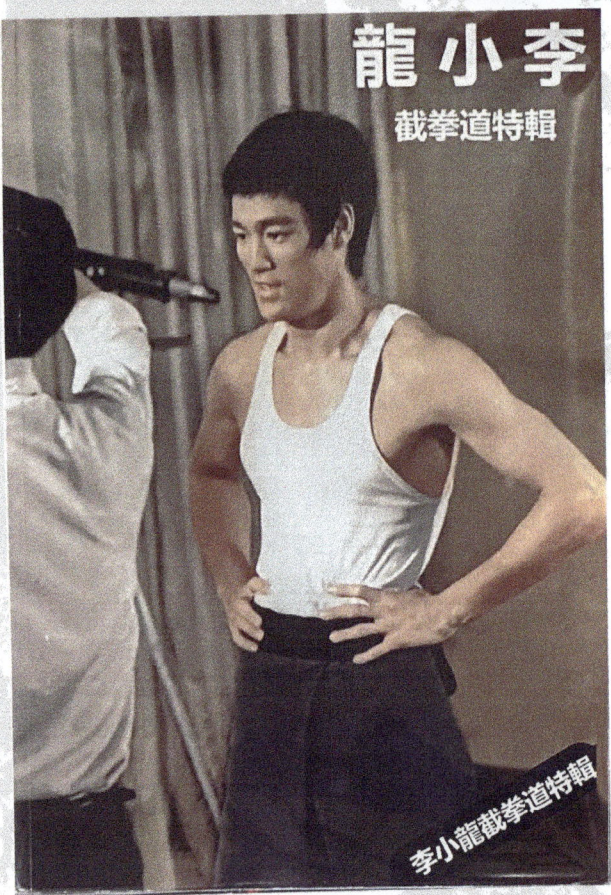

APRIL 1974 NO. 32
FREE GIANT COLOR POSTER INSIDE
the Monster Times
BRUCE LEE LIVES! PAGE 10
THE BEAST FROM 20,000 FATHOMS! P.3
QUESTOR! P.20
THE "BIG G" SPEAKS! P.25
MARVEL'S MIGHTIEST MONSTERS! P.6
WEREWOLF OF WASHINGTON! P.13
MEXICAN MONSTERS!

C 21672 E
karate revue
Jetzt 84 Seiten
BRUCE LEE:
„Game of Death" endlich vollendet
Die Revolution des Kung Fu Films
DKV Premiere: Deutschland-Frankreich
NEU: Karateszene Schweiz
Poster: BRUCE LEE

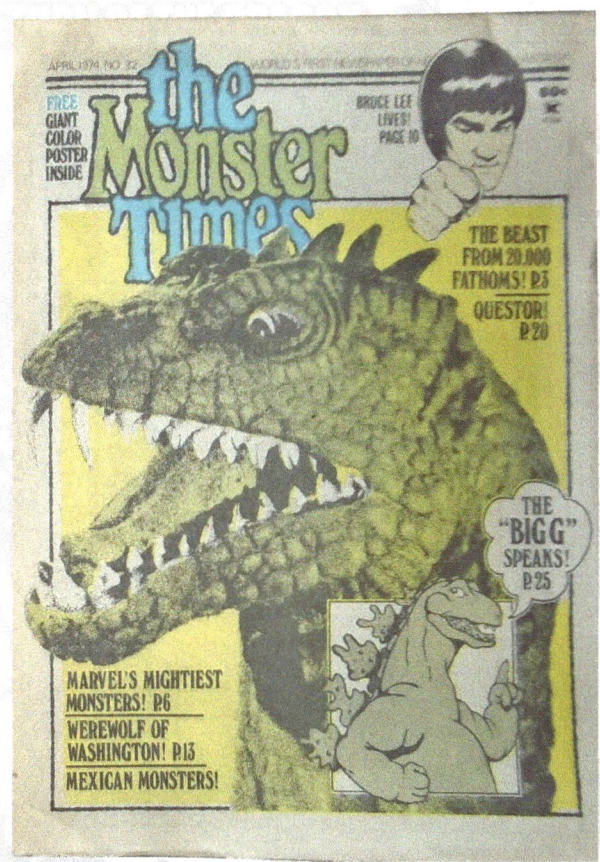

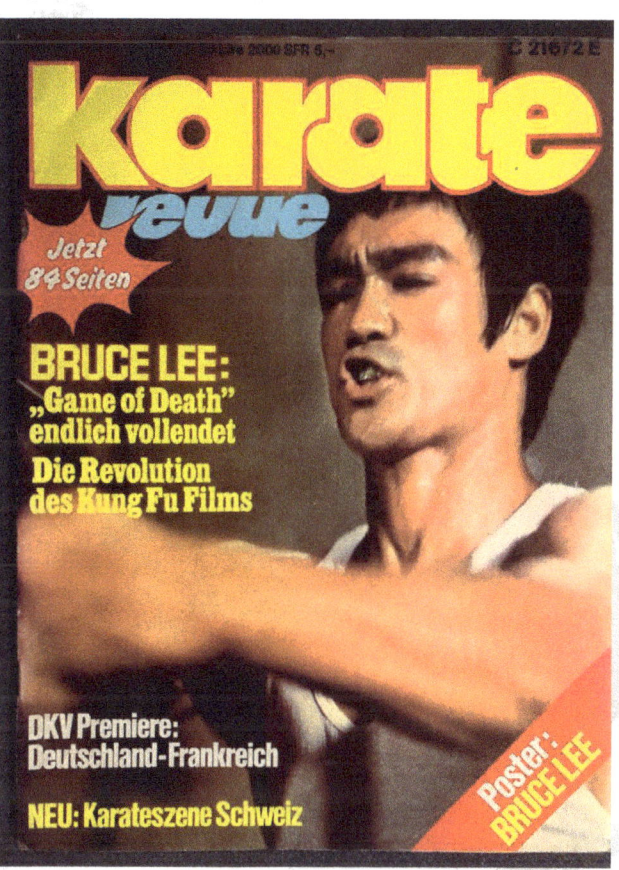

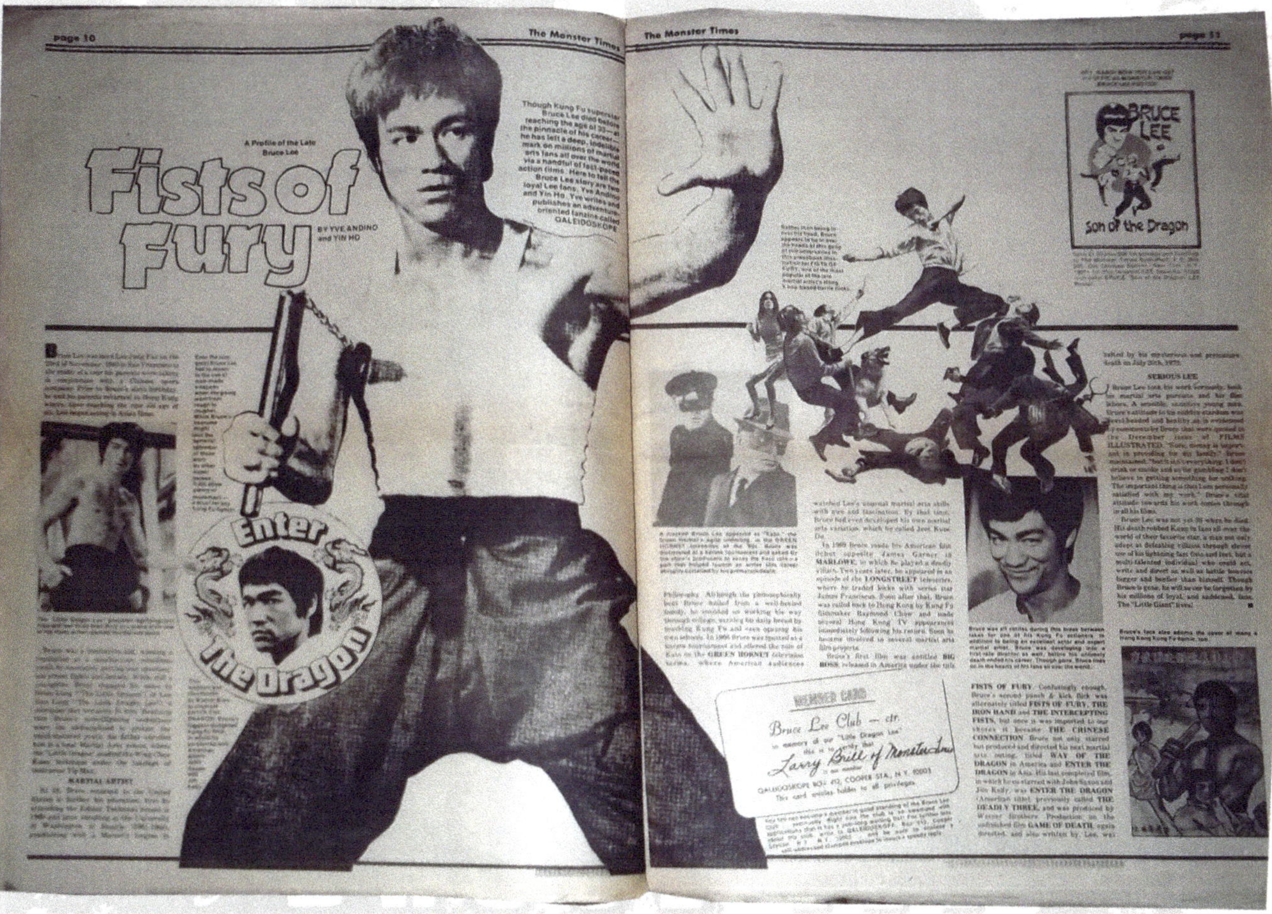
page 10
The Monster Times
The Monster Times
page 11
A Profile of the Late Bruce Lee
Fists of Fury
BY YVE ANDINO and YIN HO
Enter The Dragon
BRUCE LEE
Son of the Dragon
MEMBER CARD
Bruce Lee Club

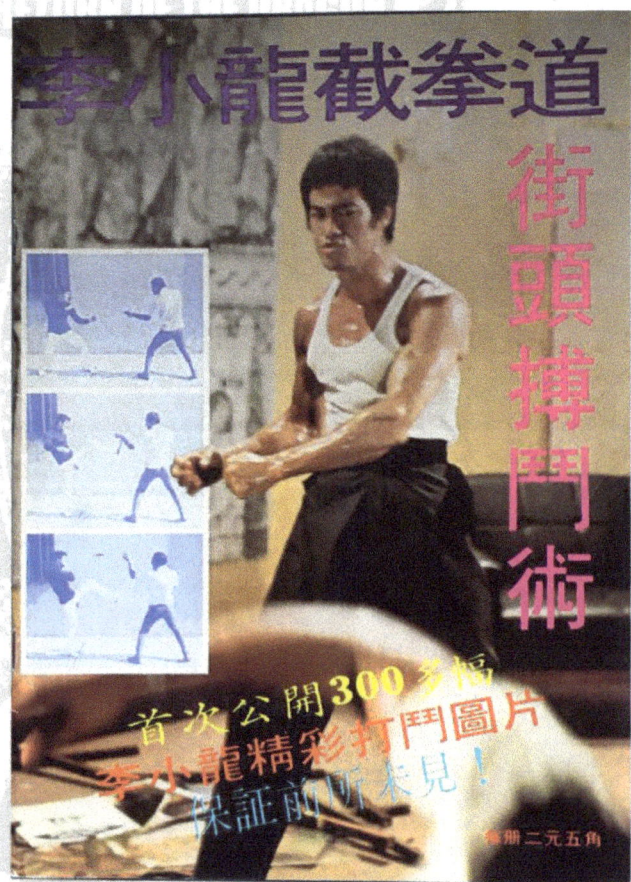

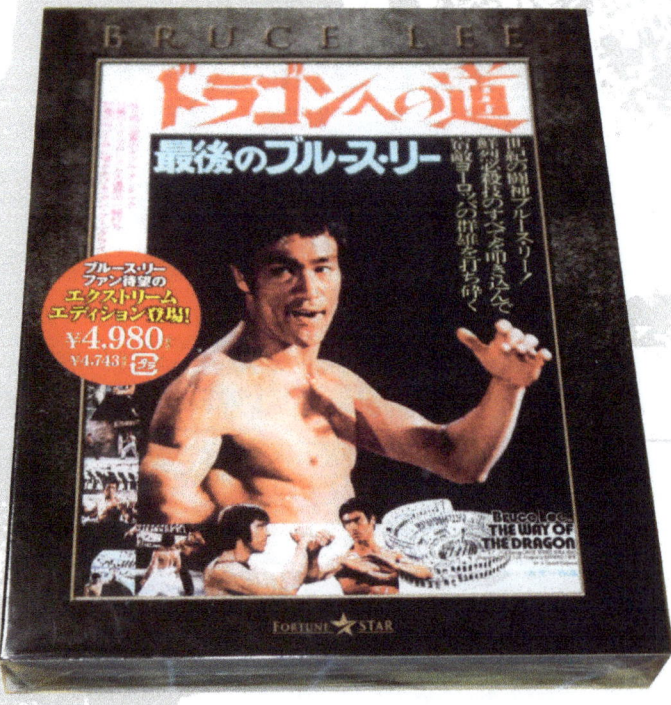

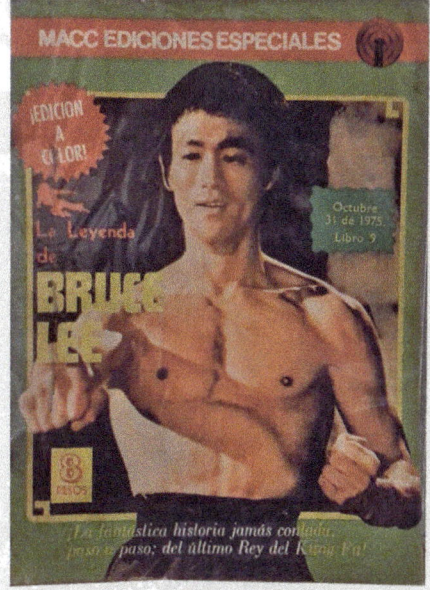

KUNG FU
Bruce Lee

CGC UNIVERSAL GRADE
9.8
Bruce Lee: The Dragon Rises #1
EMERALD CITY COMICON
LEE
KLINE
McKINNEY
ATKINSON
#1
BRUCE LEE
THE DRAGON RISES
CONVENTION EXCLUSIVE
LIMITED TO 200 COPIES

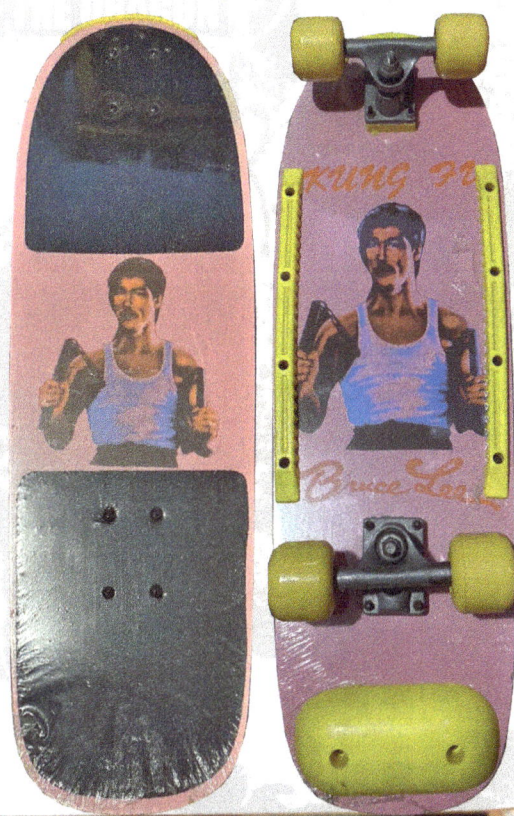

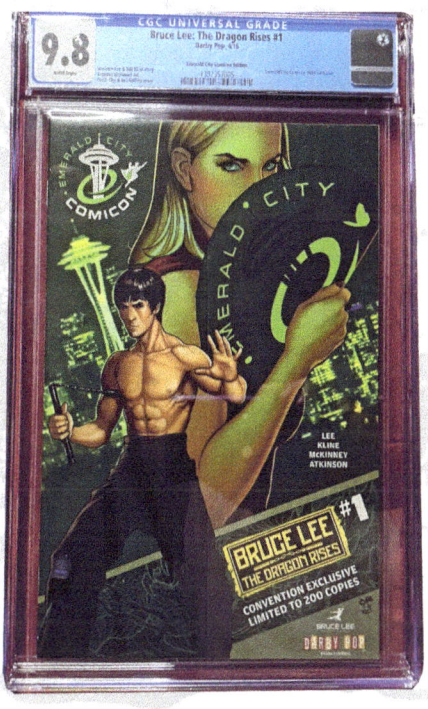

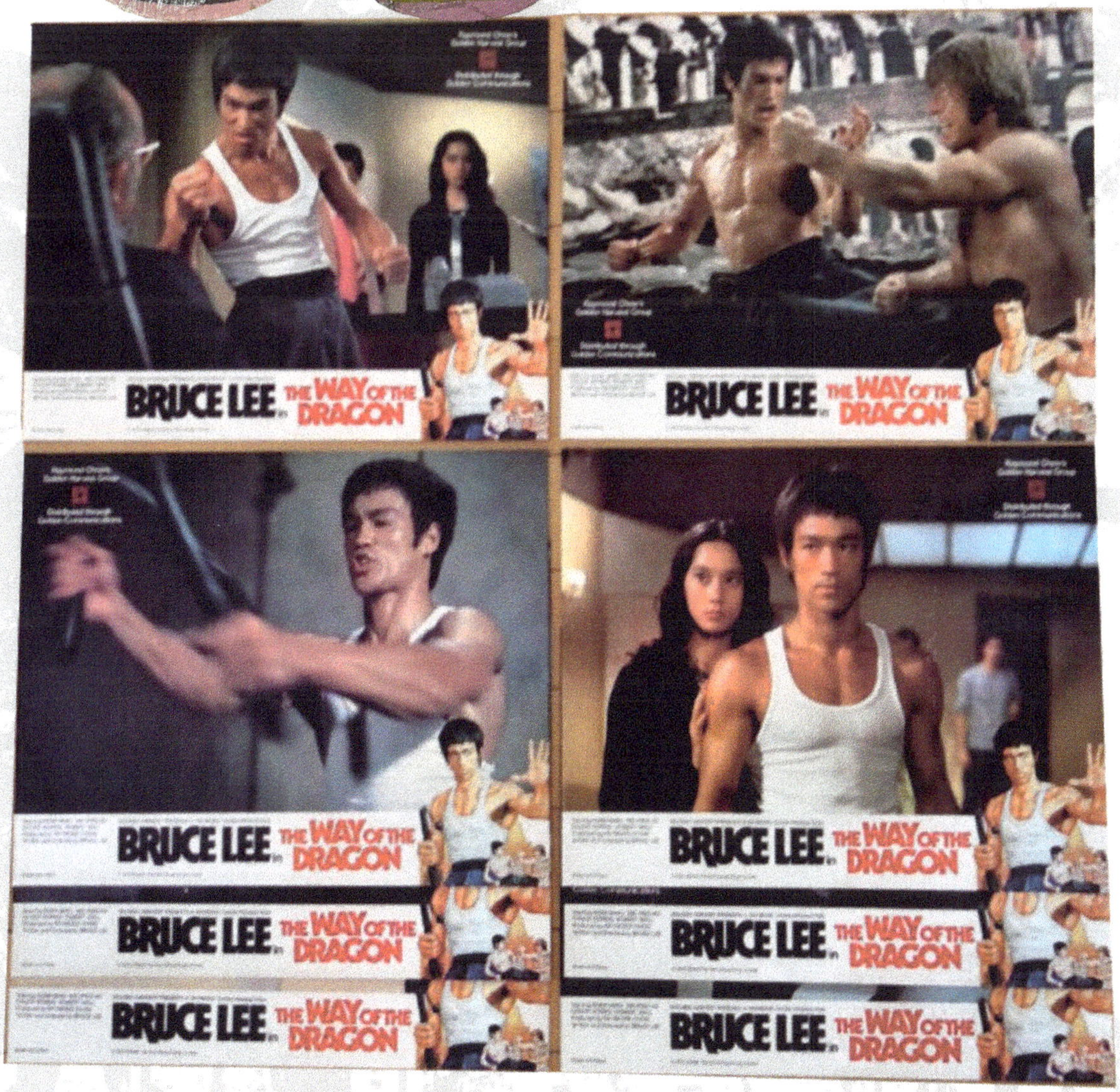
BRUCE LEE in THE WAY OF THE DRAGON

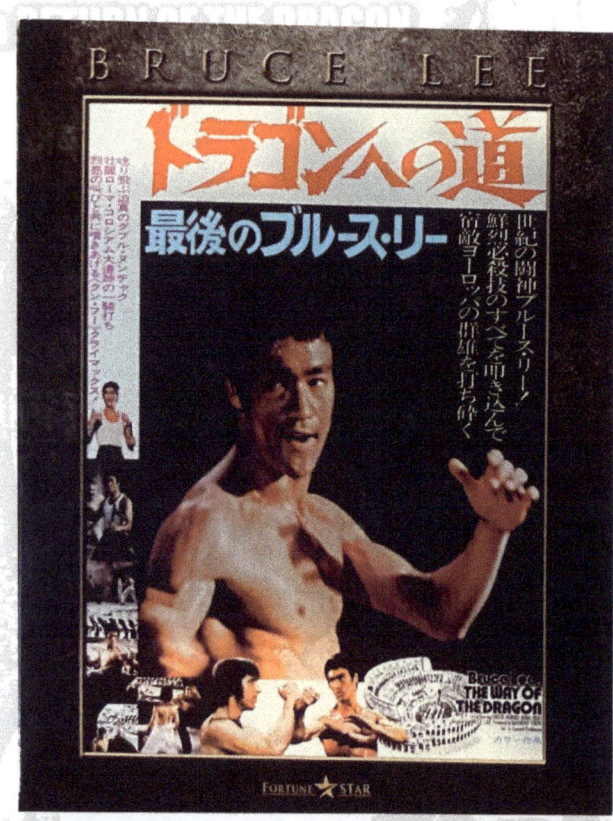

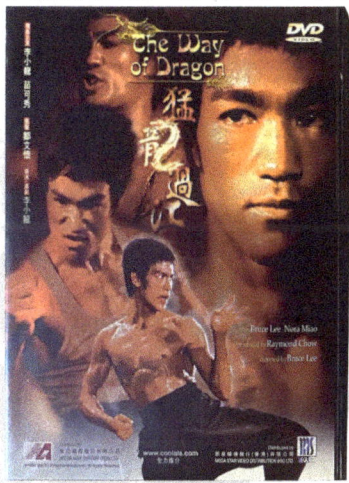

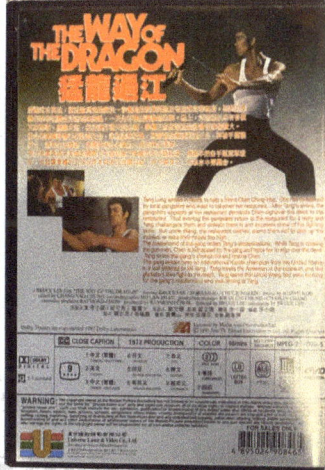

Posters & Flyers

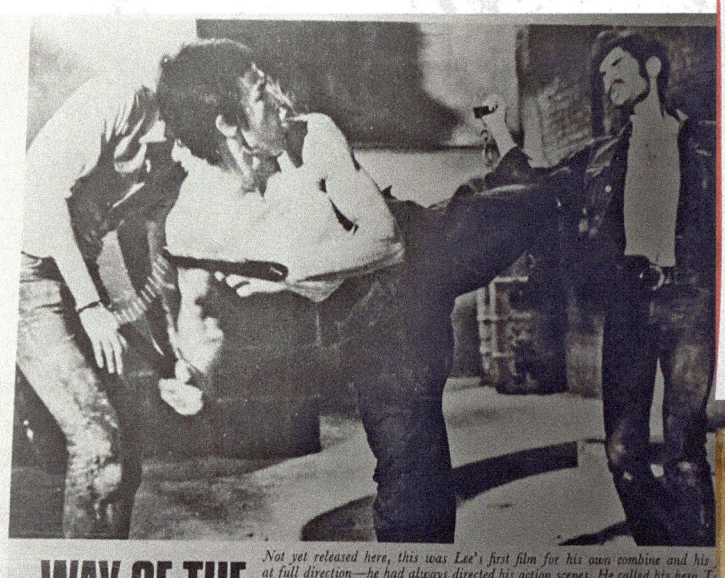

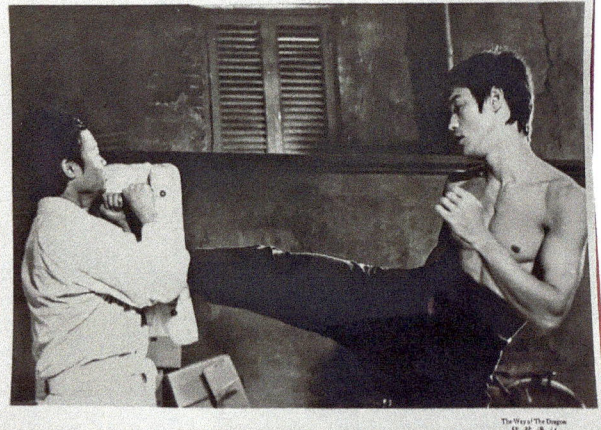

THE WAY OF THE DRAGON

猛龍過江

大滴出版有限公司
TATO PRESS LIMITED
FORTUNE ★ STAR

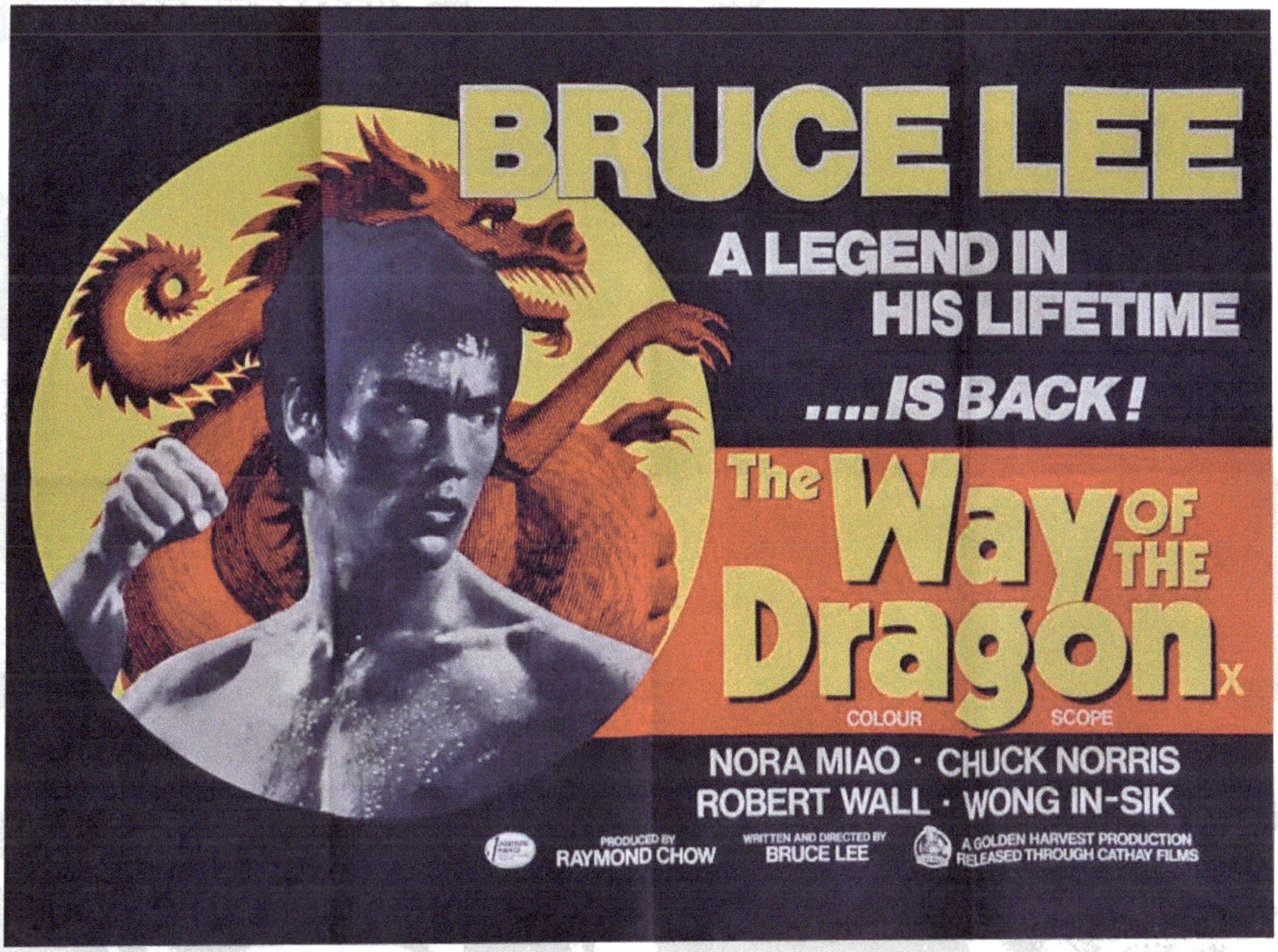
BRUCE LEE
A LEGEND IN HIS LIFETIME
....IS BACK!
The Way of the Dragon
X
COLOUR
SCOPE
NORA MIAO · CHUCK NORRIS
ROBERT WALL · WONG IN-SIK
PRODUCED BY RAYMOND CHOW
WRITTEN AND DIRECTED BY BRUCE LEE
A GOLDEN HARVEST PRODUCTION RELEASED THROUGH CATHAY FILMS

BRUCE LEE
BRUCE LEE
BRUCE LEE

BOY, CAN WE USE HIM NOW!
Bruce Lee is back in the fantastic all new adventures of the Super Hero from "Enter the Dragon"...
Bruce Lee
Return of The Dragon
R

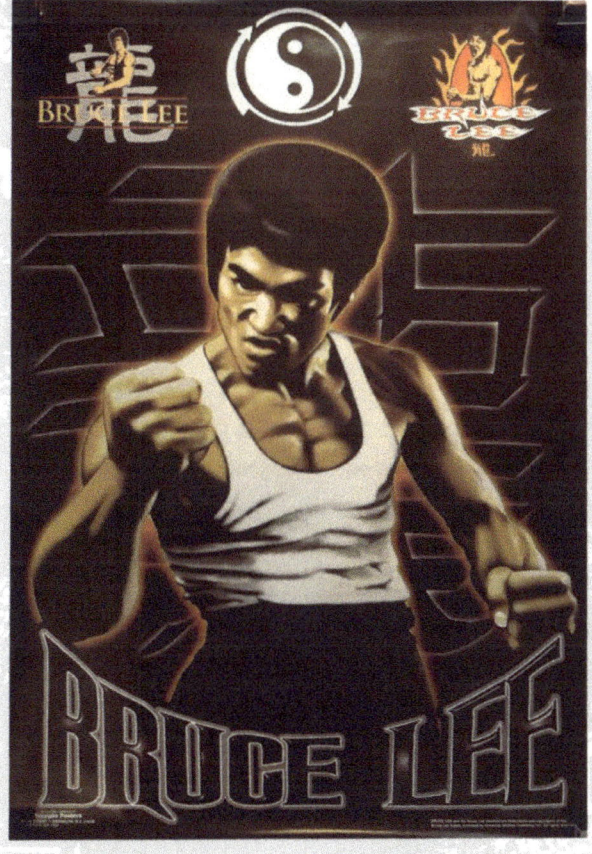

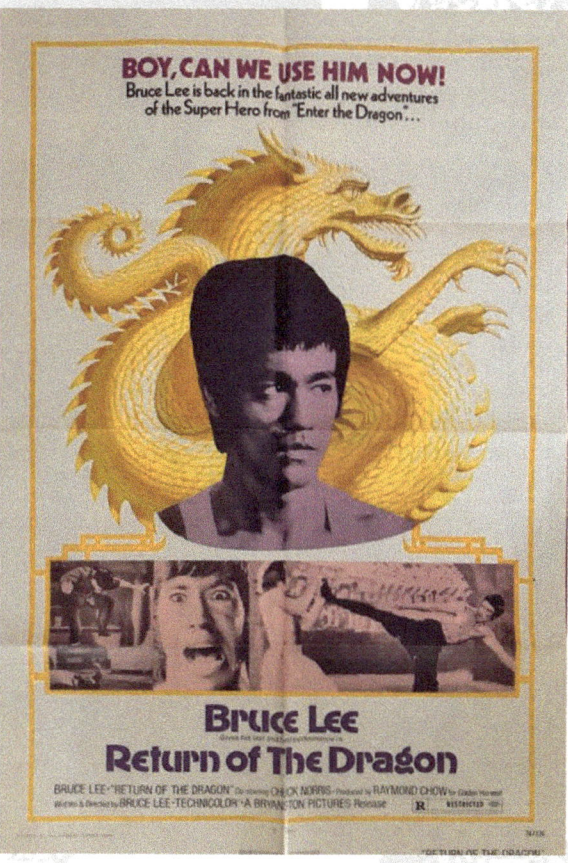

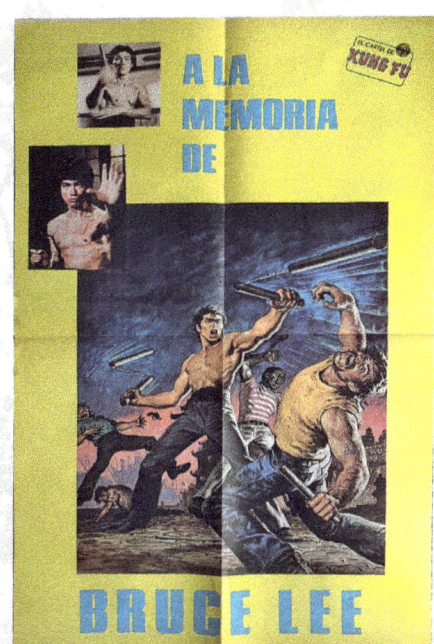

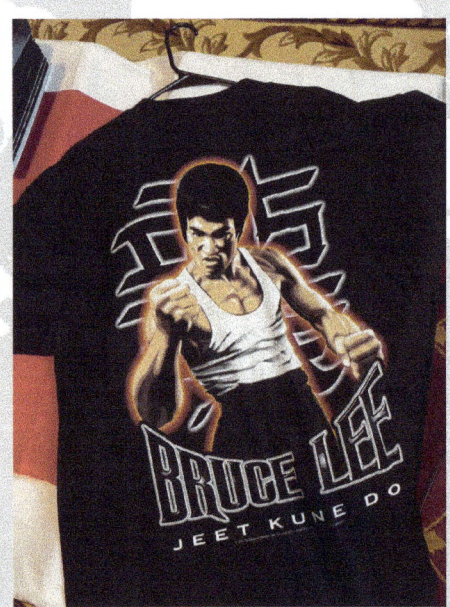

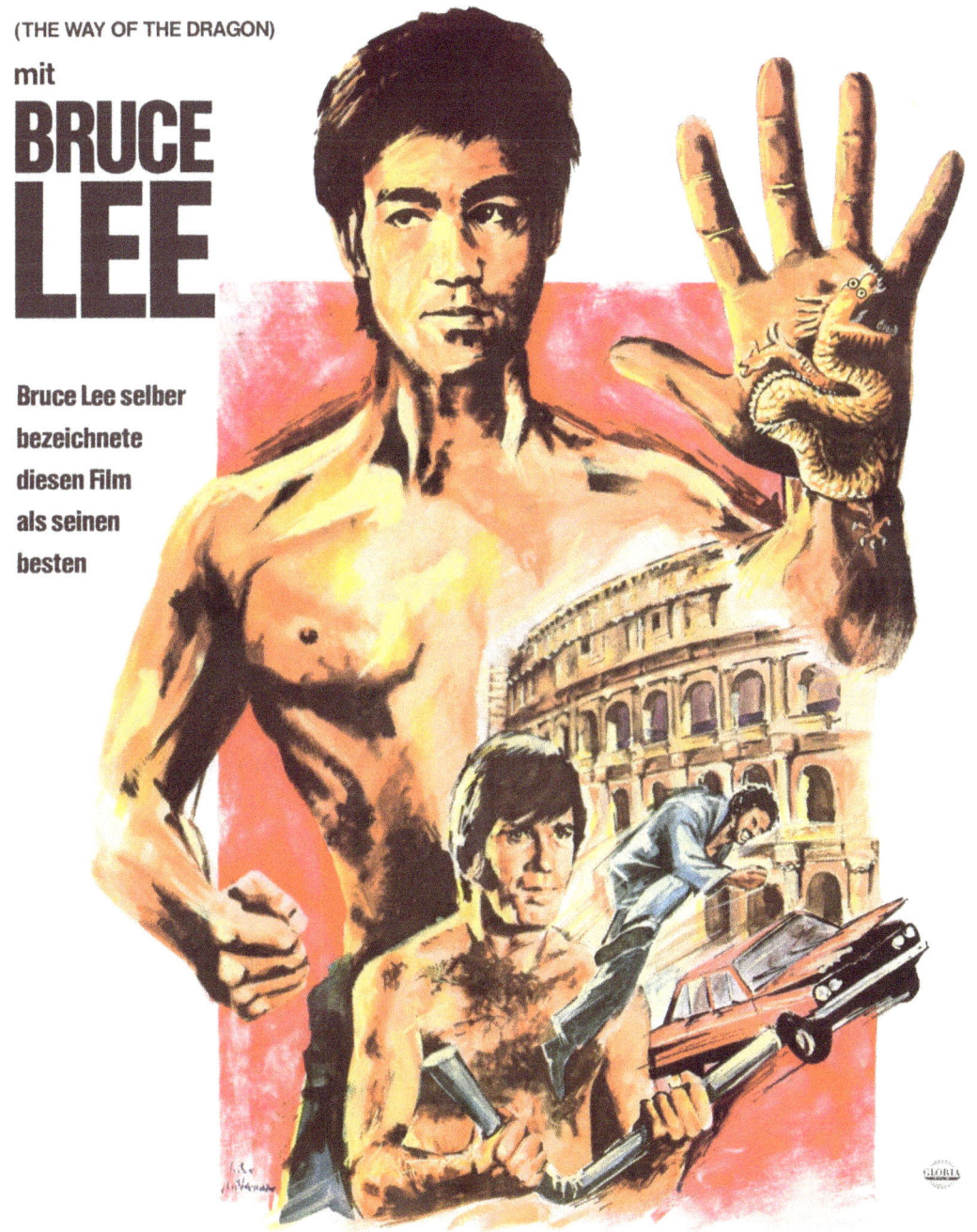

HONG KONG LOBBY CARDS

GERMAN LOBBY CARDS

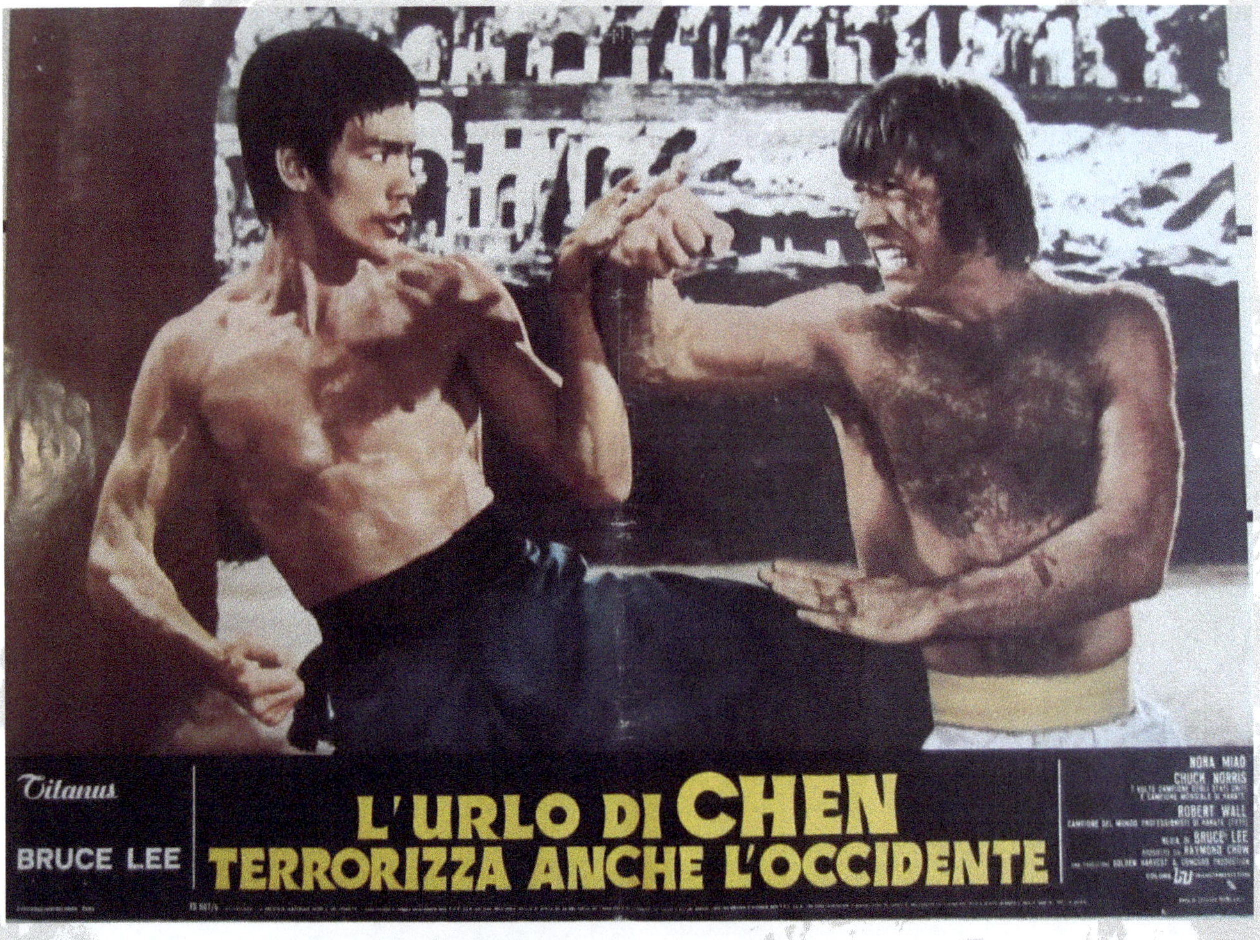
Titanus
BRUCE LEE
L'URLO DI CHEN
TERRORIZZA ANCHE L'OCCIDENTE
NORA MIAO
CHUCK NORRIS
ROBERT WALL
BRUCE LEE
RAYMOND CHOW

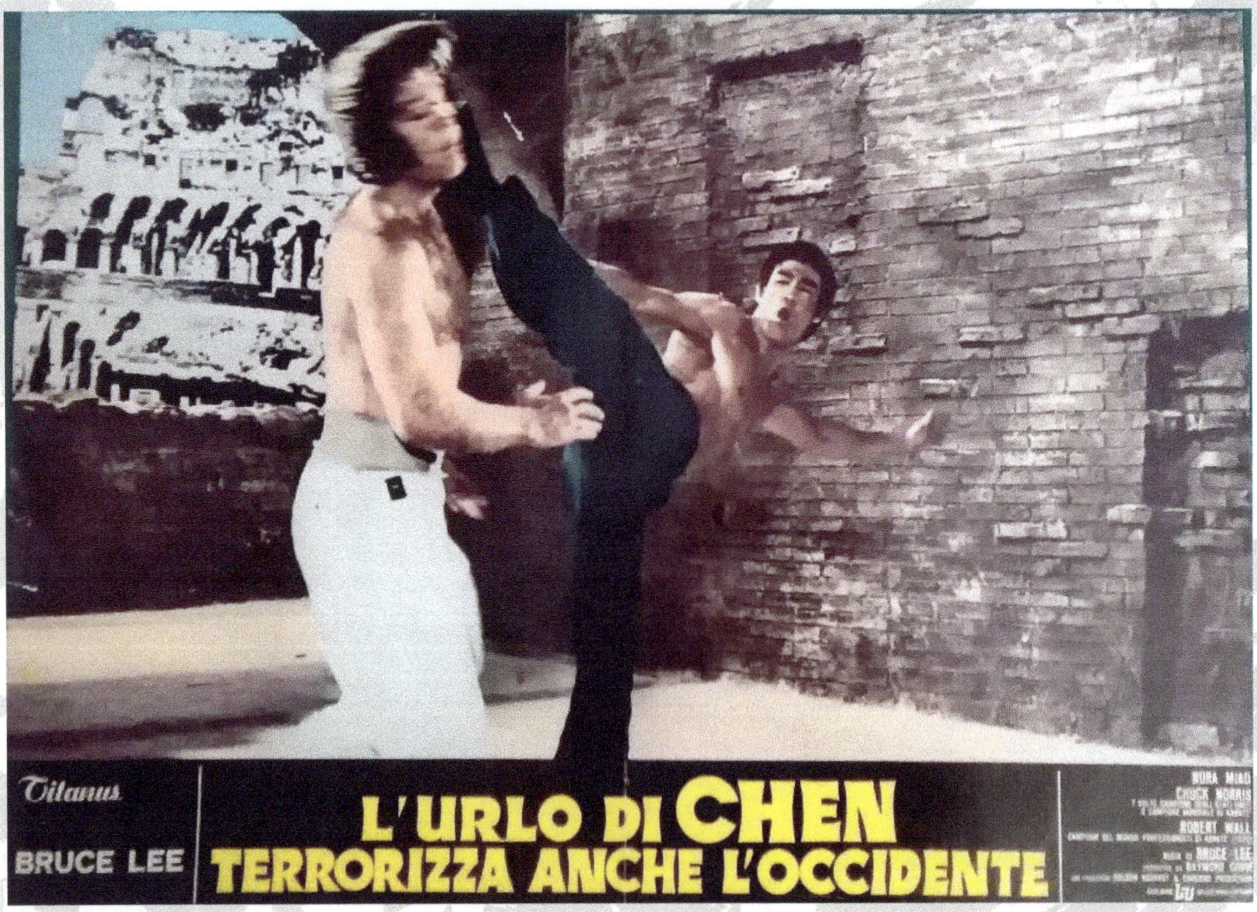
Titanus
BRUCE LEE
L'URLO DI CHEN
TERRORIZZA ANCHE L'OCCIDENTE
NORA MIAO
CHUCK NORRIS
ROBERT WALL
BRUCE LEE

JAPANESE LOBBY CARDS

JUGOSLAVIEN LOBBY CARDS

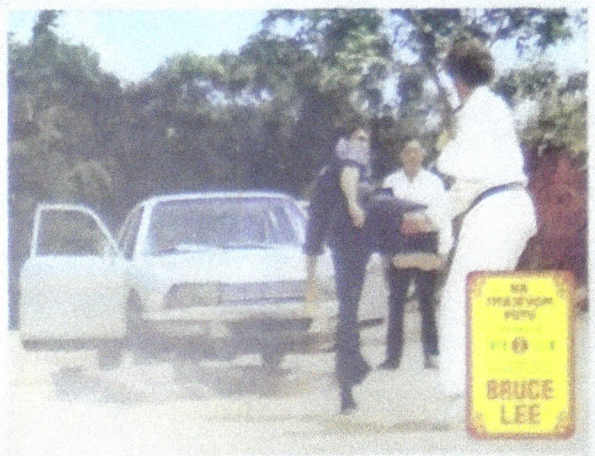

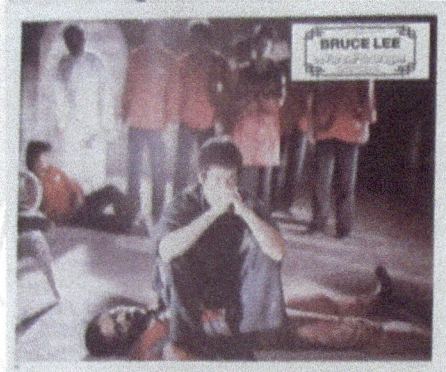

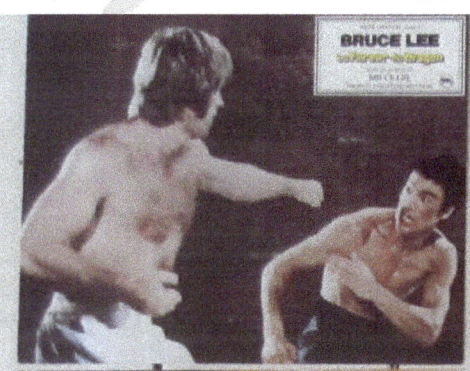

BRUCE LEE
BRUCE LEE
BRUCE LEE
BRUCE LEE
BRUCE LEE
BRUCE LEE
BRUCE LEE

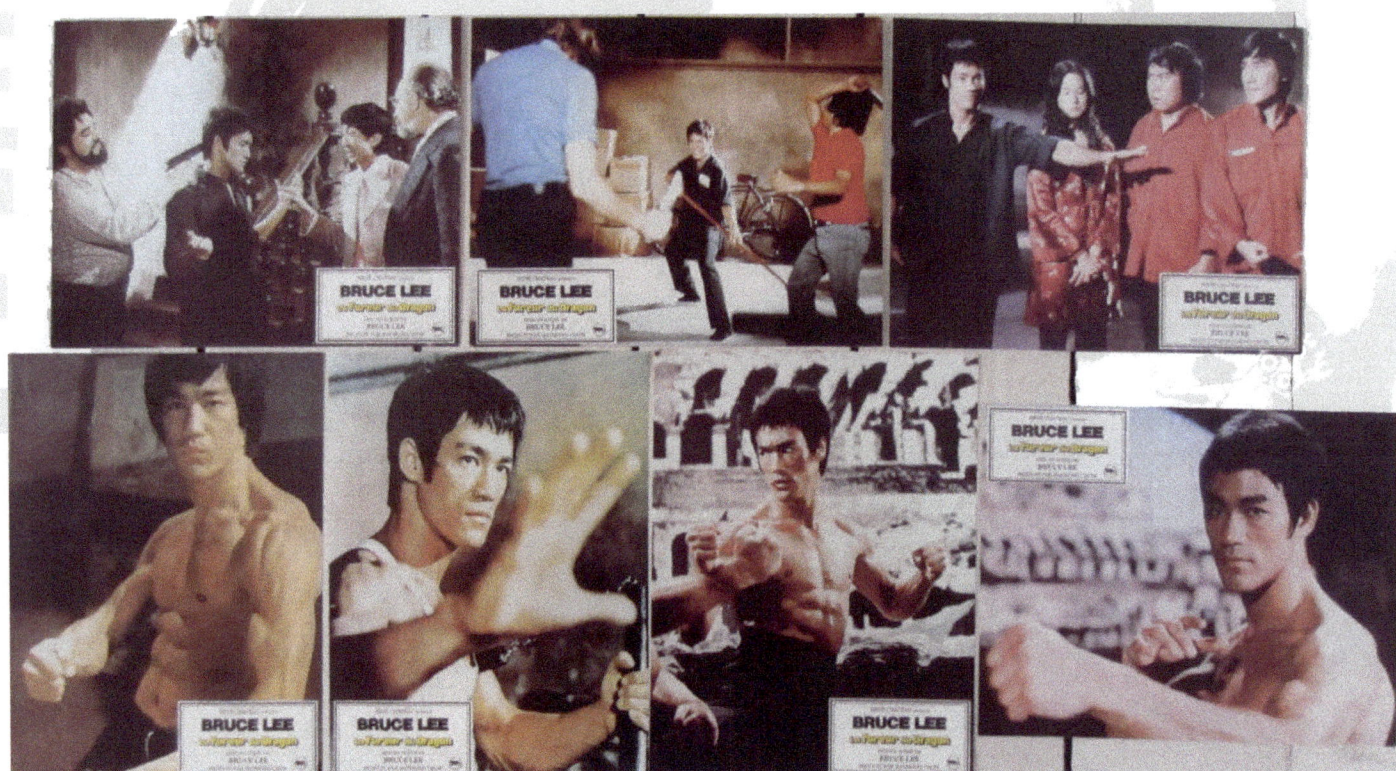

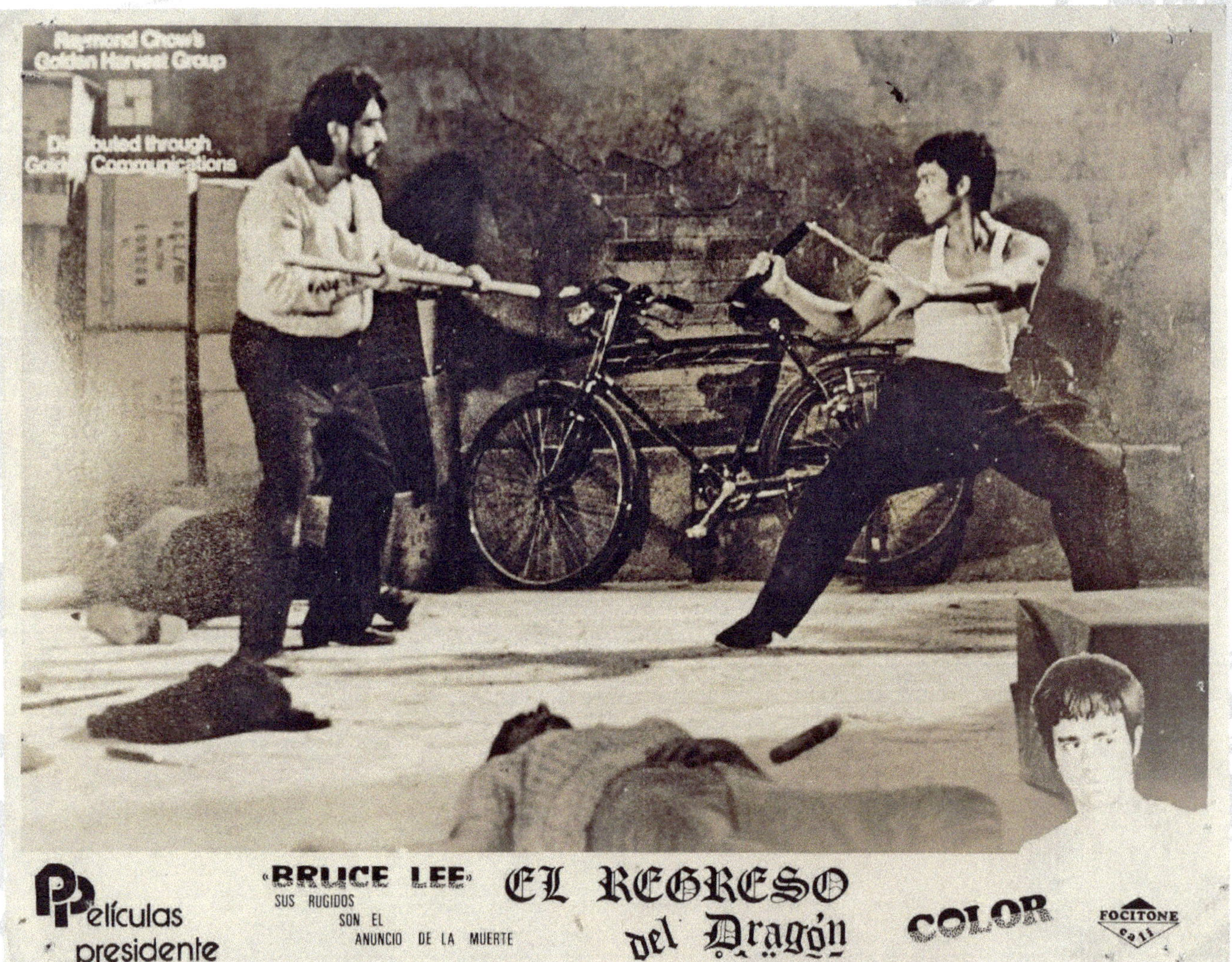
Raymond Chow's
Golden Harvest Group
Distributed through
Golden Communications
Películas
presidente
«BRUCE LEE»
SUS RUGIDOS
SON EL
ANUNCIO DE LA MUERTE
EL REGRESO
del Dragón
COLOR
FOCITONE
cali

GERMAN LOBBY CARDS

SPANISH LOBBY CARDS

MEXICAN LOBBY CARDS

SWISS LOBBY CARDS

TURKISH LOBBY CARDS

USA 8x10" LOBBY CARDS

USA 11x14" LOBBY CARDS

UK LOBBY CARDS

FRENCH LOBBY CARDS

POSTERS

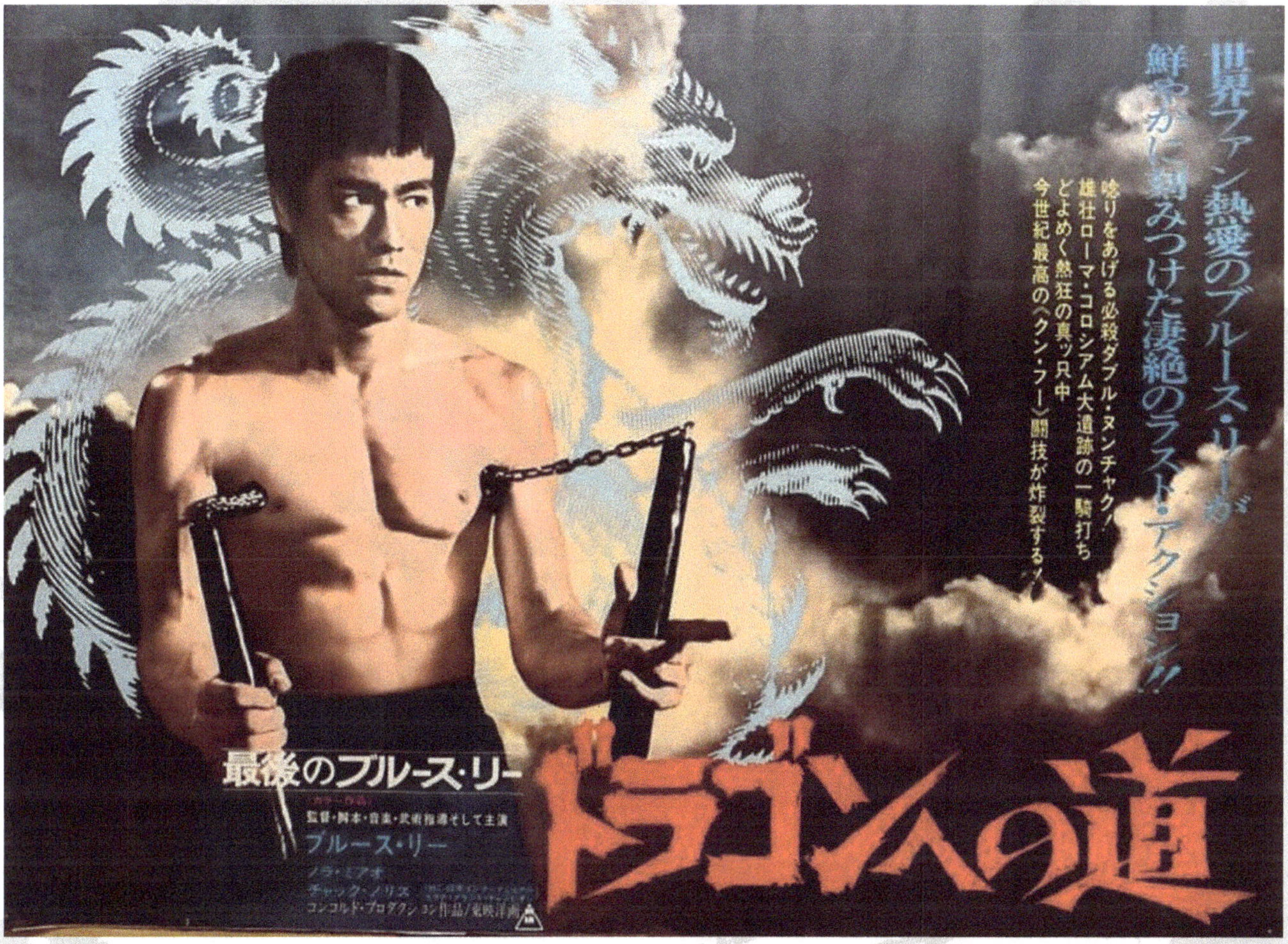

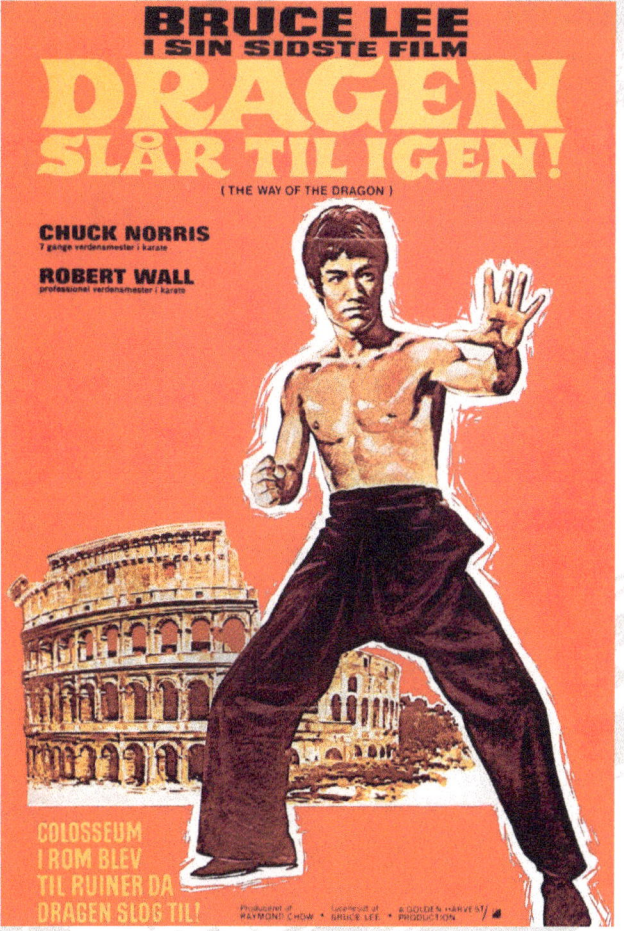

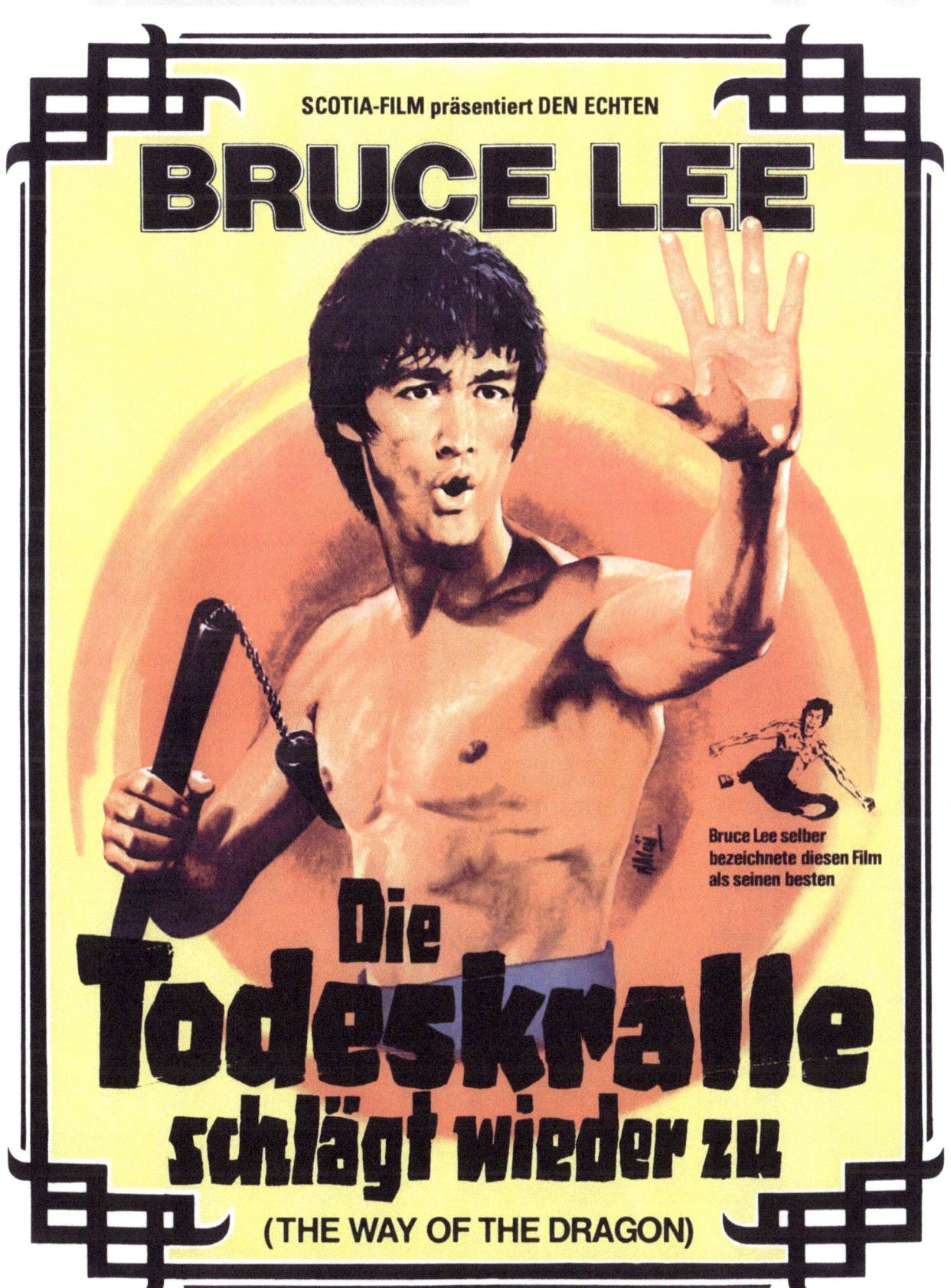

PHOTOGRAPHS

MISCELLANEOUS

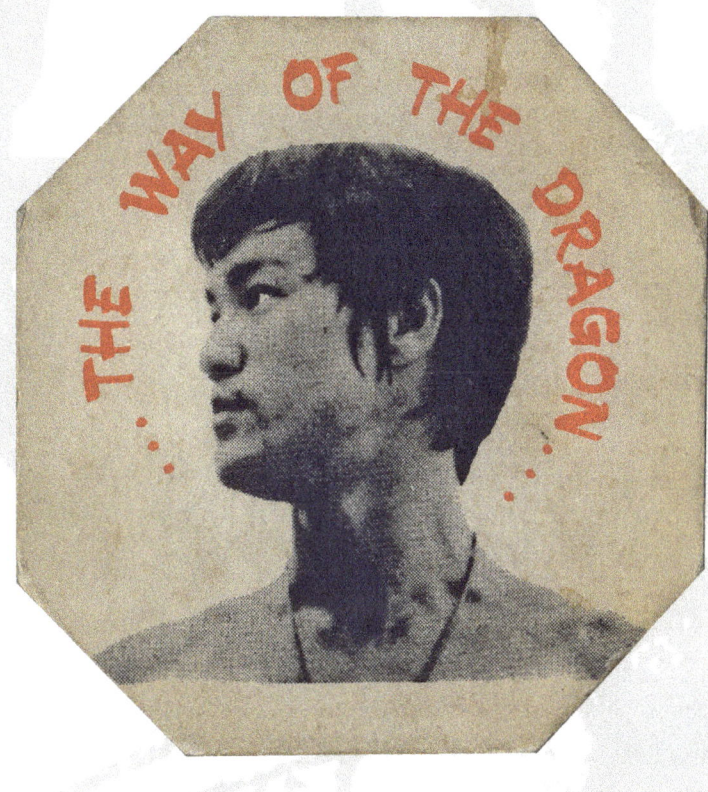

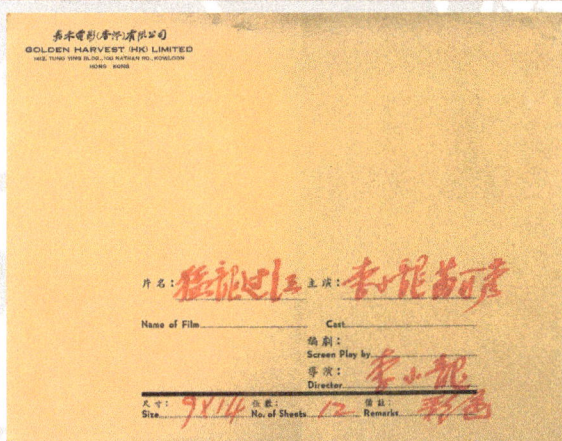

Page: 226 Eastern Heroes - Way of the Dragon Special

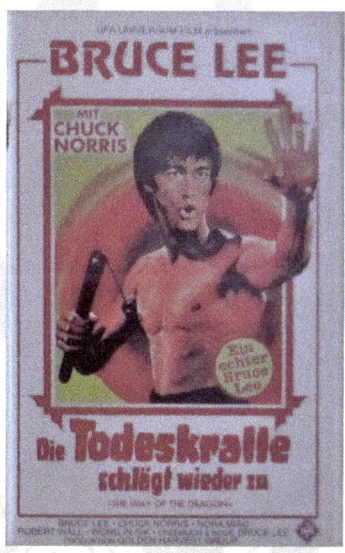

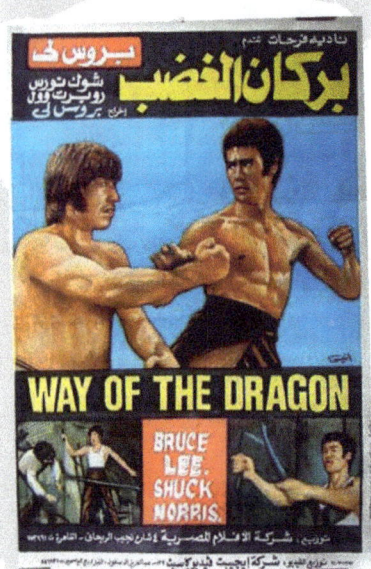

PRESS BOOKS & ADVERTS

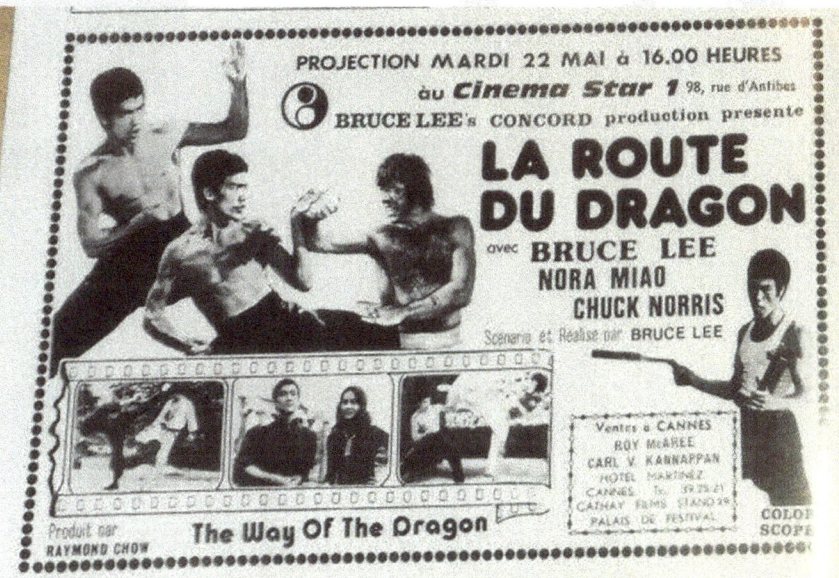

PRESSEHEFT

DIE TODESKRALLE SCHLÄGT WIEDER ZU

(THE WAY OF THE DRAGON)

Inhalt:

Ein junger Mann aus Hongkong, Tang Lung, fährt nach Rom, um einer Freundin der Familie, dem Mädchen Chen Ching-Hua, zu helfen. Sie wird von Gangstern bedroht, die ihr Restaurant übernehmen wollen. Chen und ihre Angestellten lassen sich von Tang's einfacher Kleidung und seinem Auftreten täuschen. Sie glauben, daß er nur ein Tölpel vom Land ist, der ihnen nicht nutzen kann.

Bald nach Tang's Ankunft tauchen die Gangster in der Kneipe auf. Sie verjagen die Gäste und fordern, daß Chen den Übernahme-Vertrag für das Restaurant unterschreibt. Tang, der in einem anderen Zimmer war, hat das alles nicht mitbekommen.

Die Gangster kehren am Abend zurück, um sich die Antwort abzuholen, während die Kellner boxen üben. Die Gangster lachen über ihren Kampftstil. Tang ist verärgert und besiegt alle in einem glänzenden Kampf.

Der Chef der Bande fordert Tang's Tod. Als sein Plan fehlschlägt, versucht er, Tang die Rückfahrkarte nach Hongkong zu geben. Tang lehnt ab und wirft die Bande aus der Kneipe hinaus.

Der Gangster-Boß heuert einen internationalen Karate-Meister aus Amerika an, um das letzte Mal zu versuchen, Tang zu töten. Tang trifft den Amerikaner im Kolosseum und sie kämpften wie Gladiatoren. Als Tang den Amerikaner erledigt hat, erfährt er, daß Onkel Wang die ganze Zeit für den Gangster-Boß gearbeitet hat. Nun stellt ihm der Verräter eine Falle, aber Tang wird von der Polizei gerettet.

Darsteller:

BRUCE LEE · NORA MIAO
CHUCK NORRIS – 7-facher Karate-Weltmeister
ROBERT WALL – 1970 Karate-Professional Nr. 1
WONG IN-SIK – Koreanischer Hapkido-Meister

Biographie BRUCE LEE

Der 1940 in San Francisco geborene Lee, Sohn eines chinesischen Schauspielers und Sängers, der lange der chinesischen Oper in Hongkong angehört hatte, kam dort auch in ersten Kontakt mit der Filmwelt.

Ein Studium an der Universität von Washington machte den jungen Bruce Lee dann nicht nur mit den Grundregeln der Philosophie bekannt, sondern führte ihn über den Studenten-Sport auch zur hohen Kunst der fernöstlichen Kampfsportarten, allen voran das Karate.

In Los Angeles eröffnete er eine ganze Reihe von Karate-Schulen. Die Nähe der Filmstadt Hollywood verschaffte ihm bald prominente Schüler. So hatte er schon Steve McQueen, James Coburn, Lee Marvin und James Garner unter seinen „Fittichen", um sie für bestimmte Rollen zu präparieren.

Lee war schon zu einigem Fernsehruhm gekommen, als er in den Serien „The Green Hornet", „Batman" und „Longstreet" mehr oder minder feste Stammrollen hatte.

Das Ergebnis waren mehrere Hongkong-Filme, die mit die riesige „Chinesen-Film-Welle" in der Bundesrepublik und überall in Europa initiierten.

Kurz nach Drehschluß des aufregenden Action-Abenteuers DIE TODESKRALLE SCHLÄGT WIEDER ZU, starb der 32-jährige Bruce Lee im Juli 1973 an einem Gehirnschlag.

hier in unserem Theater

So wollen ihn seine Fans sehen!

EIN ECHTER BRUCE LEE FILM

BRUCE LEE in seinem wohl besten Action-Film

Ein FARBFILM Der GLORIA

DIE TODESKRALLE SCHLÄGT WIEDER ZU
(The way of the Dragon)

DER »ECHTE« IST UNSCHLAGBAR!

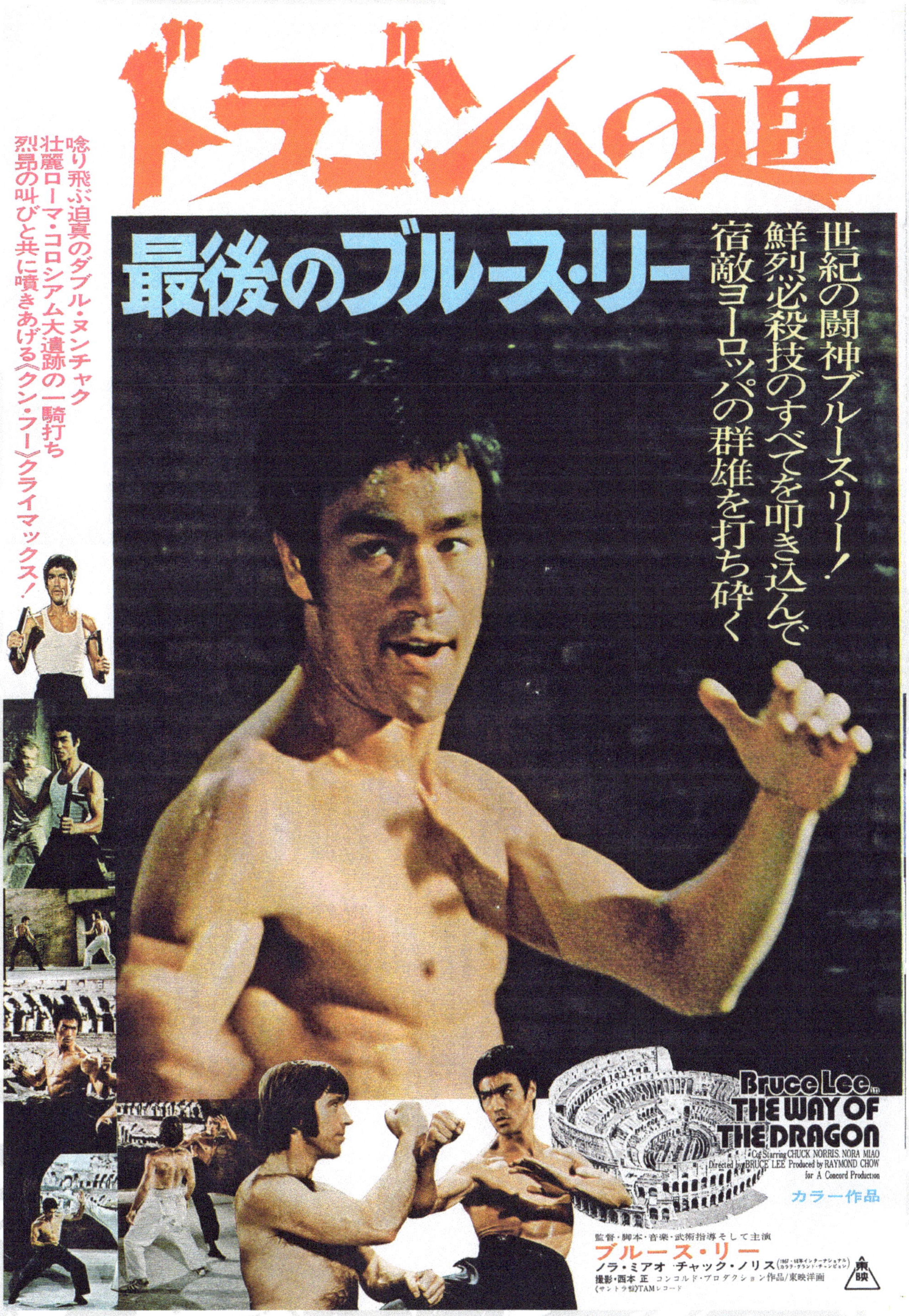

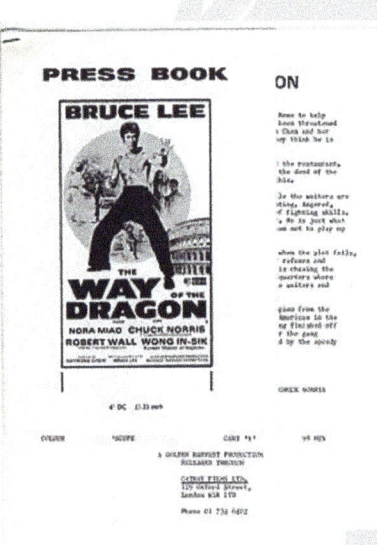

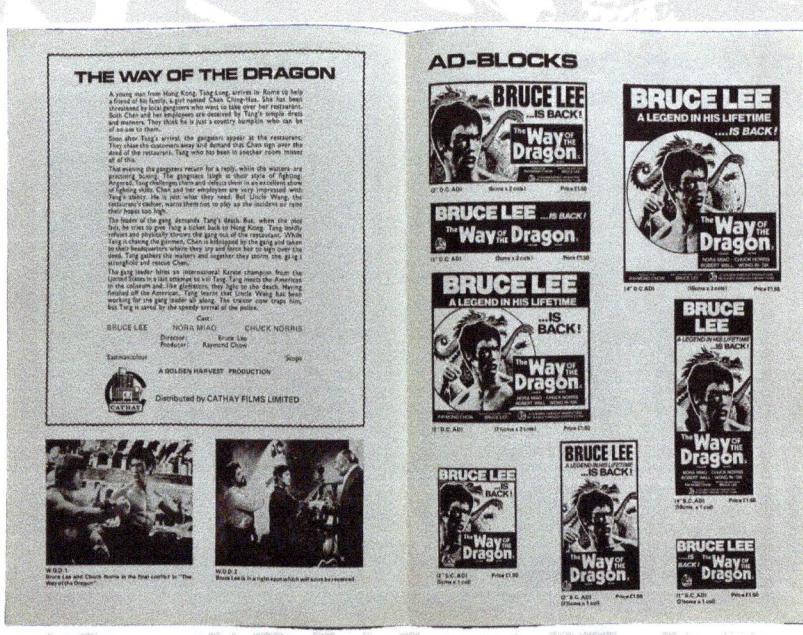

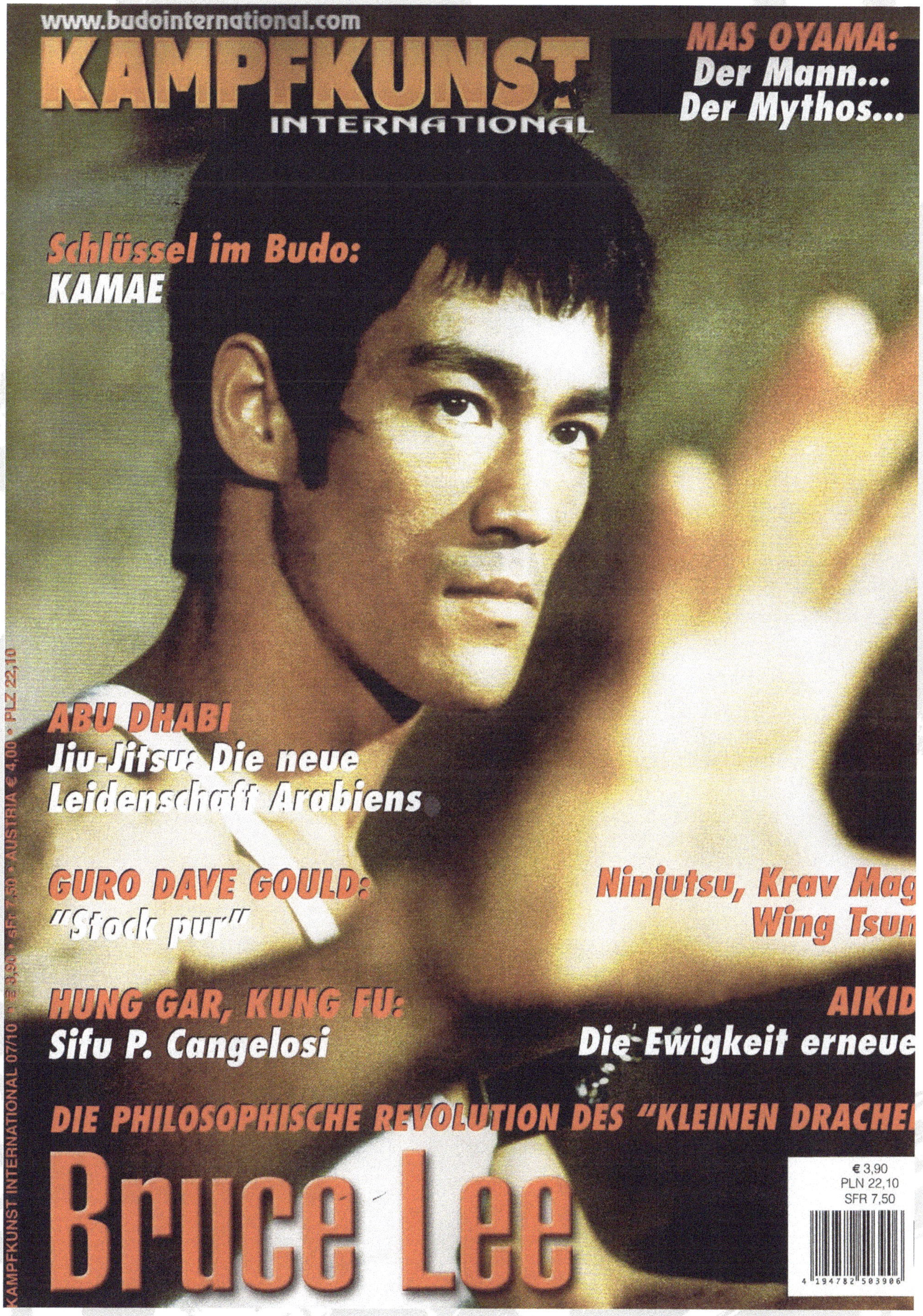

www.budointernational.com
KAMPFKUNST
INTERNATIONAL
MAS OYAMA:
Der Mann...
Der Mythos...
Schlüssel im Budo:
KAMAE
ABU DHABI
Jiu-Jitsu: Die neue
Leidenschaft Arabiens
GURO DAVE GOULD:
"Stock pur"
HUNG GAR, KUNG FU:
Sifu P. Cangelosi
Ninjutsu, Krav Mag
Wing Tsun
AIKID
Die Ewigkeit erneue
DIE PHILOSOPHISCHE REVOLUTION DES "KLEINEN DRACHE
Bruce Lee
€ 3,90
PLN 22,10
SFR 7,50
KAMPFKUNST INTERNATIONAL 07/10
AUSTRIA € 4,00 • PLZ 22,10

SYNOPSIS

A young man from Hong Kong, Tang Lung, arrives in Rome to help a friend of his family, a girl named Chen Ching-Hua. She has been threatened by local gansters who want to take over her Chinese restaurant. Both Chen and her employees are deceived by Tang's simple dress and manners. They think he is just a country bumpkin who can be of no use to them. Soon after Tang's arrival, the gansters appear at the restaurant. They chase the customers away and their Chinese interpreter demands that Chen sign over the deed to the restaurant. Tang who has been in another room misses all of this and, as the gansters are leaving, he bumps into one of them and politely apologizes. This infuriates Chen and the waiters whose opinion of Tang is very low by now.

That evening the gansters return to the restaurant for a reply, while the waiters are practising Chinese boxing. The gansters laugh at the Chinese style of fighting. Angered, Tang challenges them and defeats them in an excellent show of his fighting skills. Chen and her employees are very impressed with Tang's ability. He is just what they need. But uncle Wang, the restaurants cashier, warns them not to play up the incident or raise hopes too high.

The leader of the gang orders Tang to be murdered. But when his plot fails, he tries to give Tang an airplane ticket back to Hong Kong. Tang boldly refuses and physically throws the gang out of the restaurant. While Tang is chasing the gunmen, Chen is kidnapped by the gang and taken to their headquarters where they try to force her to sing over the deed. Tang gathers the waiters together, then storms the gangs headquarters to rescue Chen.

The gang leader hires an international Karate champion from the United States in a last attempt to kill Tang. Tang meets the American in the coliseum and, like gladiators, they fight to the death. Having finished off the American, Tang learns that uncle Wang has been working for the gang leader all along. The traitor now traps him, but tang is saved by the speedy arrival of the police.

Special Thanks to

Without valuable contributions "Eastern Heroes Magazine" would not have the informative information that we use to compile and make this great read.

Tim Hollingsworth (Designer UK)
Rick Baker (Editor in Chief)
Alan Canvan (USA)
Michael Worth USA)
John Negron (USA)
Thomas Gross (Germany)
Simon Pritchard (UK)
Michael Nesbitt (UK)
Alan Donkin (UK)
Johnny Burnett (UK)

www.ingramcontent.com/pod-product-compliance
Lightning Source LLC
Chambersburg PA
CBHW051323110526
44590CB00031B/4451